THE ROAD TO THE 707

The Inside Story of Designing the 707
William H. Cook

With editorial help from
Tandy Y. Cook

TYC Publishing Company
Bellevue, Washington

Published by TYC Publishing Company
875 Shoreland Drive S.E.
Bellevue, WA 98004

Historical photos: Peter Bowers
Boeing photos: Boeing Archives

Design and production by Merle E. Dowd & Associates

Library of Congress Catalog Card Number: 91-90998

ISBN 0-9629605-0-0

Printed in the U.S.A.

Contents

PART III—The Long-Range Swept-Wing Airplane

Acknowledgments

Aviation is blessed with worldwide enthusiasts who have photographs of airplanes and accounts of their operations. What is missing in this history of the engineering of the transports is the reasoning behind the designer's decisions. I had to fill this in based on the personal experiences of many old-timers , who were very helpful. I received a lot of information from my friends, a few of whom were in aviation before 1930. Dredging up anecdotes was a lot of fun. Knowing that there was a lot more to be lost was sorrowful.

I have received the most help on Boeing airplanes from Marilyn Phipps, Paul Spitzer, and Tom Lubbesmeyer of Boeing Archives. They provided photographs, microfilmed drawings, and engineering documents from their vast files. Finding where to look took a lot of Marilyn's time. The book *Boeing Aircraft* by Peter Bowers was indispensable in my attempts to maintain accuracy. Peter is an outstanding historian on worldwide aviation. He has one of the finest collections of historical photographs of airplanes, and he provided many of those included here.

Ann Rutledge of the Museum of Flight in Seattle was of assistance on material on non-Boeing airplanes.

Howard Fox of the Seattle Public Library is an expert on the documentation of aviation and was very helpful.

Harry Gann, historian for McDonnell Douglas, provided me with a very complete set of letters between Douglas and TWA, Wright, Pratt & Whitney, Hamilton Standard, and intra-company correspondence that did much to explain the engineering of the DC-1, a very interesting subject that has been obscured by writings on the great success of the DC-3. Dick Shevell, aerodynamics engineer at Douglas, wrote me a fine letter explaining the difficult decisions that delayed the DC-8 and thus aided Boeing's position.

Rea Goodrich of Pratt & Whitney and Anne Millbrooke, archivist for United Technology, provided valuable information on the J-57 engine.

Eric Falk of GE Aircraft Engines provided information on the TG-180 engine. In 1978 I received a letter and much material from Bill Traverse of GE and from Glenn Warren, the head of design team on the TG-180. This engine started the design of the modern type of engine in the U.S.

It is a shame that corporations do not require their engineers to write up the engineering background behind their decisions while the subjects are hot. I was helped by many in filling in what seemed reasonable.

If you can understand the contents of this book, credit is due to my daughter, Tandy. My original draft sounded like an old Western Union telegram where I tried to save words in cryptic messages. Engineers seem to develop a language of their own that inhibits their communications, and they rely too much on secretaries to make themselves understood.

Finally, I appreciate the help of Anne and Merle Dowd in transforming my manuscript into a professional book.

Preface

This book outlines the critical engineering discoveries leading to the jet transport age. Starting with the Wright brothers, it traces a path to the Boeing XB-47 swept-wing jet bomber, which was a catalyst for major developments that replaced the piston-engine transport with the jet. It ends with the first generation of commercial jet transports: the Comet, the Convair 990, the DC-8, and the 707. Although all airplanes in history contributed, even those that reached an impasse and were never developed further, only those airplanes that were in the direct line of progress are included here. Nevertheless, it is important to remember that the engineering failures were extremely useful in providing confirmation to the designers as to which was the right track to be on.

As this account nears the point in time when pistons gave way to jets, more detail is included to explain the criticality of the engineering decisions. Aviation history is most interesting in the interactions between designers, pilots, and the airline operators. Engineering has usually existed in the middle, between the top management on the one hand and the customer on the other, be that customer a branch of the military or a commercial airline. Rather than being isolated or set apart, engineering groups made decisions that often played a key role in determining other decisions relating to design or marketing. I have attempted to explain the engineering decisions to the reader in order to bridge the gap between the various airplanes that lined the road of aviation progress.

The elements of engineering design are explained so that they can be understood by airplane enthusiasts without resorting to technical terms. Mechanisms are explained by diagrams, with text to explain the logic and the course of events. The object is for the reader to enjoy the book and feel like an expert when finished. Perhaps the reader might be interested in comparing this history to those produced by company or government public relations departments.

The success of Boeing in achieving its present position of pre-eminence in the jet transport industry is due to many factors and events, and cannot be explained simply in terms of management, technical genius, size, politics, financial power, salesmanship, or any other over-simplifications.

Some of the factors that appear to have been helpful were: Boeing's continuous accumulation of experience as a business organization since 1916; its geographical isolation with respect to competitors which helped to keep the work force stable; the environment of the Puget Sound area, which tended to help the company retain skilled personnel because they wanted to live here; the long distances to other major cities, which helped to further motivate the search for improvements in airplane speed and range; Boeing's lack of political clout, which promoted a corporate attitude that stuck to business fundamentals rather than wasteful maneuvering; the failure to win some key military contracts, which left a vacuum in the factory at fortuitous times; the greatly enlarged engineering and manufacturing capabilities resulting from WWII and the Korean War; the lack of other high technology industry in the Puget Sound area in the early years, which otherwise might have bled off engineers and skilled mechanics; and lastly, an intense interest in airplanes especially during critical times which prompted people to invest their talents and money in the company.

The genius category is reserved for the developers of the first jet engines, Whittle of England, and von Ohain of Germany, and the source of the swept wing concept, Adolph Busseman, a German professor, all of whom came to the U.S.

after the war. The history of transport aviation spans 50 years in a long climb up to what might be called the "jet plateau." I was fortunate in arriving on the scene at Boeing in the lean years in the 1930's because this enabled me to appreciate aviation before the big-time business started, especially to be able to see how many engineering functions could be accomplished with simple tools and procedures. This early arrival also enabled me to be in the middle of the intense action during the transition to the jet age.

The competition between airplane companies had much of the elements of a ball game, in which respect for the capabilities of one's opponent is important. Success bloomed best in democratic organizations, where the worker had an opportunity to argue his case up to the top. As one engineer put it, we made a lot of mistakes, but we made them fast. Mistakes were mostly caught in time.

The design of such a complicated article as an airplane should be credited to the organization rather than to individuals. Almost every startling success on the way to the 707 was the result of a debate in which those who were at first on the losing side more often than not contributed as much towards the final solution as the winners. Where I have used the first person, it is only to indicate that I was in the middle of the action. I had a few good ideas and quite a few bad ones. After the 707 became acclaimed, the national technical societies had to find recipients for their medals and framed certificates. I received a couple of these, but the engineers I worked with know better.

This book is mostly a success story with little view of the vast number of pitfalls that bordered the path. Developing formulas for winning and for perpetuity may be attempted by business schools. But as you read this book, keep an eye for the difficulties that intelligent designers and pilots had to resolve by actions, often via the hard way.

Part I

From the
Wright Brothers
to the B-29

XB-47 Over Snow and Sagebrush—1948, Moses Lake

Pilot— Bob Robbins   Co-Pilot—Scott Osler

1

The Pioneers

By 1967 IT WAS CLEAR that the jet transport had taken over long-range travel. At that time most of the luxury Atlantic Ocean liners had been converted to cruise ships, and the luxury trains between New York and Chicago, the Twentieth Century Limited and the Broadway Limited, had all ended service. In addition, all first class mail had been transferred to the airways. This situation may have been predicted by aviation enthusiasts in the 1940's when the four-engine transports with piston power plants were operating, but it took the demonstration of the jet transport's comfort, speed, and long range capability in the mid 1950's to bring the idea of mass transportation by air to general acceptance.

　　The development of aviation from the first manned flight to the jet transport follows a long trail with numerous by-paths, and with many dead ends. From the perspective of the modern engineer, the main path of development has followed the scenario outlined in Figure 1, from the year 1799 and the first airplane concept using fixed wings and separate propulsion, to 1903 when the Wright brothers demonstrated sustained powered flight with three-axis control, on through the biplane development of World War I and up to the first trans-Pacific flight in 1928 using the Fokker tri-motor. The experiences of the experimenters along the way formed the logic behind the final ac-

Airplane Concept With Fixed Wing and Separate Propulsion—Cayley, 1799

First WindTunnel—Wenham, 1870

Four-Stroke Internal Combustion Engine—Otto, 1876

First Man in the Air—Lilienthal, 1894

1900

Sustained Powered Flight With Three-Axis Control—Wright Brothers, 1903

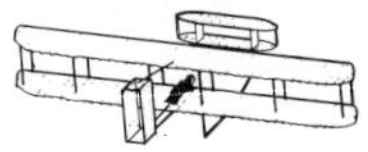

Wilbur's Demonstrations in France and Italy—August 1908 to May 1909

Bleriot Channel Crossing—July 1909

First Air Meet—38 Entered—23 Flew—9 Types—Reims, August 1909

1910

1918 Models   Sopwith Camel   SE-5   Spad

World War I—The Biplane Development—219K Built—100+ Types

All-Metal Cantilever Monoplane—Junkers—1918

1920

Ethel Anti-Knock Gasoline—1923

Fokker Tri-Motor Transport—1925

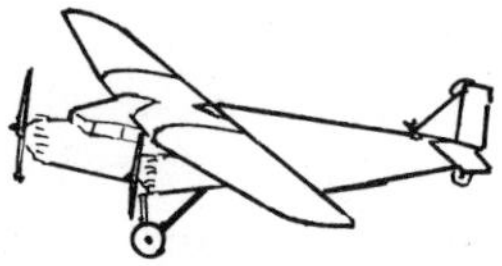

Ford All-Metal Tri-Motor Transport—1926

Solo Trans-Atlantic Flight—Lindberg—May 1927

Trans-Pacific Flight—Fokker Tri-Motor—Kingsford Smith—May 1928

1930

Figure 1—Era of the Pilot-Designer, 1900-1930

complishment of the jet transport. The intent of each designer to create unique and different designs was fundamental to finding the best engineering solution. The meager theories of the early period were often erroneous. Intuition played a major role in the creative process. As new ideas were developed and tested, new theories were developed to explain the successes and provide a key for optimizing performance even further. The negative side of experimentation also provided a fertile breeding ground for new development, as repetitive crashes gave rise to various theories to explain the reasons behind the failures.

The history of this long path of development can be most interesting in appreciating the final product. It is easy to view today's jet transport design as very obvious, but a long time was required to arrive at what has become a standard configuration. A body of critical experience on all sorts of airplanes was gradually accumulated. Although early airplane designs seem awkward and primitive by today's standards, they provided many lessons that firmly apply to the modern jet transport.

Long before the time of the Wright brothers most of the basic mechanical theories necessary for flight had been discovered and enjoyed widespread application, including those relating to Newton's laws of motion, heat engines using gaseous expansion, structural properties of trusses, beams and columns. The applications of these basic principles to flight required the integration of five basic requirements: (1) wings to provide lift greater than the airplane weight, (2) propellers to provide thrust greater than the airplane drag, (3) engines of sufficient power to turn the propeller, (4) a three-axis control mechanism to govern pitch, roll, and yaw to permit maneuvering and to counteract gusts, and (5) an overall arrangement of the airplane components to locate the airplane center of gravity near the center of lift.

The individuals who experimented with applying these basic principles to flight were probably regarded as eccentric in that they were interested in something that was considered to be dangerous, impractical, or impossible. At first they received no help from the academic or political arenas. Only after they had built prototypes and conducted demonstrations did they finally receive help. The pioneers had to support their own experiments which were performed in isolation. This was ben-

eficial in that they were left alone, uninhibited by the precon-
ceptions of others. Their isolation ended when they had to go
outside to try out their creations. Although their limited financial
means could be viewed as restrictive, it actually motivated
simplicity and highly creative approaches to problem solving. A
saying in the days of the biplane was that the job of the designer
was to "simplicate and add more lightness." A modern saying is
"given time, the engineers will find ways to complicate most
everything."

Historically experimentation has led theory in terms of
discoveries: the development of the jet engine and the swept
wing are among the very few exceptions to this maxim. It is
almost impossible to trace a scientific development back to the
first time an important idea appeared in any mind. Bird watchers
like Leonardo da Vinci [1452-1519] tried to impose the principles
of avian physiology onto a mechanism for flapping wings that
could be operated by humans, but this approach was doomed to
failure. The bird's powerplant is ideally located with the breast
muscles contained within a streamlined body. The span of the
flapping wing is equivalent to a large diameter propeller,
yielding high propulsive efficiency.

A bird such as the duck is efficiently proportioned for long
range flight at high speeds. The duck's fat reserves, which are
used for fuel, have about the same energy as gasoline according
to the calorific measurements found in household cookbooks.
The conversion efficiency of the energy contained in fat to
muscle power for flapping the wings is similar to that achieved
by mechanical engines. There is not much to eat on the duck at
the dinner table except the breast, the powerplant. The legs
contain the minimum amount of muscle tissue needed to waddle
around or to paddle when floating. The proportion of the breast
muscle weight to the total weight of the bird is similar to that of
the engine weight to the gross weight of an ordinary airplane.
Leonardo, being a student of anatomy, and maybe having had
duck for dinner, must have been impressed by the size of the
bird's breast muscles because he tried to utilize the maximum
human potential for movement by mechanizing the use of both
legs and arms in his drawing of a flying machine.

A bird's wing provides both lift and propulsion. Useful
ideas on human flight did not begin until the effort to mechanize

the wing flapping of birds was abandoned in favor of approaches that separated lift from propulsion. In 1799 Cayley [1773-1857], a well-to-do imaginative and enthusiastic Englishman conceived this idea and published it in London in 1809 in the *Journal of Natural Philosophy*. Cayley's designs had curved wing sections rather than flat. They were nearly square in planform rather than being tapered like the wings of soaring birds which seem to fly with the least effort. The very early glider designers must have been afraid of risking their necks on slim structures. The hollow bones in the bird wing and the long primary feathers presented a very difficult structure to imitate. Cayley suggested oars rather than propellers, although they had been accepted by would-be aeronauts for some time.

Leonardo da Vinci used two 4-bladed propellers for his helicopter. By the middle 1800's the propeller was the accepted means of propulsion in steamships. In 1871 Pénaud [1850-1880], a French pioneer in aeronautics, built a small rubber band driven model airplane with a propeller. It was the first example of stable powered flight. The development of the condensing steam engine by James Watt [1736-1819] in 1796 must have been of some encouragement to those who were experimenting with designs for powered flight. But the early steam engines were so heavy that it would have taken a lot of imagination to come up with a design light enough for flight, although some tried.

The missing link in all these early airplane designs was the internal combustion piston engine. In 1860 a Frenchman, Lenoir, built several hundred engines operating on illuminating gas, one of which was installed in a road vehicle. In 1868 a four-cycle engine was run in Germany by Otto and Langen. In 1885 the first gasoline engines were run in Germany by Daimler and Benz, famous for their Mercedes line of cars and aviation engines. The gasoline may have come from Baku on the Caspian Sea, where oil was in large production for kerosene lamps. The first oil well in the U.S. was drilled in Pennsylvania in 1859. Kerosene was the first widely used petroleum product for use in lanterns. Gasoline was initially considered to be a dangerous by-product. Explosions occurred when the kerosene was diluted with too much gasoline. Maybe these experiences lead to the idea of an engine that could utilize explosions.

The Wright brothers drew upon a substantial background of experiments and ideas from the previous hundred years. They became aware of German glider flights by Lilienthal [1848-1896], an engineer from Berlin. Lilienthal was the first to take a technical approach to flight. He developed a method of plotting lift and drag that is still used today. He was killed in his hang glider due to a loss of control that resulted in a stall. In addition to Lilienthal's data the Wrights also benefited from the publications of the Royal Society of London, the oldest scientific society in the modern world and a focal point for information among aeronautical enthusiasts.

From the perspective of a modern engineer, the Wright brothers' high school education was sufficient for what they were to accomplish in life. Had they received a college education in engineering at that time, they might have become gainfully employed in designing bridges instead of using their imagination to explore the possibilities of flight. They were both well read and had early ventures in the printing business in a small newspaper. They kept up with all the literature they could find on subjects pertaining to flight. In August 1900 they wrote to Octave Chanute [1832-1910], a civil engineer who had been conducting gliding experiments on the dunes of Lake Michigan. From then on Chanute provided valuable assistance and encouragement. Wilbur had studied trigonometry after high school, and this probably aided him in designing their biplane for sufficient structural strength while achieving light weight. Any other engineering knowledge of that period might have inhibited their imaginations, since education is largely an exploration of the past rather than the future.

It would have been interesting to have witnessed how the Wright brothers got along with each other. Each seemed to regard the other as an equal. There must have been many arguments. Most every problem in design has two or more possible solutions. They probably settled differences by taking the most direct approach. A new design that does not go through this process is likely to fail. Many airplane developments in the history of aviation have failed because of an autocratic chief designer who didn't have the optimum solution.

The first flight of the Wright brothers is a logical point to define the start of the build-up of ideas that culminated in the jet transport. Besides being the first to accomplish sustained manned flight with positive control and high maneuverability, the Wright brothers were the first to use "complete engineering," that is, engineering specialties that were sufficiently integrated to work together. For example, they designed the structure for both adequate strength and tolerable weight using biplane truss construction with wooden beams and columns and wire tension members. They realized the need for a three-axis control system, particularly after Lilienthal's death in his hang glider. Through flight testing they developed a very effective mechanical control system to maintain attitude even in strong gusts [Figure 2].

Because all flights tests were flown purposely at low altitudes, they survived numerous crashes. They would analyze the cause of each crash and then make ingenious corrections in design. When they found that the published data on the lift and drag characteristics of wings was questionable, they built a wind tunnel and devised clever instrumentation to measure the aerodynamic forces. Crucial to their success was the considerable flying time they accumulated on the Kitty Hawk dunes while gliding and soaring, and later while testing powered flight. With this experience the anxieties that are often characteristic of first flights changed to confidence so that they could analyze their experiences clearly and without emotion [Figure 3].

The structure of the Wright Flyer was based on Chanute's biplane gliders. The propeller drive system used roller chains with sprockets and long shafts to drive two counter rotating pusher propellers. This propeller configuration had three purposes: a high disc area to produce high thrust, counter rotation to cancel torque, and aft location to minimize any effect of the propeller slipstream on controllability, which was their primary concern.

In the final steps of designing their airplane, the Wrights calculated the power that would be necessary, and then designed the propellers and the gasoline engine to meet this requirement. These engineering disciplines are no different today. What is remarkable is the relatively short time that was required for the Wright brothers to construct their airplane: only three and a half years from the first glider flight to the first

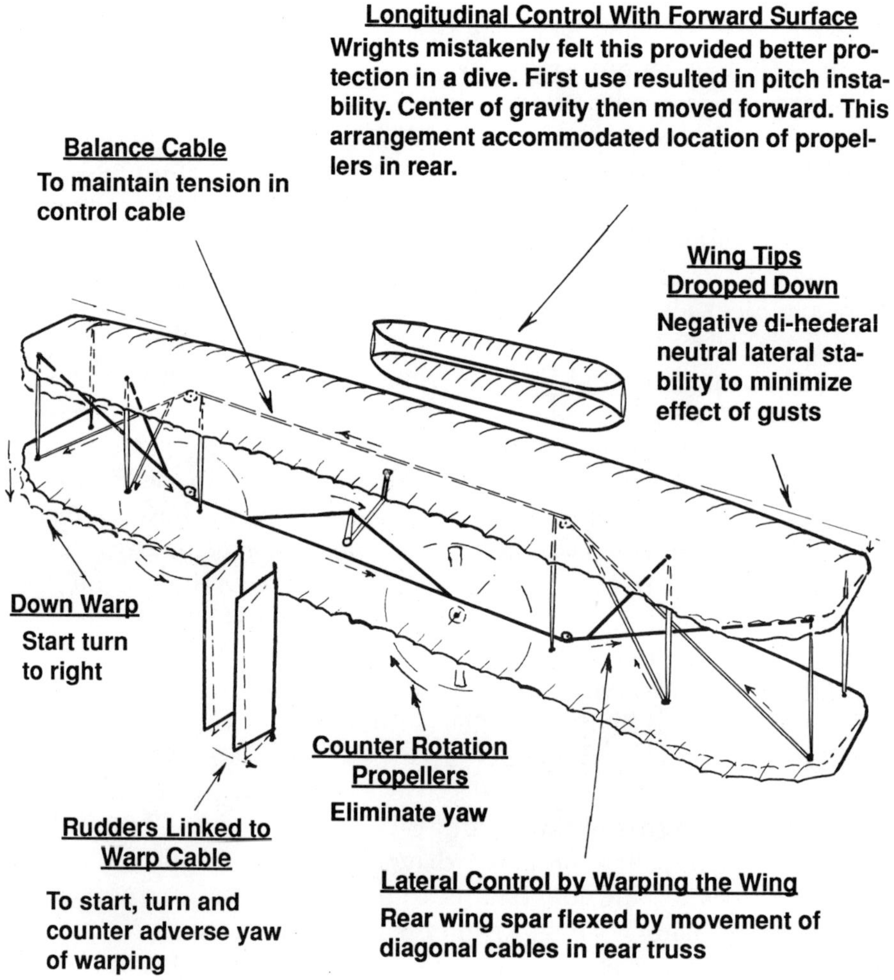

Longitudinal Control With Forward Surface
Wrights mistakenly felt this provided better protection in a dive. First use resulted in pitch instability. Center of gravity then moved forward. This arrangement accommodated location of propellers in rear.

Balance Cable
To maintain tension in control cable

Wing Tips Drooped Down
Negative di-hederal neutral lateral stability to minimize effect of gusts

Down Warp
Start turn to right

Counter Rotation Propellers
Eliminate yaw

Rudders Linked to Warp Cable
To start, turn and counter adverse yaw of warping

Lateral Control by Warping the Wing
Rear wing spar flexed by movement of diagonal cables in rear truss

Prehistoric Note: Leonardo da Vinci was a bird watcher for technical ideas to design an airplane. He recognized that all forces must go through the center of gravity for trim. For longitudinal control the tail could be deflected up or down, or the wings could be swept forward or back. For lateral control, wing warping or folding of a wing could be used. (Circa 1505)

Figure 2—Wright Flyer Controls

Huffman Prairie
Dayton, Ohio
Sept. 28, 1905

Land in Front of Shed

Headed for Thorn Tree

Stalled and No
Lateral Control

Nose Down to
Crash Land Short
of Thorn Tree

Control Recovery
Turn to Right

Grazed the Ground

Wing Tip Rips a
Branch Off Tree

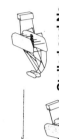

Figure 3—Orville's Recovery From a Stall

powered flight. Interestingly, this is about the same amount of time that is required today in a well run new jet airplane program. When the Wright brothers finally arrived at a design they felt would work, their first complete Flyer performed as expected, proving that their analysis had been highly accurate.

After their first flight at Kitty Hawk in 1903, they made some flights near Dayton, Ohio. During the course of these tests they made some improvements to their design. Unfortunately, there was a period during which they were secretive, and made no attempt to examine alternate configurations that might simplify the construction and improve performance. Every airplane company has made the same mistake. A most significant activity was a 10-month period between 1908 and 1909 when Wilbur Wright demonstrated the Flyer in France and Italy. The French aviation enthusiasts, who previously had been doubters, were amazed at Wilbur's ability to fly in strong winds, to perform precision maneuvers and to fly tight circuits of the landing field. During this period Wilbur flew with many passengers, and with flights as long as one and one half hours and distances up to 80 kilometers. These demonstrations were a tremendous impetus to European aviation. The motivation for the European demonstration was to sell their patent. However, it turned out to be mostly a public relations effort, and in this regard it was very successful.

The Wright brothers were the first to appreciate the necessity of lateral control. They first tried to patent their whole airplane, but were only successful in patenting their wing warping lateral control system, which was finally approved by the U.S. Patent Office in May 1906. They felt that their patent covered all means of lateral control, including movable surfaces between the wings as used by Curtiss [1878-1930] and ailerons as used by the French. The Wright brothers spent most of their efforts in protecting their patent and thus stopped development, a mistake that can be found regularly in the course of aviation history. Their patent might not have been granted from today's perspective. A fundamental principle of patent law is that a means found in nature can not be patented, only the mechanization of that means. Thus lateral control cannot truly be patented, only a specific mechanism can be patented.

Looking back, the Wright might have been rejected on even

more obvious grounds. Leonardo da Vinci had described wing warping in birds, the subject of the Wright patent. His descriptions of bird flight were appropriated by Napoleon during his campaign in Italy but were not translated into English until 1924.

Moving rapidly away from the Wright configuration, the French made numerous improvements and simplifications. Among the most notable of these were by Bleriot [1872-1936], who made a fortune manufacturing automobile head lamps. He put the propeller in front on the engine crankshaft instead of behind the wings, as on the Wright's Flyer. Bleriot accepted any effects of the propeller slipstream, which must have been minimal. The pusher configuration of the Wrights' was soon abandoned by other Frenchmen. The Wrights' propeller chain drive system probably required continual maintenance and care and was hazardous, as evidenced by Orville's accident in August 1908 when his passenger, Lt. Selfridge, a U.S. Army observer, was killed. A propeller blade split and the resulting vibration caused the failure of a wire brace supporting a drive shaft bearing, quickly resulting in failure of the aft rudder structure, with loss of control.

Bleriot is said to have crashed more airplanes than anyone else, but resumed flight testing as soon as he recovered from his injuries. Bleriot's airplanes partially enclosed the pilot in the "fuselage," the term to describe the central body of an airplane, derived from the French word *fuselé* meaning spindle-shaped [Figure 4]. Many aviation terms in common use today are of French origin. It has been said that one can not invent anything new, as a Frenchman has always thought of it first. After Wilbur's demonstrations in France the development of aviation continued entirely in Europe. Significant contributions by the U.S. were not made until 1925 when the first large reliable radial air-cooled engines were developed to power the postwar new designs.

At the very start of WWI, on August 4, 1914, the airplane played a very important role in reconnaissance. The British regularly observed the German army's advance through Belgium and western France, probably with the deHaviland BE-2 two-seater tractor biplane. It had a 70 hp air-cooled Renault V8 engine with a four-bladed propeller, giving a maximum speed of

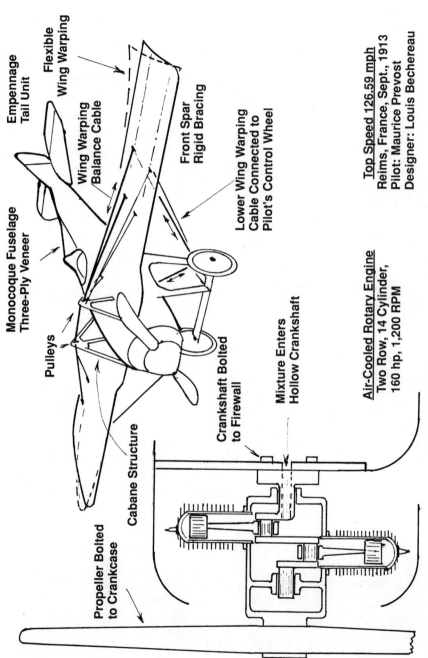

Figure 4—French 1912 Deperdussin Racer

Observation Planes at Start of World War I

British Observation Plane

RAF BE-2 with a Renault air-cooled V-8, 70 mph max. speed, 3 hours' endurance. Probably used to observe German Gen. von Kluck's army sweeping through Belgium and western France, August 24, 1914.

Morane Saulnier Type L, Gnome Rotary, 71 mph max. speed, 2 1/2 hours' endurance. Probably used to discover Gen. von Kluck's turn east, and so aided French Gen. Gallieni to organize the Paris taxis to take soldiers to the Battle of the Marne that saved Paris, September 6, 1914.

French Observation Plane

Last Allied Fighters in World War I

British Fighter

Sopwith Camel, 9-cylinder air-cooled rotary, 115 mph max. speed, 2 1/2 hours' endurance; 5,490 built; highest score of victories.

SPAD SXIIII, Hispano-Suize V-8, 234 hp, 138 mph max. speed, 2 hours' endurance. In the picture—Eddie Rickenbacker, American leading ace; 8,472 built. Bechereau designed the Deperdussin Monoplane Racer of 1913 but designed the SPAD for high stiffness.

French Fighter

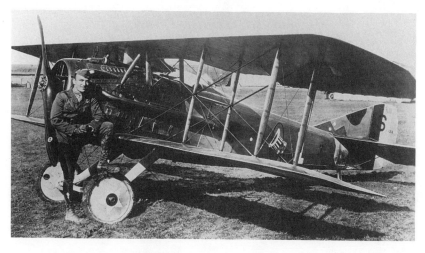

70 mph and an endurance of three hours. The French closely observed the German advance on the east. An important reconnaissance occurred during the few days preceding The Battle of the Marne of September 6, 1914, which was the critical engagement that saved Paris. The turning of the German army which exposed the German flank was observed by French pilots, possibly flying the Morane-Saulnier wire-braced monoplane. Built in 1913, it had a Gnome rotary 80 hp engine, giving a maximum speed of 80 mph and an endurance of 3 hours 26 minutes.

Airplane bombing was attempted early, but was mostly a token effort. The German Taube, a wire-braced monoplane, was used to bomb Paris for a few days starting late in August 1914. Before the war the French had plans for an air force of 3,000 planes. By the time the war ended, the French had actually built 68,000 airplanes, the British 58,000, the Germans 48,000, and the U.S. 15,000, a third of which were Jenny trainers. Combat operations cost the Allies 70 percent of the total they had built by the end of the war. During critical periods new pilots could arrive at the front with only 15 to 20 hours total flying time. Many did not survive a week [Figure 5].

World War I was a period of rapid development in aircraft design, particularly with regard to biplane structures, which could be analyzed for consistent strengths. The Wright brothers and other early designers may have used the safety factor applied to bridges, where the maximum load at failure is about six times the dead weight of the bridge plus the live load on it. The actual loads occurring in accelerated flight during tight turns and dive pullouts must have been learned the hard way, after repeated structural failures, each requiring structural analysis that resulted in improved techniques to stiffen and strengthen the aircraft components. The early monoplanes with their thin wings and wire bracing were too flexible in torsion, although this flexibility was built in for the specific purpose of creating lateral control through wing warping. The wings could suddenly twist-off during a dive at only 1G because the center of the wing stiffness was too far aft of the center of lift. At dive speeds a small change in angle of attack could twist the wing, thus changing the lift [Figure 6].

As a result, the monoplane was replaced by the biplane

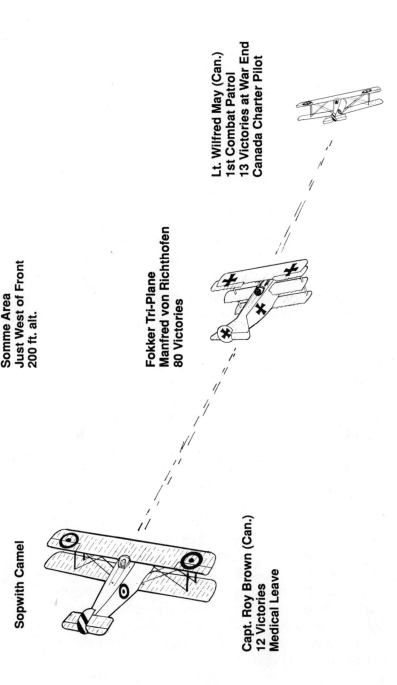

Northern France
Somme Area
Just West of Front
200 ft. alt.

Fokker Tri-Plane
Manfred von Richthofen
80 Victories

Lt. Wilfred May (Can.)
1st Combat Patrol
13 Victories at War End
Canada Charter Pilot

Sopwith Camel

Sopwith Camel

Capt. Roy Brown (Can.)
12 Victories
Medical Leave

Figure 5—Death of the Red Baron, April 21, 1918

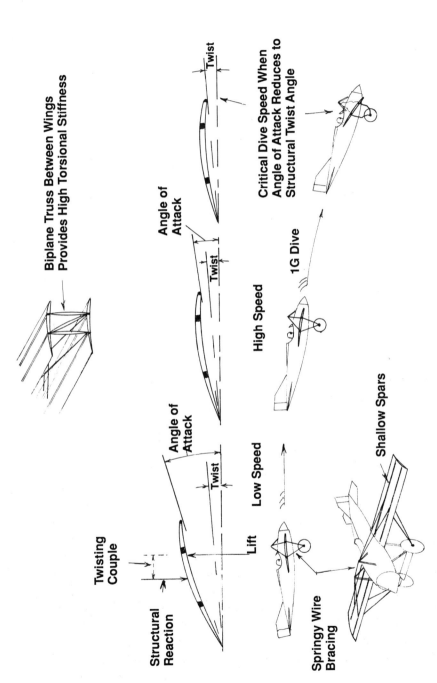

Figure 6—Early Monoplane —Twisting Failures, 1912, the Reason for the Change to Biplanes

with diagonal wire bracing between the wings that formed a truss to provide high torsional stiffness. The new, stiffer biplane structures utilized ailerons instead of wing warping as a means of achieving lateral control.

An exception to the wire-braced biplane design was the Fokker D-1 triplane and the D-V11 biplane. They had thick cantilevered wings with deep beams to take the lifting loads so that no diagonal bracing wires were required. However, they still had vertical struts between the wings near the tips, so that the wings worked together to increase torsional stiffness. The need for these struts was deduced from structural failures in flight, several of which probably resulted in the sudden loss of the wings. In his autobiography Fokker [1890-1939] describes twisting wing failures on his last fighter, the D-V111 cantilever parasol monoplane. It did not have sufficient torsional stiffness until modified. Unfortunately, Fokker devoted most of his autobiography to self aggrandizement, giving little credit to his designer and no mention of the pilots who were killed while attempting to test various solutions to the structural problem, without the safety of parachutes.

The parachute was used during exhibitions in 1797 by the French balloonist, Andre Garnerin. During World War I parachutes were available to the observation balloonists, but not to the Allied airplane pilots. The Germans started using parachutes in their fighters near the end of World War I. The talk among the British pilots at that time was to blame the War Office, "who felt that so convenient a facility for escape might invite pilots to abandon their aircraft without a determined fight!" This attitude was doubly unfortunate because the airplane designers could have benefited greatly from the accounts of pilots who might have thus survived.

Popular aviation writers have often described the World War I planes as flimsy, probably because they were covered with fabric rather than metal. However, the fabric-covered truss of the fuselage is easy to design for strength. In addition, it is easy to repair. Airplanes of today such as the popular fabric covered Piper Cub and the small aerobatic sport biplanes have this same type of structure. By the end of the war new airplane models were substantially stronger and more sophisticated in terms of strength analysis. These biplanes formed a basis for peace time design for the next 10 years or so until the aluminum sheet monocoque structures took over, wherein the covering forms a tube that is strong in bending and stiff in torsion.

The first large use of aluminum alloy in thin sections was in the framework of the Zeppelins, the first of which flew in July 1900. The Zeppelins bombed Britain during WWI. Out of a total of 123 ships in the military, 79 were destroyed. The damage to England was slight. Although their military usefulness was limited, the Zeppelins probably had a major effect in advancing aluminum fabrication techniques later employed in airplane manufacture.

A considerable amount of aluminum was being produced during WWI. Aluminum sheeting was used for cowling in the wartime airplanes. Aluminum castings were used in the engine cylinder blocks of the Hispano-Suiza V-8 that powered the French Spad fighter flown by Rickenbacker and also that powered the British SE-5 fighter. The German Mercedes airplane engine had a cast aluminum crankcase. The basic electrolytic process for aluminum ore reduction was discovered in 1886 independently in Ohio by Hall [1863-1914], who started Alcoa, and by Héroult in Paris. By 1910 a total of 49,200 tons were produced per anum worldwide. This rate of production increased rapidly after 1920. High strength aluminum alloys were developed in Germany between 1903 and 1914.

The first all aluminum airplanes were the work of Hugo Junkers [1855-1935], a professor at the University of Aachen, Germany, where he taught the only course in aviation. In 1915 he designed a structural test specimen for a thick wing that had a smooth outer skin riveted to an inner corrugated skin in which the corrugations ran the length of the span. This provided the column stiffness to be able to take compression loads in a monocoque structure. The Boeing B17 has similar construction. However, in 1918 Junkers abandoned this concept as being too complicated to build and instead designed a cantilever low winged monoplane, the D-1, where the skins were corrugations and roll-formed to the thick airfoil shape, the corrugations running in the direction of the wing chord to provide stiffness so as to eliminate the need for closely spaced wing ribs. The spanwise wing bending forces were resisted by truss spars. Junkers built less than 100 airplanes during the war. This same type of construction was used in the tri-motored Fords of the 1920's.

Junkers was the pioneer in the use of the thick airfoil sections that make cantilevered wings possible by providing the combination of sufficient bending strength and high torsional stiffness. In 1912 he built a wind tunnel where he tested over a hundred wings between 1913 and 1917. Based on the data he thus obtained, he was able to design thick cantilever wings which eliminated the need for external bracing. This also provided space for fuel tanks. He and another German, Rohrbach, were lone pioneers in the design of all-metal sheet aluminum structures for airplanes. Their work received little attention until the mid 1920's when more powerful engines permitted larger airplanes that in turn required metal structures.

Junkers may have been the first airplane designer to understand the vortex theory of airfoil lift which had been published as early as 1903. This theory demonstrated that the part of the total airplane drag resulting from lift decreased as the wing span was increased. Accordingly, the monoplanes he designed had higher spans than the biplanes. He was also familiar with the thick airfoils sections that had been mathematically derived by the famous Russian Professor Joukowski [1847-1921] in 1910. They may have exchanged ideas before the war.

During World War I aerodynamic theory was of limited use. Most of the knowledge for new airplane designs continued to come directly from experiences gained during actual flights. The development of aerodynamics stability and control resulted from the need to improve accurate firing during tight maneuvering in a dogfight. The optimum location of the center of gravity was found usually by experiment. This was sometimes adjusted by lengthening or shortening the engine mount. Pilots instinctively evaluated the longitudinal stability by the sensitive feel of the stick and their ability to fly in smooth curved flight paths or "hands-off" in straight and level flight. The desirability of a technical approach to stability was recognized early; reports on this subject were published in England in 1904 and 1911 by Bryan and in 1917 by the British Advisory Committee for Aeronautics. This may have helped the designers to size the horizontal tail and the fore and aft placement of the center of gravity with respect to the wing. Some of the early airplanes had no provision for longitudinal trim. The stabilizer was adjusted on the ground to provide minimum stick forces during level flight. Later on in flight trim capability was provided by a "bungee," which was a low-rate long spring on the elevator control that the pilot could adjust in flight. By the war's end the large biplane bombers could be trimmed in flight by a screw jack on the stabilizer and a cable control to the cockpit.

The wing sections changed very slowly from the thin wings simulating birds to the thick wings that were mathematically derived by Joukowski in a paper he published in 1910. Most of the very early designers and those during World War I seem to have assumed that wings should be thin and feature sharp leading edges to achieve high lift and low drag. Wind tunnel development of airfoils was attempted during the war in England, France, and Germany. These tunnels could only accommodate small model wings. Furthermore, they were capable of only low speeds. The early data showed that thick wing sections had lower maximum lift and higher drag than thin sections. Good wind tunnel data that showed the advantage of thicker wing sections were not generally obtained until after the war.

Sharp leading edges on most of the biplanes caused a sudden stall without warning [Figure 7]. This bad characteristic was aggravated by the small vertical tails which caused tendencies for the airplane to yaw in the stall when the tail was blanketed in the thick stalled wing wake leading to a tail spin. The famous Fokker D-V11 fighter that appeared in April 1918 was an exception to the conventional wisdom in that it had a thick cantilevered wing with a more rounded leading edge. The Allied pilots said it could "hang on its prop" in a tight turn or during a steep pull-up as it sought to aim its guns at its opponent in a dogfight. The thick Fokker wing had higher maximum lift potential by virtue of its rounded leading edge. Any pilot who has ever flown one of the old biplanes that had a sharp leading edge will remember that it had an abrupt stall with no warning whatsoever.

The training biplanes of WWII had thicker wings than the early biplanes. In order to make these biplanes spin like the early biplanes for purposes of military training, a sharp triangular strip was attached to the leading edge. When used as crop dusters, this strip was removed to improve maneuverability.

The early biplanes had to be landed directly into the wind

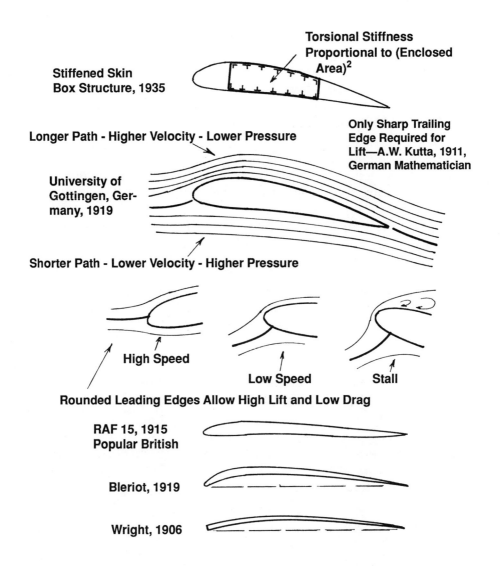

Stiffened Skin Box Structure, 1935

Torsional Stiffness Proportional to (Enclosed Area)^2

Longer Path - Higher Velocity - Lower Pressure

Only Sharp Trailing Edge Required for Lift—A.W. Kutta, 1911, German Mathematician

University of Gottingen, Germany, 1919

Shorter Path - Lower Velocity - Higher Pressure

High Speed

Low Speed

Stall

Rounded Leading Edges Allow High Lift and Low Drag

RAF 15, 1915 Popular British

Bleriot, 1919

Wright, 1906

<u>Early Designers Copied Bird Wings</u>
Thin to permit wing warping
Sharp leading edge, maybe for "low drag"
Curvature for lift

Figure 7--Thick Airfoils, a Critical Step Forward

Cantilever Wooden Wings—1918

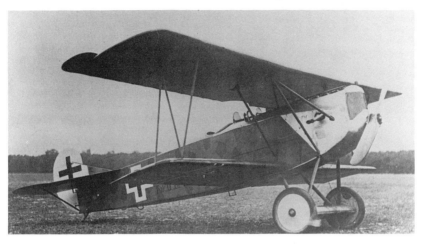

German Fighter

Fokker D-VII, Mercedes 6-cylinder, 124 mph max. speed, 1 1/2 hours' endurance; cantilever wings, wood structure; fabric covered. Note strut bracing between wing tips for torsional stiffness.

9-cylinder air-cooled rotary; 1 1/2 hour endurance; cantilever wing with plywood covering for torsional stiffness. Forerunner of postwar construction on Fokker tri-motors.

Fokker D-VIII

on three points in order to dig the tail skid in to improve directional stability and to slow down to taxi speeds. Ground loops must have been very common when the pilot failed to do so. Brakes on small planes were not required until about 1935 when tail skids were outlawed at Boston and other airports to prevent damage to the dirt and sod surfaces before the day of runways. This is a good measure on how long the wartime level of technology persisted.

In the early 1900's gasoline engine development was accelerated by the motor car industry, particularly for racers. A 1908 Fiat racer had a four-cylinder engine with four valves per cylinder, an overhead camshaft, and dual ignition. The Italians have always been fanatics on racing. It can be said that there is really nothing new in piston engines today other than optimization. While engines could be increased in power by increasing their size, the engines during WWI were handicapped because the gasoline was about 40 octane. The Germans increased the octane by adding benzol, distilled from coal. Compression ratios were limited to about 4.5 by knock. Engines using this octane lost over 25 percent of their power as compared to modern engines of the same displacement operating at the same low rpm using gasoline from a filling station. The last versions of the WWI Mercedes had a compression ratio of 6 to improve high altitude performance but had to be operated at low altitudes at part throttle to avoid detonation. Lead tetraethel additive was not discovered until in 1923 by Thomas Midgley, an engineer who worked for Delco in Dayton, Ohio, permitting higher compression and supercharging for more power at high altitudes. This greatly accelerated the development high powered engines.

The small size of the early engines necessitated very low airplane weights. This was most readily accomplished by designing externally braced wings and fixed landing gears. As a result, the drag was high and airplane sizes remained small. The top speeds were as low as 35 mph in the first airplanes. By the end of World War I, fighters had 160 hp engines and were reaching speeds of 135 mph. Power has always paced airplane development. The fixed air-cooled engines that were tried would hardly cool at all and would run only for short periods before overheating. Bleriot made his famous English Channel crossing in 1909 with an Anzani 30 hp 3 cylinder fixed air-cooled engine

Most Significant Advancements—1908 to 1919

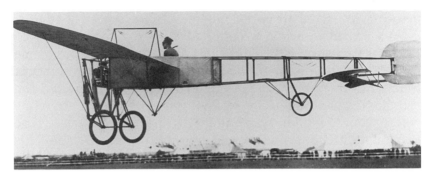

Bleriot X-25

Crossed the English Channel July 1909. Anzani 3-cylinder air-cooled 25 hp; max. speed 46.6 mph. Wire-braced monoplane with wing warping lateral control. This was Louis Bleriot's 11th try, starting in 1901.

Alumnium cantilever structure. Only 47 built before the end of the war. Comparable in weight and performance with biplanes but needed retractable gear and drag reduction to take advantage of the new construction.

Junkers CL-1

that was near overheating, with the possibility of seizing before he reached the English shore. But this was near the limit in power for the fixed air-cooled engine. Bleriot's speed of 46 mph did not provide much of a cooling blast.

The first successful air-cooled engine was the 50 hp Gnome rotary that was prominent in the first international air meet at Reims in the 1909 air meet. High cooling airflow around the cylinders was obtained by revolving the whole radial engine where the propeller was mounted on the crankcase, the crankshaft being stationary and mounted on the fuselage. This engine was very light in weight and was comparatively reliable for those times. However, it acted as a gyroscope in a turn, causing the airplane to pitch up or down, depending on the direction. Avoiding a stall and spin in a climbing turn could be tricky. Two-row 18-cylinder rotary engines were built, but the gyroscopic torques were much too high so the rotary was abandoned. If the reader should have the opportunity of examining a Gnome engine in a museum, he will be impressed with the fine design and machining to achieve light weight.

By the end of World War I both France and England were using the French Hispano-Suiza V8 water-cooled engines with up to 230 hp in the British SE5 and the French Spad fighters. The German Fokker D-V11 and the Albatros D-111 used the 6 cylinder 175 hp water-cooled Mercedes D-111. Several V12 engines appeared by the end of the war, notably the Rolls Royce Eagle. This led to the development of the Rolls Royce Merlin engine that powered World War II fighters, including the Hurricane and the Spitfire that won the Battle of Britain and the North American P51 that escorted the bombers over Germany.

2

Airmail and Early Transports

THE FOUR YEARS of World War I were a time of change when the "pilot-innovator," who searched for an original solution to flight, gave way to the "pilot-engineer," who sought to design the best fighter. During the war research laboratories were formed to do wind tunnel and flight testing in England in 1912 at the Royal Aircraft Factory at Farnborough, and in the U.S. in 1916 at the National Advisory Committee for Aeronautics [NACA] at Langley Field, Virginia. Aeronautical engineering had become recognized as a pursuit distinct from the foundations provided by civil and mechanical engineering. In 1916 courses in aeronautics were established at MIT and the University of Michigan. Soon to follow were the University of New York, Stanford, the University of Washington, and Purdue.

After the war the full employment of trained aeronautical engineers was hindered by a lack of demand for new designs, due to a large supply of surplus airplanes that was more than enough to meet the needs of military training. In fact, the surplus airplanes and spare engines were so cheap that for nominal fees, the barnstormers would crash them. For $400 a Curtiss JN-4 "Jenny" biplane trainer could be bought new still in its crate. A new 90 hp Curtiss OX-5 V8 engine cost $50.

Postwar Surplus and a Glimpse of the New Era

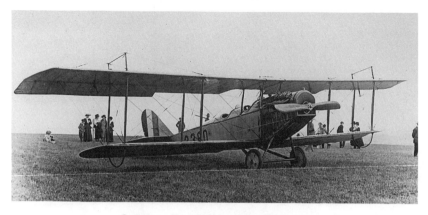

Curtiss JN-4D Wartime Trainer

OX-5 V-8 engine—90 hp—postwar surplus. Used in barnstorming shows and for ride. Plenty of struts for wing walkers to hang on to.

Curtiss D-12 V-12 engine—retractable landing gear—cantilever wing. On first flight wing fluttered, corrected by plywood wing covering. Won 1924 Pulitzer race, Harry Mills piloting. Top speed 233 mph. Designed by Albert Verville, civilian engineer in Army Air Corps. Encounter with flutter, the problem that delayed cantilever monoplanes until mass-balanced ailerons came into use in 1934. The Air Corps at McCook Field and Curtiss opposed monoplanes and retractable gears. Lt. Monteith of Cook Field wrote a textbook expressing this view. He left the Air Corps to become chief engineer at Boeing in 1926. Two years later his engineers started design of an all-metal cantilever wing and a retractable gear for the Monomail.

Verville-Sperry R-3 Racer, 1922

By 1925 these World War I trainers were being replaced by new biplanes, which had a welded steel tube fuselage, a front open cockpit wide enough for two joy riders, and a surplus engine. At this time there were at least six different makes in production. All were very similar, the pilot-designers basing their new designs on the immediately preceding designs. Engineers were hired to do the stress analysis. The first U.S. air regulations requiring stress analysis were signed into law by President Coolidge in May 1926 as part of the Air Commerce Act, which was administered by the Department of Commerce. It contained only stress analysis methods obtained from the Army. Stability and control characteristics were not specified but were left to the approval of the Department of Commerce pilots.

Pilot licenses were not issued until 1926. Les Tower, the Boeing pilot who was killed in the B-17 prototype in 1935, had License No. 30. The early pilots that were flying when the air regulations came into effect obtained their licenses under the "grandfather clause." Clayton Scott, who was head of Boeing Production Flight Test after the war, received License No. 2155 in February 1927, by which time he had accumulated 4 hours and 20 minutes of flying time, which had been spread over several months while he was working as a mechanic. For his flight check he had to circle the field once and land and then show his log book to the inspector. Herb Munter, who test flew the first Boeing airplane, the B&W, had License No. 2599. A little later on the flying time requirements were formalized, with 10 hours solo required for a private license, 50 hours for a limited commercial, and 200 hours for a transport license.

In view of all the surplus small airplanes after World War I, airmail was a sensible starting point for commercial aviation at that time. Historically, airmail started in the U.S. in August 1918, principally as a means of training military pilots for the war. The early airmail service, which was operated by the U.S. Post Office Department, served to show the inadequacies of the surplus equipment. By 1926 the WWI surplus was being replaced by higher performance airplanes with much more powerful and reliable engines. The Army and the Navy supported the development of the larger engines, both liquid- and air-cooled, to increase the power output over that of the war surplus water-cooled engines, principally the Hispano-Suiza 150 hp V-8 used in the Curtiss Jenny and the Standard trainers, and the Liberty V-12 used in the deHaviland bombers. The Navy favored the air-cooled engines because they were lighter and could therefore take off in a shorter distance on aircraft carriers. This was of great concern to the Navy because some of their airplanes were so underpowered for their weight that they would have to lose altitude beyond the end of the deck to attain sufficient airspeed to initiate the climb.

The Navy also favored air-cooled engines for carrier operations because one fifth of all their engine failures were due to water cooling problems. Although the Army favored liquid-cooled engines to obtain higher speeds, S.D. Heron, one of their engineers at McCook Field in Dayton, Ohio, pioneered the development of the air-cooled cylinder construction now universally in use. He patented the hollow exhaust valve to improve cooling. Liquid sodium was used in the hollow valve to transfer the heat from the valve head to the valve stem where the heat was conducted to the cooling fins on the cylinder head. The first promising air-cooled engine in the U.S. was the Lawrance-Wright J-4 200 hp nine-cylinder radial with a displacement of 788 cubic inches that appeared in 1924.

In September 1924 the Wright Company president, F.B. Rentschler, was impatient with the Wright board of directors for not expeditiously exploiting the principles demonstrated in the J-4 to achieve higher power outputs. He resigned and took the top Wright engineers with him to Pratt & Whitney in Hartford Connecticut, which at that time was a machine tool manufacturer with machine tools capable of building engines. Rentschler and his team had as their first objective the design and production of a 400 hp engine with 1,340 cubic inches displacement, the "Wasp." In 1926 it was successfully tested at the desired power output. The Wasp became famous for its reliability. It was selected for new airplane designs as late as 1951.

The subsidizing of the mail by the U.S. Post Office was an incentive for designing larger and faster airplanes. These were made possible by the more powerful Wright and Pratt & Whitney radial air-cooled engines. In 1927 Boeing produced the Model 40A biplane with an enclosed cabin with seats for two passengers along with the mail. During that same year John Northrup

[1895-1981] broke away from the traditional biplane to produce the Lockheed Vega, the first clean commercial passenger plane. It had a high cantilevered wing and a round monocoque four-passenger body. In 1929 Northrup made giant step ahead of most everybody in the design of the all-metal Alpha, a single place low wing mailplane with unique sheet-metal construction with stiffened wing skins instead of the traditional truss spars to taking the wing bending loads. His wing construction was called "multi-cellular," with six equally spaced light spars instead of the usual two heavy spars. The sheet metal on the wing surface was stiffened by many small "hat" sections that prevented the skin from buckling under compression loading. From an engineering standpoint John Northrup was unique. As a self-taught man, he was not inhibited by the traditional approaches usually taught in college.

In 1926 4.6 million miles were flown with 433,000 pounds of mail and 5,782 passengers. In 1929 20.2 million miles were flown with 7 million pounds of mail and 165,000 passengers, or 122 miles per passenger. This increase provided financial encouragement for future development of passenger transports. In the meantime, military production was keeping most airplane companies alive, especially after the stock market crash in the fall of 1929. With the new, more reliable Wright and Pratt & Whitney engines, over-ocean flights appeared to carry a reasonable risk to the adventurous pilots. Lindberg's solo flight from New York to Paris in May 1927 attracted financial support across the aeronautical industry. Aviation stocks on the New York Exchange soared, and along with these the stock of Seaboard Airlines, a southeast coastal railroad, which eager investors assumed to be an aviation company.

Civilian racers were designed to exploit the new engines. The first of these, the Travel Aire Mystery S, was designed and built in Wichita by two engineers in a remarkably short time during the summer of 1928. Travel Aire was the forerunner of Beech. This low-winged wire-braced fabric-covered monoplane with a Wright 300 hp engine beat the Army pursuits at the Cleveland Air Races in August 1929, where the fastest lap around the race course was 208 mph. Its manufacturing required only simple tools, such as an acetylene welding torch to assemble the tubular fuselage structure and woodworking tools

Break From Tradition by Independent Designers

Lockheed Vega
Cantilever plywood-covered wing—Monocoque body—First flight
July 1927. Designed by John Northrup. Won 1928 air races. Wiley
Post around-the-world flight in 1931.

Travel Aire Mystery S
Wire braces—Designed by Rawdon and Burnham in Wichita. Won
1929 air race against Army Pursuits.

All metal—First flight late 1929. Later model had landing gear
fairings. Pilot in photo is Eddie Allen.
Northrup Alpha Prototype

to build the wing ribs and spars. The relative ease of designing and manufacturing racers attracted many pilots and engineers to this area of prides and thrills.

Shortly after the war the British and French began modifying the large wartime biplane twin-engine bombers into transports that carried up to 10 passengers for service on the short routes in western Europe and across the channel. Larger biplane transports followed with as many as four engines, mounted in various locations. In the U.S. the cruising speeds were less than 100 mph.

The multi-engine transport era was started by Fokker whose tri-motor was to become famous with the North Pole flight by Admiral Byrd in May 1926 and the trans-Pacific flight of Kingsford Smith in June 1928. The tri-motor was the result of adding two engines out under the wing to a Fokker large high monoplane that had been developed in Holland shortly after the war for long distance operation between Amsterdam and the Dutch East Indies. The plywood covering on the thick wing section provided the high torsional stiffness that was necessary in the high span cantilevered wing. This was close to the ultimate design in wooden wings (up to the wooden deHaviland airplanes: the Comet racer and the Mosquito bomber) and pointed the way to the monoplane, as the biplane formula was near its limit. The Fokker era came to an abrupt end in March 1931 when the Notre Dame football coach, Knute Rockne, was killed in a crash on a TWA flight over Kansas, due to a wing failure which was attributed to rot.

The Fokker tri-motor competed in the Ford Reliability Tour, a 1,860-mile circuit in the central U.S. Henry Ford was sufficiently impressed to build a transport similar to the Fokker but with aluminum construction resembling the Junkers structure, using corrugated skins and truss spars. The Ford tri-motor had very high drag, and a ride felt like going through "glue" compared to a modern airplane. The engine in the nose had less thrust than the wing engines due to the drag of the large body in the slipstream. The first Fords were powered by the Wright J-5 220 hp Whirlwind and could hardly maintain level flight with a failed engine. The cruising speed was maybe 120 mph and the range was 600 miles. A transcontinental trip took a day and a half if the weather was favorable. The flight altitudes were near the cumulus clouds and often bumpy.

The Tri-Motor Era—1925-1934

Fokker FVIIB Tri-motor with 3 Wright J-5 engines

Cruising speed, 110 mph —range, 1,600 miles—8 passengers. Wing engines added to single engine FII for Ford 1925 Reliability Tour. Famous flights: Byrd to North Pole, Kingsford Smith, San Francisco to Australia, 1928. Right man in photo is famed PAA pilot Musick; Havana 1928.

Last model with P-&W Wasp. Cruising speed, 113 mph—13 passengers. Operated by major airlines in U.S. until the B-247 and DC-2.

Ford 5 AT

A sleeper train took three days coast to coast, but because the train passengers might have been in so much better shape upon arrival, air travel might have been of little or no advantage. Furthermore most passenger trips were between major cities less than 400 miles apart. A total of 194 Ford tri-motors were manufactured at a maximum production rate of four a week, when the end came in June 1933, five months after the first flight of what was to be the modern airliner, the Boeing 247. However, although the Fokkers, the Fords, the Curtiss Condor twin-engine biplane, and the Boeing 80 tri-motor biplane added little to the state of the art in engineering, all served to increase passenger travel and establish the airlines and airways.

3

The 247 Airliner

IN THE LATE 1920's the airplane designers broke out of the doldrums in terms of performance. Racing planes, such as the British Supermarine S-5 Schneider Trophy Winner had increased the top speeds to over 300 mph, although they had thin wire-braced wings and a general configuration that was obviously limited in size. Despite these limitations they indicated possibilities to the more imaginative transport designers. It is hard to determine the sequence of thoughts of the designers as they examined each other's creation. The outstanding airplanes provided the challenges as time went on. All of the airplanes that advanced the state of the art had thick, cantilever wings and were powered by radial engines. These features had been well proven by Junkers, Fokker, and Ford, although their transports lacked aerodynamic streamlining. Some of the more notable airplanes that combined advancements in structures and aerodynamics were the works of inspired individuals [Figure 8].

> 1927 - Lockheed Vega - Wood monocoque body - High
>   wing - Fixed gear
> 1929 - Northrup Alpha - All metal- 6-Spar wing - Low
>   wing - Fixed gear

Verville-Sperry Racer
Retractable Landing Gear
Curtiss D-12 Engine
233 MPH   1924

Lockheed Vega
Monocoque Body
Fixed Landing Gear
Wood   1927

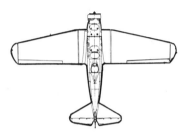

Boeing Monomail
Retractable Landing Gear
All Metal   P&W Hornet
1930

Northrup Alpha
All Metal
Fixed Landing Gear
1930

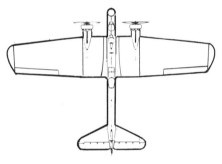

Boeing B-9 Bomber
Retractable Landing Gear
Nacelles on Leading Edge
All Metal   P & W Hornet
1930

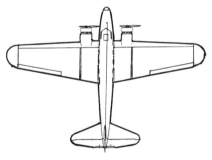

Boeing 247
P&W Wasp
10 Passengers
February 1933

All Shown to Same Scale

Figure 8—Cantilever Monoplanes That Influenced the 247

October 1929 - Consolidated Fleetster - All metal - High
wing - Fixed gear
May 1930 - Boeing Monomail - All metal - 2 Truss Spars
- Low Wing - Retractable gear

These planes could be classified as high performance single-engine demonstrators and had seats for four to eight passengers. They were designed and built with private financing for a precarious market, as the transport business was tending towards multi-engine types. A high performance multi-engine airplane had yet to be designed. These single-engine airplanes showed the advantages of competition and freedom of thought unhindered by specifications from the Army and Navy, who were supporting a large part of the airplane industry. Many Vegas were built and were widely used. Wiley Post [1899-1935] made his 1933 solo flight around the world in a Vega. The Northrup Alpha was notable in demonstrating aluminum sheet metal construction with smooth surfaces as compared with the Ford tri-motors with corrugated skins. The Monomail added the retractable landing gear to the metal cantilever wing.

This change from the Boeing biplanes was attributed to Eddie Hubbard, a very early Boeing pilot, and Claire Egtvedt, the chief designer-salesman at Boeing. He graduated from the University of Washington in Civil Engineering and was hired by Boeing in 1916. Pilots like Hubbard had fewer inhibitions than engineers when it came to visualizing new designs. They tended to circulate more freely within the aeronautical community to see what others were doing, thus instigating competition between the designers of the airplane companies scattered over the U.S. Breaking a designer loose from a traditional approach required outside interference, and Hubbard may have been impressed by the Vega and the Alpha.

The Monomail had a low cantilever wing that provided room for a relatively short lightweight retractable landing gear. The low wing seems quite logical now but some of the early designers had a false notion that high wings were more stable laterally. This belief was based on an erroneous idea of "pendulum stability." Stinson, who built popular cabin airplanes in the early 1930's, claimed this feature. Low-winged airplanes attain lateral stability equivalent to that achieved in the high-winged

Truss Type Wing Rib

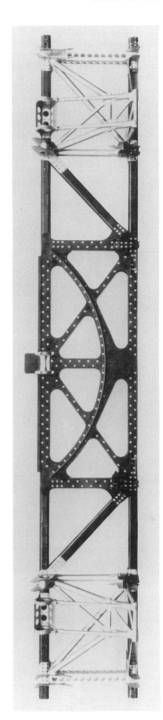

Landing Gear Supports

Body Centerline

Truss-type front spar—spars carry all wing bending loads.

Landing Gear Supports

Monomail Wing Structure—Similar on B-9 and 247 Airliner

airplanes by having about six degrees of dihedral angle in their wings, which corrects side slips.

The Monomail was so aerodynamically clean that the engine would over-rev in level flight at full throttle because the propeller was adjusted on the ground to a low pitch to provide high enough rpm for take-off. Achieving the highest possible cruising speed would have required a controllable propeller, which was not yet available. Only two Monomails were built, since the single-engine mail-plus-passenger plane was giving way to multi-engine designs. In 1934 the Department of Commerce made multi-engine configurations a requirement for passenger transports.

What had been learned on the Monomail regarding low wings, retractable landing gears, and all-metal structures was soon applied to the Boeing B-9 twin-engine bomber. This was a corporate venture that started with some Air Corps encouragement that was probably influenced by the high performance of the Monomail. The reduction in drag from the old tri-motors required a completely new multi-engine airplane configuration. The transport designers in the industry asked the NACA to run wind tunnel tests on the wing-mounted engines because they felt that the tri-motor nacelles had excessively high drag.

Preliminary tests were run during October 1929 at Langley Field, Virginia. By moving the nacelle up from under the wing where they had been installed on the tri-motors to where the engine thrust line was centered on the airfoil, the nacelle drag was reduced from 152 pounds to 25 pounds at 100 mph. Further wind tunnel tests confirmed this location as having the lowest drag, and thus the mounting of nacelles on the wing leading edge became a standard configuration. This experience marked the beginning of reliance of the designers on wind tunnel testing for drag reduction. The first application of the new nacelle location was on the Fokker XB-8 bomber. Fokker lost the production contract because XB-8 still had the traditional Fokker wooden wing and steel tube fuselage as compared to aluminum sheet-metal construction that had been demonstrated in several new airplanes.

The detail design of the Boeing B-9 bomber was started about six months after the NACA tests were completed. Its first flight was in April 1931. The B-9 derived much of its design from the Monomail, including the structure and the retractable

1933 Airliner and Its Precursors

Monomail—1930—Retractable landing gear—All metal

B-9 Bomber—1931—Nacelles centered on wing

Model 247

landing gear. In June 1931 the prototype was flown to Wright Field. The B-9 was a revolutionary airplane and had a top speed of 188 mph, which was faster than the contemporary U.S. Army pursuits. It was the obvious replacement of the U.S. Army Keystone biplane bombers that had a top speed of 121 mph. However, only seven B-9's were built. Boeing lost the large production order to the Martin B-10, which started out as a private venture like the B-9. The B-10 had a larger bomb bay, more powerful engines, and an enclosed cockpit.

Despite its early termination the B-9 program contributed additional technical advances, including control surface trim tabs and servo tabs to reduce pilot forces that resulted from the increase in size and speed. It also uncovered a new high-speed problem, control surface flutter. To correct this, mass balancing of control surfaces about the hinge line became required. The B-9 had tail flutter which was aggravated by the torsional flexibility of the long slim body and by the cut-outs in the monocoque body structure for the open cockpits.

Soon after the B-9 high-speed performance had been demonstrated, the possibility of applying the B-9 developments to a twin-engine transport was considered. This resulted in the 247 airliner, which established the configuration of transports up to the time of the jets. The 247 was advertised as having a speed of "three miles a minute." Performance far above that of the existing airliners was achieved through the combination of an all-metal aerodynamically clean airframe, low drag nacelles, sufficiently large engines, and retractable landing gear.

The 247 first flew in February 1933. The end of the slow tri-motors transports could not come too soon for the airlines in the U.S. The changeover in Europe was slower. After the introduction of the 247 and later the Douglas DC-2, an American aviation writer wrote that the slow British biplane transports had a "built-in headwind," causing quite a fuss in the loyal British aviation magazines. The 247 set the pattern in the world, especially in the DC-3 and the four-engine transports that followed. As a result of the improved performance, the transport business expanded to the point where the introduction of the jet transport became economically feasible.

While the 247 introduced the combination of a low drag airframe and an all-metal structure, a high drag problem remained in connection with the cooling of the radial engine. The cylinder head temperature on the early slow airplanes were high and this limited the power output. Therefore, the early engines were installed with bare cylinders out in the air stream without cowling. The air-cooled engine had long been recognized as needing cowling.

Not until 1934 was the problem solved by the combination of a long ring cowl plus tight baffling around the engine cylinders. This development occurred in time for the Douglas DC-1 but was too late for the 247. Up to that time there was poor cooperation between the airplane and engine designers, dating back to WWI. The rotary engines in the biplane fighters had a ring cowl to protect the pilot from the engine exhaust and the liberal spray of the castor oil lubricant then in use. The ring cowl on the rotary engine was sealed at the top and with an exit on the bottom. Castor oil could stand higher temperatures than the early petroleum oils. While this cowl reduced the drag below that of a bare engine, the power being absorbed by the whirling engine cylinders was unknown. The engine designer would claim a high power output, based on the test stand where the torque of the stationary crankshaft was measured. But the airplane designer would claim that the low airplane top speed that was measured in flight was due to low engine power, since they had estimated that the airplane drag must be low. The differences of opinion were due to the uncertainty in the drag associated with cooling the engine.

The fixed-radial engines that followed the rotary were hard to cool at the low flight speeds and high powers in a climb, and the cylinders were left exposed without cowling. In 1928 the NACA developed a long cowl in a wind tunnel at Langley Field to measure drag and cooling effectiveness. This cowl partially smoothed the airflow around the cylinders, thus reducing drag. Although long cowls had been tried before, they had been abandoned because of high cylinder temperatures. The NACA cowl was used on fast racing planes as early as 1929, but on the slower planes it restricted the airflow over the engine cylinders too much. Because of this the Boeing Monomail and the B-9 bomber had a much shorter ring cowl, named the "Townend Ring," after its British inventor. This same cowl was used on the 247's when they were delivered to United Airlines early in 1933.

The final resolution to the drag problem was achieved by a joint effort between Pratt & Whitney and Chance Vought Corporation, the builder of single-engine airplanes for the Navy. The Vought plant was located next door to Pratt & Whitney in East Hartford. Both were subsidiaries of United Aircraft Corporation. One can imagine that the chief engineers of each organization would occasionally have lunch together. When they ran out of pleasant things to talk about, the subject of drag resulting from cooling might come up. One can also imagine that they finally tired of this discussion and decided to resolve the issue once and for all by running flight tests on a Vought airplane that was powered by a Pratt & Whitney engine. They took the direct approach by simultaneously measuring engine cylinder temperatures and airplane speeds in flight. The challenge was to decrease drag as determined by airplane speed, and at the same time lower the cylinder temperatures.

The solution they finally arrived at after much testing was the combination of the NACA long cowl with very refined tight baffling around the engine cylinders that guided the air through the cylinder cooling fins. The gaps between the cylinders were blocked to prevent wasted airflow, as this would result in turbulence and more drag. The air that cooled the cylinder was only that which passed between the cylinder fins. This system was named "pressure cooling."

The first use of this was on a racing plane. Prior to the test flight the designer did not realize that the ram pressure inside the cowl nose lip in front of the engine would be high, causing a forward thrust on the cowl. The cowl was weakly mounted on the cylinder head rocker boxes, and when this failed, the cowl moved forward into the propeller with a "screech." This evidence of drag reduction was too good! Today this engine installation looks very reasonable, but aviation history is full of "obvious" design configurations that took a long time to discover. These flight tests required many changes in the cylinder baffling. In recounting the improvement, a bare cylinder lost 16 percent of its power due to drag. The final solution reduced this to 6 percent while increasing the speed of the Vought observation plane 15 mph over that with just the bare cylinders. At the same time, the cylinder head temperature was lowered 15° F. This was a considerable improvement, as the tests were run using a biplane with high inherent drag. The baffling was found to be absolutely necessary on twin-row engines that were used later on the DC-3 and on all future installations of air-cooled engines. The tests were conducted from June 1931 to January 1933, too late for the 247.

The higher speeds that were being attained in the 247 era brought on a new technical obstacle, known as "flutter." This was a divergent vibratory oscillation of the hinged control surfaces in which the aerodynamic forces on an aileron would cause the wing to bend and twist. The amplitude of the oscillation could increase to the point where the control surface separated from the airplane. In the worst case this oscillation could result in the failure of the wing. Some small monoplane racers were the first to experience this phenomena. Early attempts to build cantilever military pursuits failed because of aileron flutter. This accounts for the long epoch of the torsionally stiff biplane.

The cure for aileron flutter was simple, requiring mass balancing about the hinge line. The theory of flutter first showed up in the U.S. in an NACA report in 1928 [Figure 9]. However, the engineering solution derived from the theory was only partially used on the 247, where the aileron control system had a worm drive that was almost irreversible. While this prevented flutter, it doubled the pilot forces and prevented hands-off centering of the control wheel. The 247 elevator utilized leading edge mass balancing to prevent flutter.

By the time the 247 was being designed, the longer airline routes had been consolidated into four major airlines, American, TWA, Eastern, and United. This was the work of Postmaster General Walter Brown of the Hoover administration. Boeing had founded United Airlines and operated it in the early years. Boeing had a strong incentive to design a revolutionary airliner after the experience with the B-9 bomber. At that time Boeing was a part of United Aircraft and Transport Corporation, a holding company formed by National City Bank of New York. This consortium included Pratt & Whitney and Hamilton Propellers. One would have expected that this organization would have provided large benefits in contributing to the design choices that were made on the 247, especially since Phillip Johnson, the president of United Aircraft Corporation, had

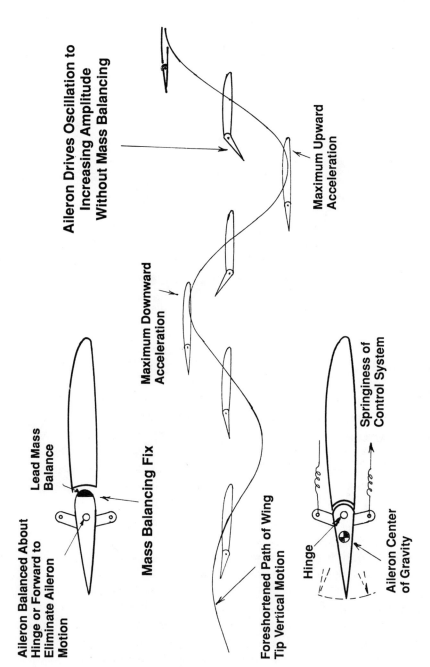

Aileron Drives Oscillation to
Increasing Amplitude
Without Mass Balancing

Maximum Upward
Acceleration

Maximum Downward
Acceleration

Aileron Balanced About
Hinge or Forward to
Eliminate Aileron
Motion

Lead Mass
Balance

Mass Balancing Fix

Foreshortened Path of Wing
Tip Vertical Motion

Springiness of
Control System

Hinge

Aileron Center
of Gravity

Figure 9—Control Surface Flutter

formerly been president of both Boeing Airplane Company and United Airlines. But in fact, the opposite proved to be the case. The holding company must not have had a knowledgeable staff which could mediate differences between the designers and the airline, and so the final design of the 247 was marked by several disagreements.

At that time United was flying 18 passengers in the Boeing 80A tri-motor, and wanted the 247 to have a much bigger capacity than the 10-passenger design that was finally built. However, Boeing was concerned about speed, weight, single-engine ceiling, and cost, and so kept the size small. Pratt & Whitney urged Boeing to use the larger Hornet engine which had 575 hp, the same engine that was used on the B-9 and the Monomail.

Instead, Boeing wanted to use the 525 hp Wasp, which was 4 1/2 inches less in diameter. This engine was more highly developed than the Hornet, producing more power in relation to its weight. In addition, the United pilots much preferred the Wasp because of its reputation for dependability. While these decisions on the 247 were being made, both Pratt & Whitney and Wright were working on larger engines, so the question was whether to build an airplane around an engine whose performance was assured or delay the development of the 247 until larger engines were thoroughly tested.

Unfortunately, the corporate lock-up between Boeing and Pratt & Whitney prevented Boeing from considering a forthcoming more powerful Wright 1820 engine that was later used on the Douglas DC-1 and the Boeing B-17. An interesting question was whether Pratt & Whitney gave Boeing the benefit of future development projections, or whether Boeing simply had a fear of attempting too much at one time. Perhaps Boeing could not imagine any competition from the tri-motor manufacturers. These may have been factors in Boeing's decision to build a transport that turned out to be small in comparison with the DC-1.

The use of the controllable propeller was another critical design decision. This would permit maximum engine rpm for minimum distance take-offs and improved climb, and then higher pitch for cruise. Full throttle could be used at high speed without exceeding the maximum allowable engine rpm. The

Martin B-10

Enclosed cockpit—Large internal bomb bay. Won the production contract over the Boeing B-9, 1932. Loss left the Boeing factory open for the 247 airliner.

247 had the ground adjustable propellers like the Monomail and that were commonly in use. The pitch could be set on the ground by rotating the blades in a clamp on the hub. Boeing's experiences with the clean Monomail had indicated the desirability of a controllable propeller. When the Monomail first rolled out of the factory, the pitch was set so high in anticipation of a high top speed that it would not even taxi, much less take off. In order to have a reasonable take-off rpm, the pitch had to be decreased, resulting in considerable loss in cruising speed to stay under the engine rpm limits. With the compromise fixed propeller pitch, the Monomail had a reputation for excessively long take-off runs at high altitude airports in Montana, particularly on hot days.

Various mechanisms for controllable pitch propellers had been investigated by the Air Corps. Hamilton Standard Propeller Corporation, a unit of United Aircraft along with Boeing, had developed a hydraulic pitch changing mechanism in which the engine oil pressure acted on a piston in the hub. The oil went through the propeller shaft. This development required the cooperation of Pratt & Whitney to modify the propeller shaft to permit internal oil passage. This propeller mechanism was patented in 1929 by Frank Caldwell of Hamilton Standard. A two-bladed controllable propeller was successfully flight tested in 1933, which was during the 247 detail design phase. However, the 247 was designed to use a three-bladed propeller to permit a smaller diameter than was possible with the two-bladed propeller. The clearance between the propeller tip and the side of the body was too small on the 247 for a two-bladed propeller.

The Hamilton Standard three-bladed controllable propeller was not expected to become available until maybe five months after the first flight of the 247, which occurred February 8, 1933. Another factor was the lack of service experience on controllable propellers. The Boeing chief engineer rejected it as being heavier and complicated. As it turned out, the three-bladed controllable prop was first used on the Douglas DC-1, which flew July 1,1933, with the controllable propellers arriving just in time. Controllable propellers were finally installed on the 247D, which was certificated in October 1934, long after Douglas had the business.

This decision to use fixed-pitch propellers on the 247 resulted in a single-engine ceiling of only 2,000 feet. The single-engine ceiling in turn was another reason for limiting the size of the 247. When the controllable propeller was finally installed on the 247D, the single-engine ceiling was raised to 4,000 feet. However, it was not until 1938 when the feathering propeller became available that single-engine performance of the twins was satisfactory.

The last mistake in the 247 program was in marketing. The first 60 247's were scheduled for delivery to United Airlines without regard to the requirements of the other airlines. TWA could not wait for 247 deliveries and so ended up at Douglas after contacting the other manufacturers. Interestingly, during the introduction of the 707, TWA tried unsuccessfully to obtain a very large block of 707's near the start of the program, in order to get the jump on the other airlines. TWA was under the control of Howard Hughes during the time of the 707. The many lessons learned from the 247 were not lost on the jet transport competition.

4

The DC-3 and the Four-Engine Transports

THE TIMING OF Douglas's entry into the transport business with the DC-1 could hardly have been better. The 247 outdated the slow Fokker and Ford tri-motors and the Curtiss Condor twin-engine biplanes. The initial production of 60 247's had been allocated to United Airlines, and this put the other airlines at a considerable disadvantage. When Boeing told Jack Frye, the president of TWA, that he could not obtain 247's until the United order had been filled, Frye wrote to several airplane companies enquiring about a transport to fill his needs, with requirements on speed and range, but most important, he emphasized the ability to complete a trip between any two stops on the TWA route after an engine failed in flight. New Mexico and Arizona were critical due to the higher terrain. Douglas alone responded and developed the DC-1 in close cooperation with TWA.

Frye was an experienced pilot who stated what he wanted irrespective of the engineering difficulties. This engine failure requirement proved to be crucial in projecting the DC-1 performance ahead of the 247. The close timing of the DC-1 behind the 247 raises some interesting conjectures.

Boeing

B-9 first flight April 1931

Seattle to Dayton flight
June 1931

247 Preliminary Design
started September 1931

Wind Tunnel model shipped
to Cal Tech December 31,
1931

Detail Design started
February 1932

Wind Tunnel Report June
1932

247 First Flight February
1933

First delivery to UAL
March 30, 1933

Douglas

Jack Frye (TWA) letter to
Douglas August 2, 1932

DC-1 First Flight July 1, 1933

DC-2 First Delivery May 1934

DC-3 First Delivery December
1935

The story went around Boeing that Douglas acquired the 247 wind tunnel data before Boeing. The 247 data would have been of considerable interest to the Cal Tech staff to verify the success of their new wind tunnel. Some of the staff were consultants to Douglas, but the importance of any transfer of 247 data was probably exaggerated. Numbers are not as important to a designer as knowing that an attractive idea really works. However, the Douglas engineers might have been thus brought up to speed.

Frye obviously wanted to match the high speed of the 247, but initially assumed that a tri-motor would be necessary to satisfy his requirement that flight be maintained with an engine failure on the high part of the TWA route. Frye's logic was that Fokkers and Fords could not maintain 6,000 feet on a hot day with one failed engine out of the three on the tri-motor. Douglas was well aware of the low drag of the 247 twin-engine configuration and the superior environment of the twin for the pilots without a hot and noisy engine in the nose blocking the forward view. The Douglas engineers probably considered that the lower drag of the clean 247 concept might permit a twin to meet the engine-out requirement, and thus proceeded to examine the possibilities.

Before the DC-1, the Douglas airplanes were quite ordinary. Douglas had built a twin-engine bomber, the Y1B-7, that had a strut-braced high wing with engines hung under the wing. It flew in 1930 and was completely outclassed by the Boeing B-9 bomber that flew a year later. The technical revolution at Douglas was aided by the proximity of the Cal Tech wind tunnel. It had been completed in 1929 and was a superior facility for testing complete models. After the tunnel machinery was checked out and the force measuring balances were calibrated, a model of the Northrup Alpha was tested in order to compare the drags obtained in the wind tunnel with the drags that had already been obtained from performance in flight. The 247 must have been tested shortly afterwards. These tests must have generated confidence among the Cal Tech Staff in the accuracy of the tunnel measurements. So by the time the model of the DC-1 was being tested, Douglas had a good tool to aid design.

Arthur Raymond was the technical leader on the DC-1 and was the negotiator between TWA and the engine and propeller companies. Douglas hired Bailey Oswald, an aerodynamicist on the Cal Tech staff, to analyze this difficult single-engine performance problem. Douglas also had the assistance of other Cal Tech consultants, including Theodore von Karman [1881-1963], famous in aerodynamics and rockets. The Cal Tech wind tunnel was used extensively in the development of the DC-1. The large fillet between the wing trailing edge and the body was developed in the tunnel to avoid airflow separation and buffeting. Tests of longitudinal stability showed the need for slight sweepback of the outer wing panel for longitudinal balance. Split flaps were added to try to satisfy Frye's landing speed requirement. Another aerodynamic contribution of the DC-3 was the development of control surface leading edge aerodynamic balancing. The enthusiastic cooperation between Cal Tech and Douglas must have contributed to the rapid start of the DC-1.

The timing of the DC-1 benefited from several recent advancements, notably larger engines. Engine cooling improve-

Douglas DC-1
Prototype of DC-2, July 1933. Body widened and wing tips extended for DC-3.

ments made possible by the combination of the long NACA cowl and the inter-cylinder baffling were well proven and were available in time for the first flight of the DC-1. This decreased the drag as compared to the narrow Townend ring cowl used on the initial 60 247's that were delivered to United Airlines. Douglas pitted Wright against Pratt & Whitney to achieve sufficient power for single-engine flight. The nine-cylinder Wright Cyclone 1820 engine with an initial rating of 710 hp received its type certificate in 1932, in time for the first test flights. There were negotiations on the propeller reduction gear ratios and supercharger blower gear ratios, which were important for maximum power at the higher altitudes on TWA's route in New Mexico. The controllable propeller proved essential for this requirement. At the start of the DC-1 design it was doubtful if the Hamilton Standard three-bladed two-position controllable propeller would be delivered in time for the first flight, but the delivery was speeded up by insistence from Douglas.

A demonstration flight was made on the critical leg of TWA's route. The DC-1 was able to climb to 8,000 feet from a take-off runway altitude of 4,500 feet and go a distance of 280 miles when, after lift-off, the ignition was cut on one engine. When the Boeing chief engineer, Montieth, was told, while visiting Cal Tech during the design of the DC-1, that Douglas intended to satisfy Frye's engine failure requirement, he was reported to have scoffed at the idea of exceeding the existing single engine ceiling requirement of the Department of Commerce. In 1931 multi-engine aircraft were required to be able to maintain level flight at 2,000 feet above sea level with full load and one failed engine. After 1934, fuel dumping to lighten load was permitted, and an additional requirement was made that the transport should be able to climb to 1,000 feet with an engine failure after take-off. In view of the long stretches of high ground on TWA's southwestern route, it was easy to understand Jack Frye's demand for 10,000-foot single-engine ceiling. Douglas's efforts to satisfy this resulted in a big advance in transport aviation.

The DC-1 was maybe the first multi-engine airplane with a modern wing structure. The conversion of Douglas to advanced metal structures on the DC-1 has been attributed to John Northrup. He had moved from Lockheed, where he designed the Vega, to his own company, which in turn was bought up by United Aircraft. He soon went to Douglas, in time for the DC-1. Douglas had to deviate from Northrup's "multi-cellular" wings to allow space for gas tanks by using three spars with stiffeners on the skin between the spars. This was an advancement over the 247, where all the wing bending loads were resisted by truss spars.

The idea of using the metal covering to help carry the wing bending loads goes back to Germany in WWI. Junkers and Rohrbach concentrated on cantilever metal wings while others were building biplanes. After WWI Rohrbach built six tri-motor transports using stressed skin construction for Lufthansa. However, neither Junkers nor Rohrbach combined their advanced structures with clean aerodynamics, and therefore were left behind. The conversion to metal structures took considerable testing where lead shot bags were loaded on top of the wing in an inverted position to simulate loads in flight. The buckling of thin wing sheet and reinforcing angles under compression could not be accurately analyzed, and therefore, the structure had to be tested to failure. Also the design of sheet metal airplanes so as to be readily manufactured was an equally difficult problem. Access to rivets inside of a box brought on the "inside of the egg" situation in design.

The DC-1 prototype performed so well that the production

version, the DC-2, was ordered by all the U.S. airlines except United. When orders for the DC-2 were coming in and the Douglas factory was jammed, C.R. Smith of American Airlines "twisted" Donald Douglas, Sr.'s arm for a sleeper version, urging that the DC-2 body be widened for sleeper berths on one side of the aisle for the more affluent passengers, as the American's Curtiss Condors had been so equipped. The berth idea was later dropped and the extra width was used for another row of seats. The DC-3 ended up with a new body and an extended wing. It flew one year after C.R.'s request, an excellent accomplishment. Thirteen thousand DC-3's and the military equivalent, the C-47, were built, and were eventually used all over the world. The structural design of the DC-3 was so conservative that they were operated indefinitely and wore out multitudes of engines.

This was a formidable experience facing competitors, such as Boeing and Lockheed. The 247 could not have been stretched to meet the competition of the DC-2. It was fortunate for the industry that the 247 was not delayed for improvements just coming into view, as demonstration of the modern transport concept would have been slowed [Figure 10].

The DC-3 was so successful that a larger four-engine transport seemed logical. Douglas's first attempt was the 52-passenger DC-4E prototype which was built in cooperation with several airlines. However, it was too big for the power of the available engines. Then a smaller and refined 44-passenger four-engine transport was built. The DC-4 had a tricycle landing gear and nose wheel steering. The military version, the C-54, was the principal long range transport during the war, displacing the large flying boats that Pan Am had been operating in over-ocean routes. The C-54 had a tremendous effect during the war in transporting critical personnel all over the world. C-54's were used to bring back wounded to have a better chance of survival in the U.S. hospitals. The C-54's were flown by the Air Transport Command, the Navy, and civilian airline contractors. President Roosevelt's C-54 was named the "Sacred Cow." It became a status symbol. MacArthur, Eisenhower, and maybe Churchill, each had a C-54. Over 1,300 were built. After the war the large passenger capacity and the higher speed of the DC-4 were major factors in establishing the U.S. in the air transport business throughout the world. Many C-54's were sold as

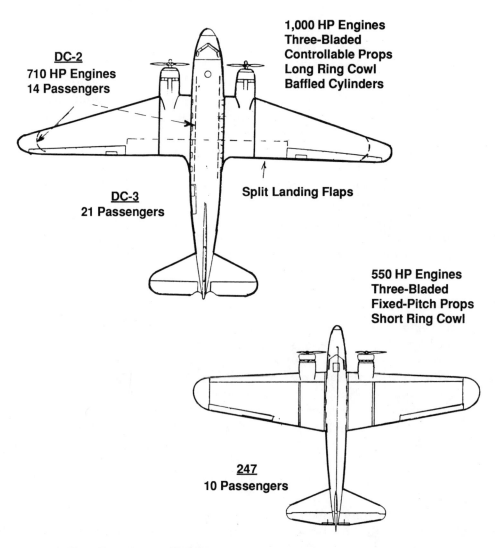

DC-2
710 HP Engines
14 Passengers

1,000 HP Engines
Three-Bladed
Controllable Props
Long Ring Cowl
Baffled Cylinders

DC-3
21 Passengers

Split Landing Flaps

550 HP Engines
Three-Bladed
Fixed-Pitch Props
Short Ring Cowl

247
10 Passengers

Both Transports to Same Scale

Figure 10—Comparison of Boeing 247 and Douglas DC-3

surplus to the airlines of the world and opened a new era in air transportation. The further development of the DC-4 into the DC-6 placed Douglas in a dominate position.

The DC-4 was originally intended to have a pressurized cabin, but the war emergency prevented this. Pressurization had been desired for some time, as the DC-3 would have to climb to 8,000 feet even to clear the Rocky Mountain passes that were north and south of the Rockies in Colorado. At this altitude some passengers could be uncomfortable. The stewardess had an oxygen bottle and mask for the occasional passenger in distress. The airlines found that the pilots should use oxygen above 8,000 feet to assure alertness. Night blindness could occur at 12,000 feet without oxygen. Flight over the numerous 14,000-foot peaks in Colorado would require cabin pressurization. In 1935 the Army contracted with Lockheed to build a pressurized body for the Lockheed Model 10 Electra twin-engine transport. The XC-35 was tested in 1937. The first pressurized production transport with a fully developed system was the Boeing 307. This was a four-engine transport using the wings from the B-17. It had a circular body to hold cabin pressure. It was designed to hold 8,000-foot cabin altitude up to 15,000-foot airplane altitude. Modern jet transports hold sea level pressure up to 8,000 ft. The development of the 307 pressurization controls made possible the pressurization on the B-29 bomber. Only 10 307s were built before the war effort ended the program. Otherwise the DC-4/C-54 was superior in most respects.

The 307 contributed to the development of flight control as a consequence of the crash of the first airplane. On a demonstration flight for KLM and TWA, the KLM pilot applied rudder at low speed. The rudder locked full over in the spin, and the control forces on the rudder were too high. Wind tunnel tests showed that a long dorsal fin would prevent the rudder locking over. A hydraulic servo on the rudder was also added. The B-17 and later airplanes benefited from the research on the 307.

In 1939 Lockheed started the design of a four-engine airliner, the 049 Constellation, which was powered by the Wright 3350, the largest engine available at that time. This project was not interrupted by Pearl Harbor, December 7, 1941, as long-range transports would be needed during the war. The first flight was in January 1943. Twenty-two were built during

Boeing 307 Stratoliner

Wright 1820 engine, B-17 wings. First airliner with a pressurized cabin; 10 built, 1938-1939. Improved vertical tail with dorsal fin to correct problem that caused the crash of the prototype.

the war and were used by the Air Transport Command. After the war the production was greatly expanded. The Constellation was used by the world's airlines for long-range travel until the jet transports took over.

After the war Douglas developed the C-54/DC-4 into the DC-6, which had a larger engine, the Pratt & Whitney 2800. The DC-6 became very popular, which to a considerable extent was due to the high reliability of the engine. After the war Boeing built the Stratocruiser, which was a derivative of the B-50 postwar bomber, with the addition of a double-lobe body and a wide upper deck. The Stratocruiser had the largest engine then available and was intended for very long range operation with a greater passenger capacity. However, very few were sold. To a considerable extent this was due to the low reliability of the powerplant, which had a Pratt & Whitney 4360 engine, four-row radial engine with 28 cylinders and 56 spark plugs, a turbo-supercharger, and a propeller that could not always be feathered when the engine failed. This may have been the largest and most complicated piston-engine installation ever installed in a production airliner. These problems had a considerable influence in the early conversion of Boeing to the idea of a jet transport [Figure 11].

Lockheed 049 Constellation Airliner

Wright 3350 engines, first flight January 1943. Three stretch versions, last of which flew October 1956, one year after PAA order for 707's and DC-8's. Total of 600 built.

Douglas DC-6

Pratt & Whitney R2800 engine. Derived from prewar DC-4/C-54. Stretched version, DC-6B; 537 built. World's most popular piston-engine airliner.

By 1955, 10 years after the war, the four-engine airliners had become so successful in generating traffic and in demonstrating the advantages of over-ocean air travel that sales of the 707 and the DC-8 commenced. The jets had to have much higher passenger capacity than the piston-engine transports in order

Boeing 377 Stratocruiser

Pratt & Whitney 4360 engine. Derivative of B-50 bomber and commercial version of C-97 cargo and refueling tanker; 55 Boeing 377 airliners built. Last delivered March 1950.

Pratt & Whitney R2000 engine. Over 1,100 built. Operated by U.S. Air Transport during WWII all over the world.

Douglas C-54

Boeing 307
Pressurized Round Body
Automatic Pressure Control,
B-17 Wings, Wright 1820 Engine, 33
Passengers, 10 Built, 1938

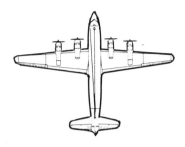

Douglas DC-4/C-54
Tricycle Landing Gear,
P&W R2000 Engine, 30-50
Passengers, 1,300 Built,
Worldwide Wartime Use, 1942

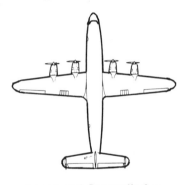

Lockheed Constellation
Wright 3350 Engine, 63-99
Passengers, 579 Built, 1943

Douglas DC-6
Pressurized Body,
P&W R2800 Engine,
54-102 Passengers,
537 Built, 1947

Boeing Stratocruiser
Double Lobe Body
P&W 4360 Engine, Turbo
Charged, 55-117 Passengers,
35 Built, 1947

All Shown to Same Scale

Figure 11—Four-Engine Airliners

to be economical. This, combined with the higher speeds of the jets, resulted in a much higher work capacity. At first it was felt that the initial sales might be limited to long ranges and luxury travel. The projection of the jet transport manufacturing business into the distant future required enthusiasm.

5

The Four-Engine
Bombers

BOEING'S LOSS of the transport business to the Douglas DC-2 was a bitter setback. To have a competitor begin exploiting the principles revealed by the 247 in a larger transport before the 247 had even been flown was a shock. A further setback came with President Roosevelt's cancellation of the airmail contracts in February 1934, only nine months after the first 247 had been delivered to United Airlines. Boeing was named a conspirator in the award of the airmail routes. Congress passed a law requiring that the airlines be separated from the airplane manufacturers. Henceforth, Boeing no longer had a captive customer. The government also forced the breakup of United Aircraft Corporation, thus separating Pratt & Whitney from Boeing. Both the engineering and manufacturing divisions in Boeing became very discouraged with the commercial business, and they wanted to revert to reliance on military contracts, which had kept the company alive since its founding in 1916.

Enthusiasm was restored as a consequence of the effort to design a revolutionary new bomber—the B-17. This airplane proved to be a vital link at Boeing between the 247 and the modern jet transport. Much has been written about its operations in WWII, but little about its origin and development or its impact on the progress of aeronautical engineering.

The requirement for a long-range bomber was opened by an agreement in December 1931 between the Army Chief of Staff, General Douglas MacArthur, and the Chief of Naval Operations, Admiral William V. Pratt. As a result of this agreement, the Army Air Corps received the role of protecting the coasts of the U.S. and its possessions. The Navy was freed from coastal responsibilities to operate in the seven seas. Nevertheless, the Navy remained convinced that the battleship reigned supreme in protecting the country by patrolling its shores. Neither the recent improvements in aviation nor General Billy Mitchell's use of Martin MB-2 twin-engined biplane bombers against surrendered German warships off the coast of Virginia in 1921 had persuaded the Navy that bombers would become effective in civil defense.

Despite the general emphasis on sea power, however, the Army Air Corps believed its role would become more important if it had a long-range bomber which could also be used for reconnaissance. The B-17 was such a high performance bomber, and it would mark a major turning point for the Army Air Corps, which had long sought to achieve power in the air that was on a par with the Army ground forces and the Navy.

In 1931, shortly before the agreement between the Army and the Navy was signed, the Boeing B-9 demonstrated a new era in airplane design and performance. By 1933 considerable numbers of Martin B-10 bombers were in service. They demonstrated the ability to fly a range of 1,240 miles at a maximum speed of 200 mph while carrying 2,260 pounds of bombs. The B-10 performance data gave considerable encouragement to the bomber enthusiasts in the Air Corps, principally General Benny Foulois [1879-1967] and General Oscar Westover. General Foulois was the Army's third pilot. He had taught himself to fly in the Army's first airplane, the original Wright biplane design that had two pusher propellers and a forward longitudinal control surface. He had made his first solo flight in 1910, after receiving some ground instruction from Orville Wright. In the following years, he had helped organize Army aviation, originally a part of the Army Signal Corps, which was responsible for reconnaissance and communications.

In 1931 General Foulois headed the Air Corps and was responsible for planning future developments. He and his assistant, General Westover, proceeded to study bombers with ranges beyond the Martin B-10. In July 1933, the engineering officers and civilians who were stationed at Wright Field issued an engineering report that showed it was possible to design a bomber to carry a 2,000-pound bomb load on a 5,000-mile mission, with a maximum speed capability of 200 mph. In response, the Air Corps submitted a proposal to the Army General Staff requesting funds for the development of a long-range bomber. In May 1934, this was approved and study contracts were sent to Boeing and Martin. In one month Boeing completed a study to design and build a large bomber. In June, Boeing received a contract to built one XB-15, a very large, four-engined airplane that would be needed to meet the 5,000-mile range requirement. Plans for its equipment and interior arrangements were quite ambitious, and they included an auxiliary electric power unit. The XB-15 design was based on an engine still in the early development stage, the Allison 3420, which was to have twice the power of existing engines. It had 24 cylinders and was the combination of two V-12 Allison 1710 engines geared together.

However, it was soon realized that the development of the 3420 was to be too far off to be used in the XB-15 as scheduled. Instead, the "chief designer-salesman" at Boeing, Claire Egtvedt [1892-1975], suggested to the Air Corps that the XB-15 be set aside for the time being and that the Air Corps revert to a more modest bomber concept using engines of lower power whose availability was assured. On August 8, 1934, a request was issued by the Air Corps at Wright Field for a bomber that would carry 2,000 pounds of bombs at a minimum acceptable range of 1,020 miles and a preferred range of 2,200 miles. The request specified a minimum acceptable speed of 200 mph and desired speed of 250 mph. A company-financed prototype was to be available for testing at Wright Field by August 1935, only one year after the issuance of the invitation to participate.

By this time, the political trends in Europe may have given the Air Corps greater incentive to initiate the development of a bomber. In April 1933, Hitler had appointed Goering as air minister, charging him to form an air force. General Foulois knew Goering quite well as a result of being sent to Germany in 1920 to access WWI German aviation in general. He spent an entire year in Germany, during which time Goering had said that he planned to rebuild the Luftwaffe and lead it to victory. With this experience, General Foulois was probably more strongly motivated to prepare for war than anybody else in the Air Corps.

Design of the German Messerschmitt 109 fighter had been started in late 1933. It flew in September 1935. Design of the British Hurricane and Spitfire fighters, both famous in WWII, had been started early in 1934. It can be assumed that Air Corps personnel at Wright Field had knowledge of the European armament build-up. The decision to develop a new U.S. bomber was made four years before the infamous Munich agreement, and two years before the Spanish Civil War, where the new military airplanes of Europe were tried out in combat for the first time. In 1934 U.S. public sentiment strongly favored isolationism. Militarism was unpopular and officers were advised not to wear their uniforms in public. Fortunately, the Wright Field visionaries ignored the prevailing mood and put the U.S. well on the way to large-scale production of effective military airplanes by the time of Pearl Harbor.

There were three entries in the U.S. bomber competition. Martin upgraded its B-10 with a more powerful engine, adding fuel capacity for longer range. Douglas built the twin-engined B-18 using their DC-2 design for the wings and other components in order to be assured of meeting the required 12-month schedule. In contrast, Boeing had to design and build an entirely new airplane, since its B-9 was outmoded.

The new design was given the designation of Model 299, which was the serial number of the Boeing designs that had reached the stage of serious consideration on whether to build or not. Although the Army had only requested a "multi-engine" airplane, the Army assumed this to mean two engines or more; a four-engine airplane was not specifically required. For its prototype, Boeing selected four engines rather than two because, during the XB-15 negotiations, the Army had clearly indicated its desire for much more range than the minimum specified. While the new requirements could be met with a twin, a four-engine configuration would yield greater performance and would also avoid direct competition with the other entrants.

The principal problem was the very short time to design and build a revolutionary airplane.

Although the engines and propellers would be furnished by the government, the additional cost of the larger airframe would further stretch Boeing's precarious finances. The engineers were probably in favor of the four-engined bomber due to their previous, preliminary work on the XB-15, from which they probably had gained confidence in their ability to design a bomber that was smaller than the XB-15. It is not hard to reconstruct the engineering logic behind the final decision. While the fruitfulness of these decisions were well proven in WWII, success in the near term competition depended heavily on matching the size and weight of the airplane to the power of the largest engines available for the Army tests that would begin in August 1935. Winning the fly-off depended on the efficiency and reliability of many detail components yet to be designed. A major defect in any component could spell failure.

Eleven months was a very short time in which to design and build the bomber. At this time, the design process resembled that of today but on a smaller scale. The dimensional accuracy on the drawings was high, but the paperwork was simplified wherever possible. The general arrangement of the airplane was conceived by the preliminary design chief, Giff Emery, and his assistant Ed Wells [1910-1986]. First Giff and Ed made freehand sketches of what they thought the airplane should look like, until they arrived at a plausible and attractive configuration. Although they were closeted, they undoubtedly asked questions of those who could provide direct answers. There was no time for research or conferences or lengthy planning meetings. It was most important to get started early on the detail drawings that would be sent to the shop.

The team was aided considerably by virtue of having just finished the basic design of a four-engined passenger transport to the point that a wind tunnel model had been designed, indicating that they could have utilized some of the passenger transport performance calculations to size the bomber around the transport wing and the Pratt & Whitney Hornet engines. In just 15 days from the start, centerline diagrams of the major airplane sections were passed out to the engineers who were to design the details. Ed Wells took on the job of designing the body. He decided upon a circular cross section for the sake of simplicity. The tapering of the body from the rear of the bomb bay to the tail was determined using a mathematical cosine function rather than the time honored "lofting" method, which is a nautical term denoting the process whereby a ship's contour lines were drawn full scale on the floor in the loft above the shop. The circular body frames were spaced at 10-inch intervals from the bomb bay to the tail, and the diameter of these could be readily framed. With only a drawing of the cross sections of the frames, the shop could then quickly start building the frames and the body assembly jig. This could be considered as a prehistoric application of CAD/CAM, the computer being the trigonometry tables and a hand-cranked calculator.

Only changes in details could be made after the centerline diagrams were issued to the shop. If a major flaw in the concept was found, then the process would have to be started all over again. It is obvious that the success of the prototype, which was designed and built in 11 months, depended heavily on the talents of the engineering leaders and the early decisions that froze the configuration. During the peak of detail design, less than 100 engineers were assigned to the project. Ed Wells put in a lot of overtime. Three weeks after the start of the design he took two days off to get married.

The detail design of the major components of all airplanes in that era was based on the Army's standard requirements. In those days the manufacturers used the Air Corps "Handbook of Instructions to Airplane Designers," referred to as HIAD, which was about two inches thick. This document contained engineering formulas, data on strengths and weights of materials, and drawings of standard accessories. Deviations from HIAD had to be negotiated with Wright Field. Ingenious, advanced features might have to be backed up with test data. Small parts like nuts, bolts, and accessories were listed in the AN Book, a product of the Army and the Navy. It was advantageous to conform to these standards, as the customer would thus better understand and hence accept the design. The manufacturer also had a "Draughting Room Manual," or DRM, that contained company information derived from the experience gained on previous airplane projects. Thus equipped, the engineer could begin the task of designing his part of the airplane, which included making a formal drawing for the shop, since being an engineer at that time entailed fully developed drafting skills. Each engineer understood the overall design and how his component fit into the whole. Today, a large library and numerous consultants would be required before an engineer could make decisions to proceed with his drawing and get it approved.

There were no specialists. The engineers were totally responsible for both the design and the functional operation of their part of the airplane. Additionally, they were responsible for its weight, its strength, and any additional drag that might be caused by some component sticking out in the breeze. Later on, there were a few specialists who had graduated from the drafting board to routinely check stresses and total weights. The chief engineer and one aerodynamics engineer would analyze performance; typically, their report was no more than six pages in length. After a final check for errors, a component drawing was released to the shop. The originating engineer had to be mostly right, otherwise the delay for redesign could be costly, or fatal in a timed competition.

A brief 1991 interlude—

Today's modern computer graphics systems provide a tool to better coordinate and expedite the engineering design phase. But errors and delays continue to plague the design process due to problems relating to data communications between dissimilar systems, manual procedures that must interface with the computer system, and software or hardware errors that are time-consuming and therefore costly to correct and which may bring into question the integrity of the electronic engineering data that was so painstakingly created. Computers by themselves have not eliminated the problems associated with transferring drawing data between engineering and the shop. Perhaps now as well as then, the key to quality design engineering which is "mostly right" the first time remains rooted within a finely honed human mind whose analytical and intuitive powers are conjunct.

Tandy Cook, Programmer

The 299 design had many interesting features. Compared to the much larger XB-15, the 299 body's interior provided for reduced accommodations and fewer number of crew. Its structure was based on the 247 in that the wing bending loads were resisted entirely by truss spars. Previously, a large amount of analysis and static testing on metal cantilever wings had been completed at Wright Field by Captain Carl Greene. In one of his test specimens the upper and lower wing skins were stiffened by corrugations. In 1932 the results of these tests were distributed to industry, and they may have subsequently influenced the 299 wing design, which included thin, corrugated sheet metal under the outer skin, both tightly riveted together to prevent the outer skin from buckling, as had been a problem on the 247. The corrugations on the 299 wing could withstand a portion of the bending loads. But this fact was not taken into account in determining whether the strength requirements had been met because a time-consuming structural test would have been needed to check for buckling under maximum loads.

In actuality though, one of the original 13 "field service" 299's that were built, designated as the Y1B-17's by the Air Corps, was highly stressed in flight to the point where the corrugations did buckle, which gave some assurance that the truss spars had the desired strength. With the increase in gross weights on the B-17E, F, and G, the corrugations were thickened so that they shared the bending load with the truss spars. In fact, this type of heavily reinforced wing skin construction probably helped in bringing B-17's back to home base after incurring severe battle damage during WWII bombing runs.

The wing airfoil section on the 299 was symmetrical, in contrast to the "cambered" airfoils on previous Boeing airplanes which had a curved centerline. The symmetrical design may have been a concession to the shop in order to halve the required number of forming dies for pressing the wing ribs. The NACA wind tunnel tests at that time indicated that thick, symmetrical airfoils had almost as much maximum lift as cambered airfoils.

The 299 wing flaps constituted another new feature. These moved on linkages which produced a small aft travel along with the desired downward deflection of air. Although far short of the modern flap, this design was more effective than the split flap used on the DC-2.

The maximum gross weight of the 299 prototype was 38,053 pounds. The last model of the B-17 had a gross weight of 65,500 pounds. But while the wing area was still adequate to carry the higher weight and the structure had to be reinforced, runways had to be lengthened to accommodate the longer take-off runs.

B Model 299—The B-17 Prototype
Pratt & Whitney Hornet engines. Note streamlined blisters for .30 caliber machine guns and small original tail, later greatly enlarged on the B-17E. Photo taken August 1935 before flight to Wright Field.

There was a whimsical explanation of why the B-17 utilized electrical power rather than the popular hydraulic method to actuate the landing gear and flaps. The story went that one of the very early Boeing engineers, Louie Marsh, had one of the best sports cars of the 1920's, a Wills St. Clair. It had hydraulic brakes, but when they failed on one of Seattle's steep hills, the decision was made to reduce the use of hydraulics on the airplane. Whatever the reason, this design decision proved to be fortunate; electrical actuation systems turned out to be less vulnerable to battle damage than hydraulics.

Another interesting feature on the 299 was an aileron control mechanism with a worm screw drive to make it nearly "irreversible" to avoid flutter. It was designed by Dick Nelson, who became project engineer on the B-17 at age 32 during the period of big production at Boeing, Douglas, and Lockheed, with all the changes brought on by the war. This control mechanism was used in lieu of mass balancing of the aileron about the hinge line. Mass balancing was not fully understood at Boeing, although the 299 had mass balanced elevators. Boeing had recently encountered the severe high-speed problem called "flutter," which can be described as a large amplitude oscillation of the wing or tail in bending and torsion. A Boeing experimental fighter for the Navy, the XF7B-1, had a cantilever wing that fluttered so violently in a dive test that loose rivets within the wing attained enough velocity to dent the upper and lower wing skins from the inside. Fortunately, the plane's damaged condition did not prevent the pilot from landing safely.

Another flutter incident had occurred in the summer of 1934 at Wichita on a Northrup Gamma, which was a low-winged, all-metal cantilever monoplane. Northrup was a part of Boeing at that time. In a dive test the Boeing pilot, Deed Levy, encountered flutter that was so violent he bailed out. Afterwards the second guessers on the ground asked why he hadn't tried to save the airplane, since the wings had not come off. It is difficult to appreciate the severity of flutter unless the experience has been gained first hand.

In the early days at Boeing the designers were supported by only one aerodynamics engineer, Ralph Cram, and a couple of assistants. The Model 299 was tested in the Cal Tech wind tunnel in May, 1935, only three weeks before first flight. No changes resulted from the wind tunnel test. At that time wind tunnel tests were mostly used to endorse the final design. Such tests did have some technical value, however, for they verified the allowable center of gravity travel and the best location of load. Additionally, early wind tunnel tests were used to check the stabilizer angle setting for better trim control on the first flight. Advanced wind tunnel test techniques to analyze control forces on full models had not yet been developed. For small airplanes this had not been a critical problem since the pilot usually had sufficient control power and strength to get through the first flight without trouble.

The tail surfaces of the 299 were comparatively small. The rudder was large compared to the fin. This might have been considered desirable for achieving better control in cross-wind landings. Servo tabs were used to reduce the control forces on the 299. These had been used on the Boeing Model 80 tri-motored transport rudder and on the B-9 bomber. Efforts to regulate the control forces to suit the pilot consumed the major part of the early 299 flight testing.

At 6 a.m. on July 24, 1935, the 299 took off for the first time on a flight which lasted one and a half hours. The next three weeks were spent working around the clock to correct mechanical problems. The tail wheel shimmied during take-offs and landings, so a lock in the neutral swivel position had to be installed. Bad brakes, leaky plumbing, failed engines and numerous control problems all had to be fixed. Engine ground runs were made in the middle of the night. These minimal flight tests were mostly conducted for the purpose of adjusting the control surface servo tab linkages and checking the mechanical operation of all systems. In Seattle, the total logged flying time was 14 hours 5 minutes and the total engine running time was 27 hours 50 minutes, which was a very abbreviated test period to meet the August delivery deadline. A final detailed inspection was completed on August 12. The 299 was not to be just a performance demonstrator; it provided for a complete set of military equipment, including a Sperry autopilot, a bomb hoist and parachute flares for night landings.

On August 20, 1935, the 299 was flown to Wright Field near Dayton, which was the Army's flight test center at that time. It attained an average speed of 232 mph at 63 percent power. Throughout the next two months the Army conducted flight tests to measure the plane's performance. On October 30 the 299 crashed on take-off due to the failure of the crew to release the control gust lock on the cockpit aisle stand. The elevator was locked in an upward angle of 12 1/2 degrees, and at an altitude of 300 feet, the 299 stalled. The Army chief test pilot, Major Hill, was killed. Boeing test pilot Les Tower was riding along as an observer. He died later of burns. Survivors were Lt. Don Putt, sitting in the co-pilot's seat, Wright Field aeronautical engineer John Cutting, and the mechanic, Mark Koogler.

While considerable performance data had been accumulated before the 299 crash, the production contract was awarded to Douglas. A total of 218 Douglas B-18A's were built. The B-18 fulfilled the terms of the competition, and it obviously could be brought into service much sooner than the Boeing entry. The B-18 served to expand the bomber branch of the Air Corps. During the war it was used to patrol for submarines. The slim Army budget during the depression probably was a factor in the award to a lower performance bomber.

There was some concern outside of Wright Field that the 299 was too much airplane for the pilots. However, the enthusiasm for the 299 was high at Wright Field, and production planning was started at Boeing soon after the crash. The Army was authorized by law to buy 13 "field test airplanes" each year without going through the process of conducting a competition, which resulted in an Air Corps order for the YB-17 two and a half months after the crash. This proved to be a fortuitous circumstance since, with such a small production run, Boeing was able to continually modify and perfect the B-17 without the building of heavy tooling at the outset, which would have had the effect of freezing the design.

The turbo-supercharger was a very important addition to the B-17 in that it permitted combat missions at 25,000 feet, which reduced the effectiveness of ground-based anti-aircraft fire. Before the turbos were installed, 1,000 hp could be obtained on each engine at 13,500 feet of altitude, above which the power fell off rapidly. With the turbos, 1,200 hp could be obtained at 25,000 feet of altitude. The turbo-supercharger was already an old idea, having been proposed in 1906 by Brown-Boveri, a prominent manufacturer of turbines and pumps in Switzerland. In France Rateau, a builder of steam turbines, had designed and built a turbo before the end of WWI. In 1919 the U.S. Army had contracted with General Electric for the development of turbos. This work was to be accomplished under the direction of Sanford Moss [1872-1946], an engineer who had started work on gas turbines as a graduate student at Cornell in 1901. In 1931 turbos were tested on a dozen Curtiss P-6 biplane fighters with Curtiss V-12 liquid-cooled Conqueror engines. (A 1990 GE television ad shows the turbo being pulled up to the top of Pikes Peak by mules for testing at altitude, with "Sanford Moss" in charge.)

In 1938, turbos were installed on the 14th YB-17. This particular plane had originally been ordered for the purpose of conducting structural tests. The turbos were first located on top of the engine nacelles, but this proved to be quite unsatisfactory, as the swirling exhaust flow from the turbo exits stalled the air flow on the wing's upper surface. A quick change to a bottom installation was successful.

Initially, the operator control procedure for the turbos was simple. It required the pilots to refer to the engine instruments to avoid opening the throttle to the point of causing detonation. However, a problem appeared after 20 B-17D's were sent to England as part of the U.S.-British lend-lease agreement that was in effect before Pearl Harbor. The British pilots were accustomed to automatic engine throttle controls which prevented them from over-boosting their highly supercharged engines at low altitudes, thereby avoiding detonation and rapid

Boeing Y1B-17

Wright 1820 engines; first flight December, 1936; 13 built. Subsequent models had GE turbo-superchargers, enlarged tail surfaces, and gun turrets; 12,726 B-17's built during the war by Boeing, Douglas, Vega.

destruction of the engine. Many of the British pilots had little concept of machinery, some being said not to have driven a car before learning to fly. When in combat, the British would often use full turbo and throttle in their B-17's, inadvertently causing engine failures. The U.S. Air Corps Wright Field liaison officer, Jake Harmon, wired back home asking for an automatic turbo control. Wright Field replied, "Service experience shows that this is not necessary." Jake wired back the message, "Service experience shows that there are no pilots with service experience."

The 299 tail control surfaces were completely revised and enlarged on the B-17E, which was developed in 1940. The larger, horizontal tail offset the center of gravity aft movement caused by the tail turret. A much larger vertical tail gave better engine-out control than was possible with the original tail. A dorsal fin was added to prevent the rudder from locking over in a severe side-slip, a lesson learned from the 307 Stratoliner accident. The B-17E had leading edge aerodynamic balances to reduce control forces that had been patterned after the DC-3. At high control surface angles these balances gave lower control forces than with only the servo tab controls that were used on the 299. The control surfaces on the B-17E were developed at the University of Washington wind tunnel with new instruments that could accurately measure the control surface hinge moments.

Although not an Air Corps requirement, the ability to trim out two failed engines on the same side was desirable. An amusing episode occurred in this connection when a British Air vice-marshal visited Seattle in about 1942. An Army Air Force officer, Carl Brandt, who was engaged in the B-17 development, gave a demonstration flight with the vice-marshal in the co-pilot's seat. Carl feathered both engines on the right side, and then took his hands off the wheel, folded his arms, and asked, "What do think of that?" The reply from the vice-marshal was, "It's a lot quieter." This refinement in pilot control paid off in combat when engines were shot out. The B-17's were superior in that they were able to hold tight formations for protection against enemy fighters even though engine thrust might be unevenly distributed.

Powered gun turrets were added in stages to the E, F, and G models of the B-17, along with much additional equipment and fuel capacity. The gross weight was increased from the original 38,000 pounds to 62,500. In a 60-degree bank at 2G's, this weight produced loads up to the structural design limit without permanent set of the wings in bending.

The companion of the B-17 in the bombing raids over Germany was the Consolidated B-24 four-engined bomber. The design was started in September 1938, three years after the B-17 was designed. The first flight was in December 1939. The B-24 wing introduced a new era in aerodynamic wing design. The B-24 had a greater range than the B-17 due primarily to a slender wing with 6 1/4 feet greater span and 26 percent less wing area than the B-17. Compared to the symmetrical airfoil on the B-17, the B-24 wing had a low drag cambered section, called the "Davis Wing." At one time Davis had been a partner of Donald Douglas.

The B-24 also had highly effective "Fowler" flaps, which moved far aft as well as down to give high lift on landing, thus compensating for the lesser wing area of the B-24. The overall wing design was a product of tests by Davis with an airfoil section mounted on his car and also tests in the Cal Tech wind tunnel. This wing concept had first been tried out in flight on the experimental Consolidated Model 31 flying boat. In fact, the Boeing B-29 wing was essentially a scaled-up version of the B-24 wing. In 1939 George Schairer came to Boeing to run aerodynamics to replace Ralph Cram, Boeing's one aerodynamicist, who was killed in the Stratoliner crash. Schairer brought with him the knowledge he had gained at Consolidated, where he had worked in aerodynamics. It was Schairer's experience with the B-24 wing design that was largely responsible for the improvements that were applied to the B-29 wing design.

The body of the Consolidated B-24 enclosed a large volume as compared to the B-17, which permitted the B-24's use as transport for passengers and cargo during the war. The B-24's versatility resulted in a much greater number being built than was the case with the Boeing B-17 series. The B-24 was preferred in the Pacific and in Africa because of its greater range. In European daylight bombing raids, the B-17 was preferred because of its superior capacity to maintain control in tight formations and to operate at higher altitudes than the B-24, which was much more vulnerable to flak. Both airplanes had engines of almost the same cylinder displacement. Moreover, their engines were equally powerful without the turbos.

The higher wing span on the B-24 should have allowed flight at higher altitudes than it did were it not for the fact that the B-24's supercharging system had longer ducts whose air inlet was located on the nose of the engine ring cowl. As a result, the B-24 superchargers suffered from a loss in ram pressure at the turbos. This contrasts to the B-17's air inlet which was located on the wing's leading edge, close to the turbos so that ram pressure could be maximized.

The success of the B-17 and the subsequent increase in range with the B-24 prompted the Air Corps to request a higher performance bomber. A more powerful engine was in sight, permitting a larger bomber to be designed. In January 1940, a new specification was issued for a bomber with a top speed of 400 mph and a bomb load capacity of 2,000 pounds that could be dropped at the halfway point on a mission that spanned a total of 5,333 miles. Possibly, the significance of this range requirement was that it would permit the bombing of Moscow on a mission that had originated in England. The new Air Corps solicitation took place during the time of the treaty between Hitler and Stalin to invade and divide Poland, indicating that Russia could be an enemy as well as Germany. This range would also permit the bombing of Tokyo from Manila. Japan had already joined Germany and Italy in the Axis, and the tension between the U.S. and Japan was mounting as a result of Japan's invasion of China.

At Boeing in 1938, after production of the 13 YB-17's was concluded, studies of a longer range bomber were already underway. The critical design factor was the selection of the largest available or "real" engine, one which would show positive signs of functioning as required while on the test stand. This was of special concern because the Boeing XB-15 had been designed around a larger engine design which failed to materialize. Likewise, Douglas had failed on the very large XB-19, designing it for the same seemingly never finished Allison 3420.

In 1936 development was started on the Wright 3350 twin-row 18-cylinder air-cooled radial engine. By 1940 it was far enough along to be considered as a practicable engine entry for an Army bomber design competition. By the time several competing bomber designs showed promise, the Army ordered a large production quantity of these new Wright engines in April 1941.

Lockheed submitted the design for its XB-30, an adaptation of the Model 49 Constellation air transport, but it was too small for the Army's needs. Douglas submitted a design for a bomber, the XB-31, which was to have twice the wing area of the B-29. It was to be powered by the Pratt & Whitney 4360 28-cylinder four-row engine, but this engine was delayed and was not ready for production until the end of the war. The Consolidated B-32 and the Boeing B-29 were designed around the Wright 3350 engine. The B-32 was the smaller entry, with about the same wing area as the B-17. The design was probably biased towards meeting the Army's 400 mph maximum speed requirement. Because the minium acceptable military payload kept growing as a result of the wartime experiences in Europe, the smaller B-32 lost out and only 115 were built. However, the larger B-29 design could meet the increased payload requirements. This design was continually changed throughout the 1940's to include radar and additional armament [Figure 12].

The top speed of the B-29 was 360 mph, compared to the top speed of the famous Japanese Mitsubishi Zero fighter, which was 350 mph. Because the Zeros might attack B-29's some distance from the bombing target, the B-29's long-range cruising speed of 260 mph was more pertinent than its top speed. Originally, both the B-32 and the B-29 were to have retractable gun turrets to avoid additional drag, but powered turrets with a low profile were installed instead because a fighter attack might start early in a mission. The turrets were directed by remote firing stations with computing gun sights, and this was more effective than the guns in the B-17's. By the time of the later B-29 bombing missions from the Mariana Islands, located 1,500 miles south of Tokyo, the Zeros had become less effective, and the losses of B-29's to fighters were low. The B-29 would have had a tougher time in Europe where enemy fighters were based near the English Channel and were active early in the bombing missions.

The B-29 was the only wartime airplane to have cabin pressurization, thus avoiding the need for using oxygen masks during most of the mission. This was especially helpful during the early bombing of Japan from China, as the B-29's ferried supplies over the Himalayas from India. Later on, the cabin pressurization was an aid to the crew during the 17-hour missions from the Mariana Islands to Japan. The B-29 operations and the final use of these airplanes to carry the atomic bombs ended the war without the need for an invasion.

Typically, the B-29's take-off weight was 140,000 pounds. At this high gross weight, the loss of an engine on take-off often meant disaster, particularly on a hot day in India. Early in the operation of the B-29's, a Wright engine field service representative named Frank Lary was sent to India to advise the Army 58th Bombardment Wing how to best operate the engines for long-range cruise. Upon his arrival the pilots told him to forget about cruise efficiency and fix the exhaust valves in the engine cylinder heads. These were overheating during the hot take-offs, breaking in two within the combustion chamber and then puncturing the piston, which caused the engine to fail. When Frank returned to the Wright plant in Paterson, New Jersey, it

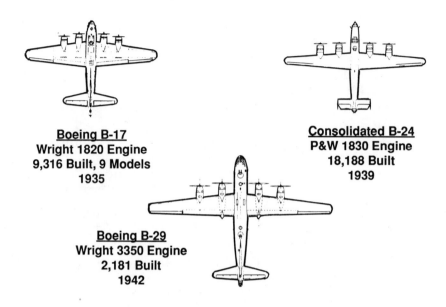

Boeing B-17
Wright 1820 Engine
9,316 Built, 9 Models
1935

Consolidated B-24
P&W 1830 Engine
18,188 Built
1939

Boeing B-29
Wright 3350 Engine
2,181 Built
1942

WARTIME MASS PRODUCTION

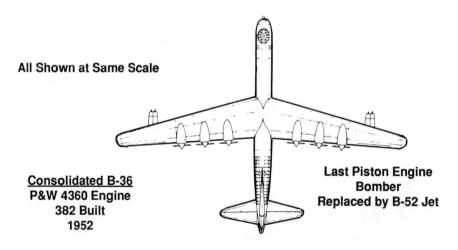

All Shown at Same Scale

Consolidated B-36
P&W 4360 Engine
382 Built
1952

Last Piston Engine
Bomber
Replaced by B-52 Jet

Figure 12—Strategic Piston-Engine Bombers

took him a week to convince the engineers that the problem was real. A new cylinder head with longer cooling fins was designed and put into production just in time for the B-29 operations in the Marianas.

The B-29 was the first Boeing airplane where significant design improvements were made using the wind tunnel. The tunnels at Cal Tech and the University of Washington were used extensively during 1940. It also signaled the beginning of a new era in terms of the special aerodynamic problems that were being encountered, an era in which the aerodynamics experts were becoming concerned about a rise in drag near the speed of sound. The Lockheed P-38 twin-engined fighter was the first U.S. airplane to seriously encounter high-speed control problems in a dive. This phenomenon was termed a "high-speed stall," and it made the pull-out difficult. The speed on the upper surface of a wing is much higher than the actual airplane speed. The airflow over the wing is aggravated by thick wing sections and also the higher angles of attack in the thinner air at high altitudes. This problem was accentuated by the high unit wing loading of the B-29, that is, the gross weight divided by the wing area. This was 80 pounds per square foot on the B-29 compared to 15 pounds per square foot on the DC-3, which was designed at a time when landing speeds were required to be low.

By 1940 the NACA, the U.S. government's technical authority, had become concerned that the Air Corps' new bombers might be so fast and so highly loaded that they might easily get into trouble. Rather thick airfoil sections were being used on the inboard wing sections to reduce structural weight and to provide a high volume to contain the fuel tanks. As a result of their concerns, the Air Corps told the heavy bomber competitors to line up for tests in the NACA high-speed wind tunnel at Langley Field, Virginia, which had an eight-foot diameter test section. Consolidated at San Diego was the first up at bat with the B-32.

In order to test airplane models at very high speeds, it was necessary to avoid the airflow interference of the conventional type of model mounting which utilized floor mounted struts holding the wings of the model. Instead, the NACA designed the tunnel to support the models by extending the wing tips through the tunnel side walls where they would be mounted on the lift and drag measuring balances. Since it was expected that the

B-29 Bomber

Wright 3350 engines. Built by Boeing at Wichita and Renton, by Bell at Marietta, Georgia, and by Martin in Omaha. Total production, 3,627. Bombed Japan first from China but later from Mariana Islands, 1,500 miles south of Tokyo. War ended when B-29's dropped two atomic bombs.

high-speed problem area would be located at the thick wing root rather than at the wing tips, this was a logical way to mount the model. To accommodate this mounting technique, Consolidated built a scale model of the B-32 which had a wing span greater than eight feet. The wind tunnel data on the B-32 showed that there was a sudden rise in drag as the predicted top speed of the B-32 was approached. The NACA then recommended that the solution was to use a new NACA airfoil.

Boeing's head of aerodynamics, George Schairer, perceived that the B-32 model had such a large cross section that the model formed a blockage, creating a "local venturi" that forced the air in this region of the tunnel closer to the speed of sound. The wind tunnel had solid walls, and the air flowing around the model was thus restrained from expanding as would have been the case in the open air. In other words, the air in the tunnel in the region of the model was really flowing at a higher speed, with respect to the airfoil surfaces, than was indicated by the tunnel airspeed meter. Perceiving this problem, Schairer had the B-29 model made smaller and the wings were extended beyond the normal tip so that the extensions protruded beyond the tunnel. With this smaller model the test data of the B-29 showed no high-speed problem. The NACA and the Air Corps erroneously deduced that the B-29 was a better design, and of course Boeing did not enlighten them that they did not understand the wind tunnel operation. Martin followed with their model of the B-33A and made the same mistake as Consolidated by testing too large a model.

Boeing introduced another innovation in the B-29 testing that neither Martin nor the NACA were wise to. Wind tunnel tests were usually started using only the bare wing; the nacelles were added in the next test run to measure the incremental effects on drag and lift. To provide room for the landing gear wheels in their retracted position, the nacelles on the B-29 and the B-33A were hung low instead of being positioned on the wing section centerlines. This configuration increased the air velocity over the airfoil's lower surface, therefore decreasing lift in the vicinity of the nacelle, which caused a slight increase in drag. To counteract this effect, a small extension to the B-29 wing's trailing edge was added just behind the nacelle at the time when the nacelles were installed. The airfoil extension at this specific location compensated for the negative effect of the nacelle.

Previously, this trick had been discovered during B-29 testing in the Cal Tech wind tunnel. The NACA observed that a loss in lift occurred when the nacelles were added to the B-33A, but that the same thing did not happen on the B-29. Their conclusion was that the B-29 design was better. The B-33A was then canceled. Aided by this misinterpretation of the wind tunnel results, the B-29 won the Army Air Corps competition.

The B-29 brought Boeing up to the level of their competition in southern California, in terms of structural design and aerodynamic refinement. The pressurized cabin that was supplied from the engine turbos was an advanced feature. The sizing of the B-29 wing and body to match the power of the Wright 3350 engines was outstanding in obtaining the optimum combination to maximize payload and range. This was the result of years of study and a great number of trial drawings that ended up in the trash. A total of 3,627 B-29's were built for the Army Air Corps by Boeing in Wichita and Renton, Bell in Marietta, Georgia, and Martin in Omaha, Nebraska.

Shortly after the end of the war a modified B-29, named the

"Dreamboat," made a long distance record of 7,916 miles between Guam and Washington, DC. The turrets had been removed and the bomb bays were filled with fuel tanks. At the time, this seemed to indicate the ultimate in the design efficiency of large airplanes. A little later on this appeared to be an impossible performance goal for jet airplanes, that is, until the 1980's when this record was exceeded in commercial jet transport operations.

6

The War Years

HITLER'S INVASION OF POLAND in September 1939 set off a rapid expansion of plant facilities throughout the aircraft industry. For all anyone knew, the war could be a long one. If this were to be the case, the demand for mass production of aircraft could exceed the capabilities of the aircraft industry even after it was expanded. In 1939 the airplane companies had very small plants. Boeing might have been able to build one airplane a week. Douglas was in much better shape, rolling out more than three DC-3's a week. In 1940 the Army ordered large production of B-17E's and Wright 1820 engines.

As an additional source of aircraft engines, the government naturally looked towards the automobile industry. By virtue of its extensive experience with machine tools, the automobile industry was judged to be best suited to the task of building aircraft engines in sufficient quantities. However, aircraft engines were required to be of much higher quality compared to the cast-iron auto engines. The manufacturer of some of the Wright 1820 engines for the B-17's were subcontracted to Studebaker. During the early days of the war against the Japanese, the B-17's were operating in the South Pacific. The B-17 pilots much preferred the engines built by Wright, as the Studebaker engines could be expected to run only 50 hours before they failed. Buick built the Pratt & Whitney 1830 engines for the B-24 and did a much better job.

The automobile companies were also asked to build airplanes. Ford erected a plant at Willow Run, west of Detroit, in order to produce B-24's. Overly optimistic schedules were made by people who knew little about airplanes. When the B-24 was finally in production, the inspectors found that some of the structural rivets which were the hardest to install were simply being omitted. In 1942 General Motors started out to build complete B-29's but ended up building just the nacelles. Even then, the first nacelles that were shipped to the Boeing plant at Wichita would not fit on the wings. Because they had been removed from the rigid manufacturing jigs before all the riveting was finished, they ended up warped. Moreover, sheet-metal aluminum used in the airplane structure and the stainless steels used in hot engine ducts were a lot tougher than the soft steels the automobile companies were used to. The automobile companies had to learn how to make dies that would press metal airplane parts without wrinkles.

Raising production levels in the airplane plants required greatly enlarged floor space to accommodate multiple bodies and wings in each position on the production line, so that the same operations could be performed on many planes simultaneously. The tooling had to be improved to achieve higher production rates as well as to effectively utilize inexperienced sheet-metal workers. In the "olden days," prior to WWII, it was most important to get the first airplane out early so it could be flight tested as soon as possible. The result was a minimum amount of tooling and a heavy dependence on skilled mechanics who could drill rivet holes neatly spaced by eye.

During the war, many unskilled workers were employed in the airplane factories to overcome the labor shortage, including large numbers of women, hence the term, "Rosie the Riveter." The original Rosie was said to have worked at Grumman on Long Island. They were provided with templates with drilled holes to allow easy, correct drill placement. A team of two assemblers would work on each side of a wing that was held in a vertical position. They would communicate by tapping on the sheet metal. Otherwise, they couldn't be heard above the loud din of the riveting that was going on all around them. In one

Rosie the Riveter skinning the B-17 body
Left to right—Naomi Ashley, Pearl Diaz, Helen Haugen

instance an operator using an electric hand drill with a long extension bit made the required hole in the sheet metal but then continued drilling through the neck of her partner. Nearby workers came to their aid and quickly loosened the chuck in the electric drill. They helped the victim walk under her own power over to the first aid station, the slender drill bit still sticking through her neck. The drill bit was quickly pulled out. It had not punctured anything vital.

Much of the high production rate tooling was thought up by experienced mechanics who were tired of doing the job manually. Giant hydraulic presses were used to form aluminum alloy sheet metal into compound curves such as those forming engine ring cowls and the body nose sections. The individual parts were located precisely in rigid jigs so that they could be riveted together. The engineers designing the parts and the engineers designing the tooling had to work closely together to increase the production rates. This was a complicated process, and many manufacturing methods had to be learned through on-the-job experiences. This was way beyond what could be taught in college.

High production rates required careful planning to determine the number of assembly positions of each part so that there would be no shortages to hold up final assembly, while minimizing requirements for excess part inventory storage space. During 1944 Boeing's Plant 2 in Seattle reached a peak production rate of 15 B-17's every 24 hours, a pace that was maintained for six weeks. Douglas and Vega also built B-17's. According to U.S. fighter pilot Don Hillman, now retired from Boeing, the German fighter pilots were astounded by the large numbers of B-17's. Don had to bail out over Germany when his P-47 caught fire after a strafing run over a German fighter airfield. The German officers at the base treated Don to a dinner before sending him to prison camp. They remarked that after having shot down many B-17's on any one day, the same number or even more would appear on the next Allied raid.

The plant expansion that was necessary to achieve sufficiently high production rates created a skilled labor vacuum that had to be filled quickly. The old-time engineers and mechanics were dispersed throughout the enlarged plant facilities in order to train the new hires. There was no time to train generalists, those who would have mastery of a broad range of complex tasks. Instead, the old-timers trained a vast army of specialists. Anybody who could draft or use a tool soon became skilled in a detail job. The expansion in the aircraft industry was perhaps more sudden than similar industrial expansions that had occurred previously as a result of the technological advances brought about by steam power, electrical power, or the automobile. The sudden demands of WWII changed the aircraft engineer from a "jack-of-all-trades" to a specialist in design and analysis.

During the war the middle- and lower-level supervisors in the engineering departments were those whose creativity had been proven on the drafting board, or by solving problems at a desk and making things work in lab tests. In other words, there were no "management specialists" who were brought in from the outside to lead the engineering troops. In 1930 there might be less than 100 engineers in an entire airplane company; each would be assigned responsibility to design a particular airplane part, section, or system. When he finished one assignment, he was given another. The most innovative designers soon distinguished themselves and became supervisors of a design specialty group. The selection process was positive. No genius was likely to be lost in the crowd. New hires were tried out in less demanding jobs to see what they could do.

When the organizations were still small, the phonies were soon discovered. Designers were discovered on the job and seemed to be born, not made. They needed only the engineering essentials they had learned in college, as technology was constantly changing, and with it the specific mechanical means of realizing engineering designs. But by the end of the war engineering organizations could number 5,000 or more, irrevocably changing the nature of the organization itself and its management. However, creativity still depended on the lone individual.

In 1939 the chief executives of all of the airplane companies were much alike. They had begun their careers in the biplane era, and they never became out of date in airplane design, as the fundamentals have remained the same. Between the two world wars they had to struggle to keep their companies alive. Early on, the careers of these future executives diverged from those of the still small engineering community as they became part-time sales engineers in an effort to win business from the military or the airlines. Trained engineers were best equipped to understand customer requirements for better airplane performance and reliability. These sales engineers had to be receptive to new ideas, especially those put forward by customers who had money.

From an engineering point of view, every wild idea might have some merit, however impractical it might seem at first. The sales engineers also had to be technically competent in order to have new engineering design options to offer their customers. When the airplane became more technical, they knew better than to try to become involved in details, but they could sense an absurdity. They could give effective orders that they knew would end up at the designer on the drawing board. And when the job was finished and the results brought up to them, they could personally sense whether their general orders had been carried out properly. During the war their job was the big expansion in production. After the war they were back in business as salesmen. When these executives with their vast accumulation of experience retired after the war, some of the airplane companies had difficulties as a result.

The Paper Mill

During the early years after WWI some airplane builders used a minimum of paperwork. A lone designer who had an idea but not much money might draw an airplane and then build some parts of it himself, using only three or four pieces of paper, based on his own ideas stored in his head and on what others had told him. If several identical airplanes were to be built, the drawings had to contain more information so that lesser skilled workers could utilize the data in performing their tasks, and as production expanded, so did the number of drawings.

The initial conception of an airplane or a major airplane component was most interesting in terms of how the graphic display of a design on paper could stimulate further ideas. A designer may have received instructions of just a few brief words from a theoretically inclined type of engineer who knew only that he wanted something designed but who did not necessarily know what it should look like. Although the designer might draw something that looked rather strange, it could turn out to be quite innovative. His work might then attract the attention of others in the vicinity who would lean over his drawing board to take a look. If a visitor wanted to add an idea he would draw his squiggles on a small piece of tracing paper on top of the layout so as not to mess it up. Such discussions could become highly enthusiastic and animated, indicating a bright new concept was about to be born.

This same type of scenario has always played a role in bringing about radical engineering improvements. The designer had to be skilled in the use of descriptive geometry so that he could conceptualize in three dimensions. It is amusing now that some would-be engineers without experience look down on graphics as a lowly trade. They would do well to consider whether Leonardo da Vinci, Michelangelo, Frank Lloyd Wright, or the pioneer airplane and jet engine designers who initially worked alone would have subcontracted out their conceptual graphics. The teaching of graphics may have disappeared in some colleges. A course in descriptive geometry is missing in the present day MIT catalog, unless it is hidden somewhere within the computer science department. The human mind is said to actually think in three dimensions but is restrained to flat land by paper and pencil. Those skilled in the rules governing the graphic representation of three-dimensional objects can overcome the mental restraints imposed by two-dimensional mediums to more fully utilize the mind's innate imaging potential.

The modern computer with its sophisticated graphics display software is a superior design tool because it can be used to completely define all three dimensions of an airplane part in a single picture or drawing. This electronic definition can then be rotated and transformed on the graphics display screen, making it appear as if it actually were being manipulated in space. A problem is that these systems are not yet portable or affordable, making them impractical for very small shops or individual inventors. Even in a big corporation there have been occasions when an airplane program has been saved by a pencil sketching that was made in a hotel room or on an airliner to convince the customer a change could be made or to start the designers on a new track.

By the late 1930's the formality of the drawing system had increased considerably. At the start of an airplane design, the designer first made one or more layout drawings. Initially, the layout was comprised of the minimum number of lines to determine size and shape so as visualize the airplane as a whole, and judge if it might satisfy basic requirements. This was the first step in making refined production drawings so that the various parts and assemblies depicted could be analyzed with regards to stress, weight, and interferences with other parts before being sent to manufacturing. It was important to adhere to this very methodical drawing system no matter how good the initial design turned out to be. Attempts to short-cut this process in order to get a prototype out quickly could pose problems if the prototype was so good as to be put into production right away.

To minimize rework and thus maximize the efficiency of production line assembly procedures, all discrepancies had to be ironed out in advance, despite the fact that a single prototype could be built without production quality drawings. A famous case was the Lockheed P-80 jet fighter produced by Kelly Johnson [1910-1990] in a secret small experimental division of Lockheed, called the "Skunk Works," a name derived from a popular comic strip, *Li'l Abner*. Redrawing for production took a lot of time, maybe a year. The British Spitfire fighter of the Battle of Britain was another example of a delay in what proved to be a critical situation. Because the design was not promptly redrawn to production standards, there was an excessive time lag between the proving flights of the prototype and final deliveries from the production line.

An airplane is probably the biggest assembly of intricate parts in any independently operational unit. The drawing system that is needed to facilitate and track the fabrication and assembly of all these parts in a continually changing environment defies a simple description. The drawing system is, in fact, the foundation of the airplane business, as every action starts from information on the drawing, whether this be raw materials procurement or final inspection. Drawing systems grew rapidly at the start of the war because of requests for more information from the various functions downstream from the designer. The drawing system on airplanes is different from that in other high production industries such as the automobile industry. Most airplane sheet-metal parts are shown only in assembly drawings instead of individually on separate sheets, and this greatly complicates the drawings. Drawing systems often differed from company to company. In southern California the engineers would often move from one company to another, resulting in some standardization.

As an odd analogy, one can wonder when and how music notation evolved. It may have become standardized about 400 years ago, before Bach. Musicians throughout Europe had to cooperate so they could read each other's music and so they could play together. Like the symphony conductor's music score, every necessary instruction about a particular airplane needed to be available on the drawing pages. The designer could be analogous to a musical composer. The drawing included not only a pictorial representation, but all dimensional data as well, plus a list of parts, materials, process specifications, and references to adjoining parts. The title block had places for numerous approval signatures from organizations whose responsibility it was to analyze the part in question with respect to its strength, weight, and mechanical function. The engineer responsible for the drawing instructed those downstream in the total process how to complete their various subtasks so the completed drawing would make sense. An occasional engineer might try to be as temperamental as an eccentric musician but would be forced to conform to the standards by a drawing checker.

WWII brought on a tremendous paper mill. Building the same airplane in widely spaced plant locations required a lot of coordination. Orders for changes to meet new combat requirements would arrive from the Air Force in a steady stream. The drawing system became considerably complicated in order to keep up with numerous design changes while maintaining an audit trail to the past. An assembly drawing might be comprised of several sheets, with a long tabulation of parts. If every airplane were the same, life would have been simpler. But the same basic airplane might carry different equipment for different uses. All of this information was tabulated on the drawing. Change notices were attached to the drawing, complicating its use. Production flow on the assembly line certainly could not be stopped just so the drawing could be brought up to date.

Drawings were so complicated that it might take a several minutes to find a particular part, and then more time would be required to check the change notices to see if it had been changed. Mistakes in reading the drawings were frequent. During the war some new hires attended blueprint reading classes. Even then, the graduates could not be trusted to use a blueprint correctly. The solution was to provide manufacturing tools to locate every part so that drawings were not needed to fabricate a part. In fact, if a drawing was seen in a production area, it signaled either a mistake or a quick mandatory change. The paperwork was so involved and time consuming that there was a joke that the belligerent who ran out of paper first would win the war. To avoid change-related production slowdowns during the war, the Air Corps set up separate Modification Centers to install radar systems and other new military equipment in the airplanes. They tended to dispense with factory drawings. When an airplane came out of "mod," it might be impossible to trace a wire or troubleshoot a system because there was no paper audit trail to track the design history. Consequently, these "mod" centers were referred to as "butcher shops."

The old airplane drawing system was developed over many years. The change-over to the modern computer is eliminating some of the drudgery and inefficiency of this old drawing system. Computers also provide much greater accuracy. Then as now, completed drawings represented security. When drawings were completed and printed, or "released to production," they could not be altered. A change required that the drawing be rerouted back through the system and reprinted, or "locked" in computer language. Whether one is talking about paper drawings or electronic drawings, the term "configuration control" is a law in production. But the paperwork associated with the old drawing system became an impediment because it absorbed so much effort. During the war, the laborious record-keeping task prevented the engineer from creating much that was new. After the war he was ready for a big change.

Part II

Technical Innovations

7

The Turbo-
Jet Engine

DURING THE WAR, while airplane production absorbed the major portion of engineering efforts, development was under-way on a key advancement, the jet engine. The jet engine was independently conceived in the 1930's by two independent students who started out with no affiliations in industry.

The turbo-jet engine was the most radical innovation affecting the concept of the airplane since the Wright Brothers. The turbo-jet is the simplest and lightest possible means of propelling air to high speeds. One could wonder why it took so long to dream up something that turned out to be so successful. In its basic form it has only one moving part, a shaft, which has a compressor rotor at one end and a turbine rotor at the other. With an enormous amount of hard work, the design of the piston engine and propeller had been refined to achieve high fuel efficiency and tolerable reliability. The thought of displacing such a successful, well established design was abhorrent to all but the most radical thinkers. Both industry and academia tended to weed out the few thinkers who might upset the apple cart. The need for higher speeds provided the incentive for overcoming this inertia.

During the 1930's airplane speeds increased rapidly. Most of the engineers did not take the time to theorize about the highest possible speeds obtainable by the conventional piston

97

engine and propeller, as the prospect of actually facing an upper limit probably seemed remote. From 1912 to 1931 the top speed records were set in the Schneider Cup seaplane races, an international series inaugurated by Jacques Schneider, an enthusiastic Frenchman. Britain retired the Cup by winning the 1931 race in the Solent with the Supermarine S-6B at 407.5 mph. In 1934 Warrant Officer Francesco Agello of the Italian Navy set a speed record of 440 mph in a seaplane racer that had been built for the 1931 race but which was not ready in time. The last Schneider racers were low-winged wire-braced monoplanes with the most powerful engines available. The propellers were wooden with very high fixed pitch. The take-off runs were very long, as the propeller blades were close to the stall until near top speed when full engine rpm could be reached.

Not until the end of WWII was this speed equaled in fighters, by which time the fastest fighter was the North American P-51H, with a top speed of 487 mph. WWII brought the piston engine to near its ultimate level of performance. For example, by the end of the war, the power capacity of both the British and German liquid-cooled V-12 engines had been doubled, to about 2,000 hp. The most notable of these were the Rolls Royce Merlin, which powered the Spitfire, and the Daimler-Benz 601, which powered the Messerschmitt 109. This was accomplished by using higher octane fuels and by improving the efficiency and capacity of the supercharging system. Towards the end of the war the Merlins were operating on 100/150 octane fuel. Engines were run on the test-stand at high powers until they failed and then run again with redesigned parts until they could finally pass the 100-hour military test. During the Battle of Britain, because the operational life of a fighter was short, peak performance rather than long endurance was the goal.

The propellers on the high-speed fighters were also near a speed limit. The propeller tips were going through the air in a 45-degree helical path as an advancing screw at speeds 40 percent greater than the forward speed of the airplane. The tips were moving very near the speed of sound, and the engine power was partly making waves rather than producing forward thrust. As engine powers and rpm increased during the war, the propeller became the limiting component that limited fighter speeds. The propeller tip speed had to be held below this tip speed limit by installing lower gear ratios to reduce propeller rpm and by installing lower diameter propellers with four blades. The high pitch of single-row propellers at high speeds resulted in a lot of the power being lost in rotating the slipstream rather than in providing forward thrust.

After the war the final swan song of the propeller on high-speed airplanes involved the addition of dual, counter-rotating propellers to reclaim the energy in the rotation of the slipstream. This was used on the Russian Tu-114, a large swept-wing tran-sport first introduced as a bomber in 1954. This large, Russian turbo-prop was frequently in the news with regards to flights to Cuba during the Cuban missile crisis. The Tu-114 had four 12,500 hp turbine engines. The logic behind this design was obviously to attain high speeds while retaining the maximum propulsive efficiency of propellers as compared to jets in order to obtain maximum range. The mechanical complications of the engine gear boxes and propellers were severe, and maybe these accounted for some of the Tu-114's presumed to have disappeared in over-ocean flights. The propeller tips were thin to permit highest tip speeds, and maybe the tips vibrated and broke due to metal fatigue. Although this was supposedly the ultimate in large long-range airplanes, one might presume that it was conceived by a Russian committee or central planning group that did not contain experience on mechanisms.

In the U.S. the development of dual rotation, propeller-powered long-range bombers after the war had been advocated by a think factory that was supported by the Air Force. Bombers to use such power plants were in the design stages when this trend was interrupted by the appeal of the turbo-jet because of its mechanical simplicity. By 1950 the turbo-jet had become standard for new fighters, but it was still questionable whether a jet bomber would have long enough range.

The gas turbine engine is an old idea; it appeared in a patent in England in 1791. The first such engine that would run at all was built in France before 1906, but the efficiency in terms of fuel used and power output was only 3 percent, as compared to 35 percent for a diesel engine. In 1907 in an attempt to identify a new means of generating electricity, General Electric investigated gas turbines as a possible alternative to the emerging steam turbines, which were then replacing reciprocating

Russian Tu-114 Transport

1957—12,500 hp turbo-prop dual rotation propellers. Derived from Tu-20 BEAR bomber of 1954. The Boeing B-52 design was headed in this direction until Colonel Warden changed the engines to jets.

steam engines. Because it was shown that the efficiency of the gas turbine was very poor in comparison to the steam turbine, gas turbine development was dropped. To achieve a comparable efficiency would have required much higher gas temperatures entering the turbine blades. The best metal alloys then available for the blades would be so weakened with the desired temperatures that they would have failed.

In post-WWI England there had been some interest in the gas turbine as a means of driving airplane propellers , but the thinking was constrained by the well developed ideas about industrial steam turbines. These turbines had cast-iron outer cases split in two halves with bolted flanges, and were therefore very heavy.

Prospects were very poor for an airplane engine based on the steam turbine concept. The aeronautical departments of U.S. educational institutions were teaching piston engines, although undoubtedly there were visionaries interested in gas turbines. At MIT in the late 1930's there was no instruction offered concerning gas turbines for airplanes. More significantly, the MIT professors regarded the turbo-supercharger, which was a step towards the gas turbine power plant, as inferior to jet stacks for the production of additional thrust from reciprocating engine exhaust. This attitude prevailed despite the turbo-supercharged bombers that had been in high production at the start of the war. Some academicians missed "the boat of a lifetime," along with most everybody else.

In 1921 a Frenchman named Guillaume patented a turbo-jet engine for the propulsion of airplanes, which at that time was brilliant forward thinking. While it had the good features of a multi-staged axial compressor, his patent depicted a very small space for combustion and a hand crank for starting, indicating little concept of the real technical requirements. This patent was overlooked until well after turbo-jets were running. The same basic idea occurred independently to two college students: Frank Whittle in England in 1929, and Hans von Ohain in Germany in late 1934.

Frank Whittle

Whittle came from a family of limited means. His father was a machinist who owned a small manufacturing concern. From him Whittle learned machine work and drafting. Whittle first attended a small college, but in 1928 he was accepted at the RAF College as a flight cadet. During the technical courses he became interested in high speeds. After four years of instruction and preparation of a thesis on high-speed flight, he became interested in jets as a means of avoiding the limitations of the propeller. In this time period the speed of fighters was still only 150 mph, and at this speed the propeller was far short of the limit set by tip speeds.

Whittle first considered the combination of a conventional piston engine driving a high-pressure fan, all enclosed in a duct. Additional fuel would be burned aft of the fan to raise the temperature and thus increase the velocity of the gas at the exit nozzle. However, his calculations showed that the performance would be very poor due to the weight of the piston engine, the low power of the existing piston engines, and the high fuel consumption due to the combustion that would be occurring aft of the fan. This combination of the piston engine and the ducted fan was later built by the Italians and installed on the Caproni-Campini airplane, which was flown in 1940. While this was the first truly "air-jet" flight, the resulting performance was poor, just as Whittle had predicted. Whittle then developed his ideas further, substituting a gas turbine engine for the piston engine to considerably increase power and reduce weight, but still with the fan being driven by a shaft from the engine.

Whittle's next thought was a stroke of genius. Why not combine into one rotor both the turbine engine compressor and the fan, since both were doing the same job of compressing the air—in other words, enlarge the compressor to do both jobs? Besides simplifying the layout of the whole scheme, the combined rotor would produce a much larger airflow than that of the original compressor, and all this airflow would go through the turbine as well. With this greater airflow the temperatures in the turbine could be lower in providing the power to drive the compressor. This would solve the high temperature problem that had previously held up the development of the gas turbine engine. The turbine would have to extract only enough energy from the gas flow to drive the compressor, leaving the remainder to produce the thrust that would propel the airplane. This reasoning took place in October 1929 after he had graduated from flying school and while he was attending Flying Instructor's School. In this duty he had leisure time to organize his thoughts and came up with a winner. Bright ideas often occur in periods of relaxation after having struggled with the mathematics of a difficult problem.

This scheme would be much easier to design and test than one with a separate gas turbine engine to drive a fan or a propeller, such as the design Dr. A.A. Griffith of the Royal Aircraft Establishment had been working on since 1926. Once his basic idea had taken shape, Whittle was faced with the problem of designing the hardware. A choice had to be made between two types of compressors: the bladed axial disc which required several stages to achieve the desired pressure, or the single rotor centrifugal compressor which was similar to those being used in piston engine superchargers. Although the centrifugal compressor might have been within Whittle's capacity to build and test, the air output pressure had to be twice that of the centrifugal superchargers then in use. At this point in his education at the RAF College, he had enough knowledge of mathematics and physics to make preliminary performance calculations and to analyze the requirements of the engine components.

Whittle applied for a patent in January 1930. His drawing depicts a ring of small exit nozzles around the periphery of the engine instead of the single large nozzle which became standard on all later jet engines. It was hard to visualize how this engine could be installed in an airplane.

Whittle's commandant at the Flight School secured an appointment for him at the Air Ministry, which controlled the British government's funding of research. However, they were negative. Whittle would have been helped by an installation drawing of the engine as it would appear in an airplane, and a performance report showing the benefit of the low weight of the engine. But at this stage, the production of these data would have been way beyond his resources. He later had the opportunity to explain his engine design to Dr. Griffith, the Air Ministry's principal expert on gas turbines. Griffith replied that Whittle's assumptions about the performance of the engine components were too optimistic. Had Griffith been a proponent of very high speed flight, his response might have been more positive. Griffith seemed to have dismissed or overlooked the central features of Whittle's radical engine concept, which were the elimination of the propeller and the alleviation of the high temperatures that posed a problem in the gas turbine.

However, a reward for Whittle's work eventually showed up. His thesis at the Flight School, entitled "Future Developments in Aircraft Design," which was finished in June 1928, and his radical engine concept that he arrived at in October 1929, resulted in his assignment in July 1934 as an RAF officer to Cambridge University for a two-year Engineering Course. Later, this additional education proved to be essential in confirming his stature as an engineer during the promotion of his new engine. Whittle's credentials also lent credence to his ability to actually help design a sufficiently reliable aircraft engine.

Whittle was concentrating on his studies at Cambridge when, in the middle of the term, he was contacted by R. D. Williams, a former roommate when both had been test pilots at the RAF base at Felixstowe in East Anglia. Williams had resigned from the RAF because of health. He and his business partner, J.C.B. Tinling, another ex-pilot, visited Whittle at Cambridge with the idea of promoting the financing of the turbo-jet engine development. Williams had retained his enthusiasm for Whittle's engine that was derived from their conversations at Felixstowe. Tinling had a family connection with a well-known aeronautical engineer, M.L. Bramson, who in turn captured the interest of a private investment banking company, O.T. Falk & Partners.

Because Whittle's technical education at Cambridge was sufficiently advanced to permit preliminary design work, he was able to start designing the new engine while still continuing his studies. Additionally, he was aided by the machine work and drafting he had learned from his father. He was given encouragement from a famous aeronautical professor at Cambridge, Melvill Jones. Whittle continued his studies at Cambridge but divided his time to help in the building of a test turbo-jet engine.

The development of such a radical engine concept from preliminary design to flight status would eventually require funding far beyond what could be expected from the private bankers. The first task was to build an engine for a test stand demonstration to prove that its thrust would be reasonable for flight. Such a test engine would provide visual proof of its small size and weight. The demonstrator also had to give sufficient evidence of high reliability characteristics. Once this was accomplished, it might be possible to attract sufficient financing to build a prototype that was qualified for flight.

The engineering design, parts manufacture, and testing was contracted for with the British Thomson-Houston Company in June 1936. This firm might be likened to GE in the U.S., due to its prominence in building machines for electric generation. The initial contact with BTH was arranged by W.E.P. Johnson, an RAF pilot who had been an instrument instructor at the Flight School while Whittle was studying there. Johnson's brother knew the BTH chief engineer, where both were at Rugby School. It is noteworthy to mention that Whittle received much of the necessary support from pilots, who were enthusiastic about the engine and who were uninhibited by engineering reasons as to why such a new and unconventional idea would fail. The sequence of the conception and the tenuous promotion of such a radical engine was remarkable, and would have been strange inside most industrial environments. Some technical types had been contacted early in attempts to obtain backing, but were initially negative. After an engine ran, the critics found ways to assist on the project—maybe to avoid embarrassments.

Three prototypes were built and tested before there was sufficient knowledge and confidence to design an engine that would be tested in actual flight [Figure 13]. The first prototype did not resemble an object that would fit in an airplane. It was used strictly to test the engine components, and remarkably, it was operational by April 1937, only 10 months after the contract signing with BTH. This first jet engine prototype was quite simple in its design, as it was best to start the project from a base of currently available knowledge. It would run on its own power after the starter was disconnected. This was encouraging and even remarkable in light of the later experiences of some large corporations' engineers who tried to build a complete engine and found that it would not continue rotating after disconnecting the starter. But Whittle's first engine operated in such an uncontrolled manner and revealed so many problems that its thrust was not reported. However, it was tested for four months before it actually failed. The test provided sufficient data to motivate the Air Ministry to initiate financial assistance.

Unlike the first jet engine prototype, the second engine bore some resemblance to a shape that might ultimately fit on an airplane. It was first run in April 1938, only a year after testing of the original prototype had begun. It ran for only one month before failure, but a thrust of 480 lbs was recorded. The third jet engine prototype became operational in October 1938. It revealed many problems but was useful throughout the long test period as modifications were made to almost every component in an attempt to overcome the major difficulties. With its compact form and single exhaust nozzle, it looked very much like an engine that could be installed on an airplane. In June 1939 the Air Ministry contracted with the company Whittle and his associates had formed, called Power Jets, for a flight-ready engine. The Air Ministry contracted from Gloster for an experimental airplane to be designed around the engine. Gloster was a builder of fighters.

An engine qualified for flight was first tested at the BTH facility near Coventry in April 1941. It was installed in a small experimental airplane, the Gloster E-28/39. The new engine flew for the first time in May 1941. Gerry Sayer, Gloster's chief test pilot, was the pilot [Figure 14]. The first flight lasted 17

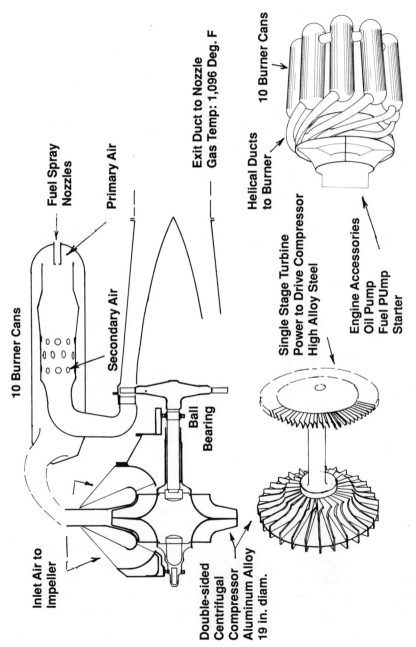

10 Burner Cans

Fuel Spray Nozzles

Primary Air

Secondary Air

Exit Duct to Nozzle Gas Temp: 1,096 Deg. F

Helical Ducts to Burner

10 Burner Cans

Inlet Air to Impeller

Ball Bearing

Double-sided Centrifugal Compressor Aluminum Alloy 19 in. diam.

Single Stage Turbine Power to Drive Compressor High Alloy Steel

Engine Accessories Oil Pump Fuel PUmp Starter

Figure 13—Whittle W-1 Turbo-Jet Used on First Flight

minutes and was uneventful. Sayer overtook some Spitfires, whose pilots were amazed at seeing the nose had a hole rather than a propeller. Later they jokingly explained this by saying that the Gloster sucked itself along like a Hoover vacuum cleaner.

From then on the development of the turbo-jet concept accelerated rapidly. Thrust was increased from the 850 lbs on the first flight engine to 1,700 lbs on the production models installed in Gloster twin-engine British Meteor fighters. These entered service in June 1944 in time to be used in the interception of the German V-1 buzz bombs.

A copy of the original flight-test engine was flown to GE at Lynn, Massachusetts, in October 1941. At that time GE was building turbo-superchargers for U.S. bombers and fighters. This corporation was therefore the logical place where the U.S. Army could get quick action in terms of new engine production. The first mass-produced U.S. turbo-jet engine was a GE design based on Whittle's concept. It generated 4,000 lbs of thrust and was installed in the Lockheed P-80, which first flew in January 1944 and later saw service in Korea.

Whittle was a true genius and what one might term a "one man gang." He understood almost every aspect of the turbo-jet design project, pushing it vigorously to success in the first flight and later into production. One can imagine that there were some people who were offended by his close attention to technical and business details. The effects of Whittle's zealousness showed up years later in situations when his advice was ignored on the use of jets instead of propellers. Whittle was a real genius, but his countrymen failed to recognize the full implications of his work, possibly because of the narrow vision of some British airplane designers on the future potential of the jet. A notable exception was deHaviland.

Whittle received only nominal monetary rewards, the excuse being that he had received military pay during the entire development period. Whittle's health was compromised by the stress of attending Cambridge for two years followed by a year of post-graduate work, during which time he labored to correct engine problems that were revealed in testing. In 1948 he retired from active participation in the project after he was assured that the turbo-jet development was well underway.

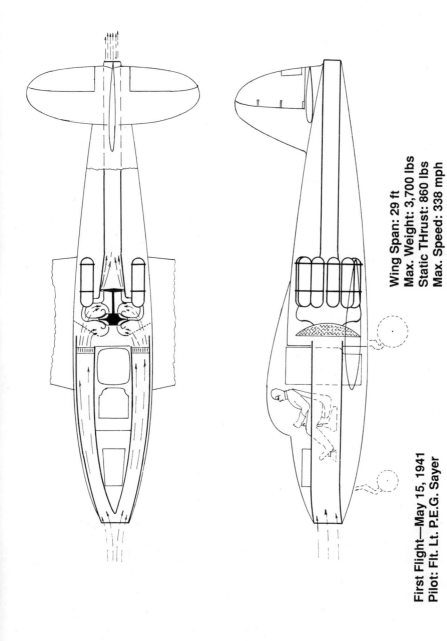

Wing Span: 29 ft
Max. Weight: 3,700 lbs
Static THrust: 860 lbs
Max. Speed: 338 mph

First Flight—May 15, 1941
Pilot: Flt. Lt. P.E.G. Sayer

Figure 14—Gloster E-28-39 Experimental

Lockheed P-80 Jet Fighter

One GEI-40 engine. First flight January 1944. Over 1,000 built. Served in Korean War. Obsoleted by North American F-86 Swept-Wing Jet Fighter.

Hans von Ohain

The German development of a turbo-jet engine was also started by an individual without the help of industry or government. An engineering student by the name of Hans von Ohain began thinking about jet propulsion in the fall of 1933, about the time Whittle was continuing his calculations and about two and a half years before Whittle finally succeeded in getting financing to support actual prototype development. In 1934 von Ohain started the preliminary design of a jet engine while he was still a student at Gottingen University.

Gottingen was famous for early wind tunnel testing and the development of aerodynamics. At the end of the year von Ohain decided to build a working model at his own expense. Apparently, he believed he had sufficient personal means to build a successful engine. It was fortunate that he underestimated the task, because otherwise he might not have started. His engine had a centrifugal compressor similar to Whittle's, but used a radial in-flow turbine, where the flow is from the maximum diameter inward to the exit nozzle.

Von Ohain had the help of Max Hahn, the head mechanic at the garage where he kept his car. Hahn was a machinist with considerable talent in design. Together they built their turbo-jet engine prototype. The compressor was formed from sheet metal. Von Ohain obtained permission from his university professor,

R.W. Pohl, to use his instruments and equipment and to run engine tests on Gottingen University property. However, the combustion of the gasoline fuel took place not in the combustion chamber as was intended, but downstream in the turbine, with flames coming out of the exit nozzle. The engine would not run without some power from the starting motor. Even though von Ohain's initial tests were disappointing, he had hardware to show for his efforts. The cost was about equivalent to $10,000 of that time period, a considerable amount for a student to spend.

In spite of the engine's failure to run unassisted, Professor Pohl continued to encourage von Ohain and offer his help, an attitude good teachers should always have. He wrote a letter to Ernst Heinkel, a German airplane manufacturer whom von Ohain had selected as the best bet for further development assistance. (Von Ohain had decided not to approach the engine manufacturers because he believed they would be negative on the idea of a turbo-jet.) Heinkel started out as an airplane designer in WWI. He built up a company of considerable size in the manufacture of military airplanes. In later years von Ohain described him as being obsessed with speed, his mission in life being to build high-speed airplanes. Heinkel had recently built a very clean single-engine, low-wing airplane, the He-70G. This was supposed to be a mailplane with seats for up to four passengers, which was allowable under the Versailles Treaty. However, the He-70G looked more like a military prototype.

Heinkel was quite receptive to Professor Pohl's letter, and he invited von Ohain to his home for a conference with his leading engineers. At the time, Heinkel was busy building a fighter prototype to compete with Messerschmitt, (the latter won with ME-109, the fighter to become famous in WWII). It seems surprising that Heinkel had time for von Ohain. The Heinkel engineers were skeptical, but with the boss showing enthusiasm, they were smart not to pour cold water on the idea. Heinkel arranged for von Ohain, with his mechanic helper from Gottingen, Max Hahn, to report directly to him. In order to demonstrate the basic turbo-jet principle in an engine that had the greatest probability of working the first time, von Ohain chose hydrogen as the fuel. Hydrogen burned more quickly than any other fuel and would tolerate wide mixture ratios [Figure 15].

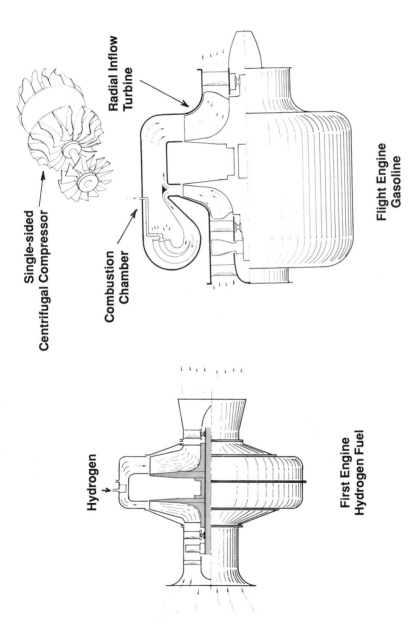

Single-sided
Centrifugal Compressor

Radial Inflow
Turbine

Combustion
Chamber

Flight Engine
Gasoline

Hydrogen

First Engine
Hydrogen Fuel

Figure 15—Von Ohain-Heinkel Turbo-Jet

After testing his first experimental engine at the university, von Ohain was left with the belief that combustion with liquid fuels would pose a major problem. Nine months after beginning the design work, the von Ohain-Heinkel collaboration resulted in a hydrogen-fueled engine that ran successfully, producing 550 lbs of thrust. The test run generated much enthusiasm among Heinkel's airplane designers. An engine using gasoline was finally run in 1939, but not before encountering considerable developmental problems with the combustion section. A specially designed airplane, the He-178, flew in August 27, 1939, before the first flight of Whittle's engine. There were only company witnesses, as attempts to attract the participation of top military observers was thwarted because this first flight was on the eve of the invasion of Poland and all military personnel were unavailable [Figure 16]. Later attempts to interest the German government attracted the bureaucrats who financed engine developments. They became very enthusiastic. However, they decided that jet engine development belonged in an engine company, not at Heinkel.

While Heinkel continued his jet engine development efforts, building and flight testing a twin-jet fighter, the bureaucrats initiated a jet engine development competition between BMW and Junkers. Even though neither firm was interested initially, the bureaucrats employed the subterfuge of telling each firm that the other was secretly busy on the development project. The result was the Junkers Jumo 004, which was selected to power the Messerschmitt 262, a twin-engine jet fighter that startled the world. It first flew in March 1943, but its use as a fighter was delayed until April 1944, because Hitler wanted it to be used as a bomber. This was a serious, tactical mistake because, were it not for this delay, the 262 could have caused the loss of Allied air superiority and possibly prevented the U.S. 8th Air Force bombing of the German synthetic fuel plants that was a major factor in bringing the war to an end. Nevertheless, 262 operations during the last stages of the war were sufficiently impressive to show the world that the piston-engine fighter was obsolete.

The experiences of both Whittle and von Ohain demonstrated the effectiveness of expedited experiments by technically trained, uninhibited minds. Theoretical studies alone

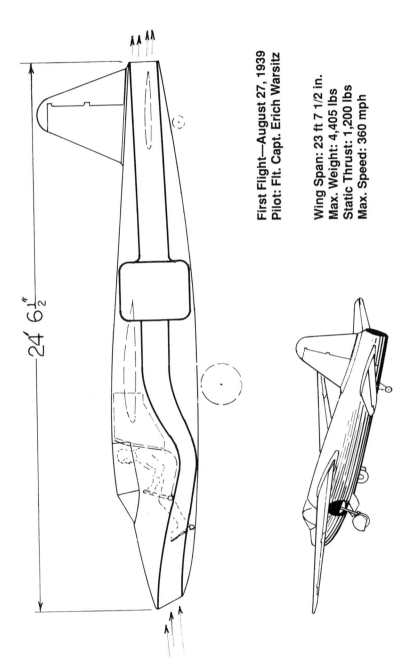

First Flight—August 27, 1939
Pilot: Flt. Capt. Erich Warsitz

Wing Span: 23 ft 7 1/2 in.
Max. Weight: 4,405 lbs
Static Thrust: 1,200 lbs
Max. Speed: 360 mph

24' 6½"

Figure 16—Heinkel He-178 Experimental

Messerschmitt 262 Jet Fighter

Two Junkers Jumo 004 engines. First flight July 1942; 1,443 built; 300 operated against U.S. piston-engine fighters near the end of WWII. Note engine nacelle location close under wing, an unfavorable location.

probably would have overlooked the turbo-jet in favor of the turbo-prop, at least for a considerable amount of time. The effectiveness of the individual thinker compared to the collective minds in industry and government was most clearly illustrated by the dual success of Whittle and von Ohain. In fact, the ability to design the actual engine hardware without complete dependence on established organizations was essential to their accomplishments in developing the first turbo-jet engines.

8

The GE TG-180
Jet Engine

THE DEVELOPMENT of the British jet engine was unknown
to the U.S. Army Air Force until 1941, even though in 1936 the
design and manufacture of the first ground test engine had been
started. A high level of secrecy surrounded the British work, but
cooperation between Britain and the U.S. on military technical
developments was opened up when President Roosevelt signed
the Lend-Lease law on March 11, 1941. This law cleared the way
for the U.S. to provide war materials to Britain to fight the Axis.
Britain wanted destroyers to defend against the German U
Boats that were sinking cargo ships crossing the Atlantic.
Britain promptly requested B-17C bombers. Twenty were ferried to England in May 1941. Because the British were unfamiliar with turbo-superchargers used on the B-17's, GE, which
manufactured the turbos, sent a technical service representative to England.

Roy Shoults was an inquisitive type, and somehow he
learned of the turbo-jet project. Possibly he visited the piston
engine manufacturers that were building the gear-driven supercharger impellers for their fighters. Since turbo components
were similar and in fact were fabricated using the same type of
machine tools, Shoults might have seen some of the larger rotors

for the British jet engines. He alerted the U.S. Army Air Force liaison officer in England, who in turn informed the Chief of the Army Air Force, General Hap Arnold [1886-1950].

In the U.S. before Pearl Harbor General Arnold was one of the very few who had enough imagination to foresee the need for a radical aircraft engine to achieve higher speeds. He graduated from West Point in 1907. One of the very early test pilots, he had learned to fly in Dayton, Ohio, in 1911, and since that time had always been a forceful promoter of technical progress. When informed of the turbo-jet, he promptly visited England in May 1941. The British informed him of the whole development. Without waiting for the first flights of the Whittle engine, General Arnold returned to the U.S. and started activities to catch up with the British. Because he did not want to overburden Wright, Pratt & Whitney and Allison, which were building piston engines for the wartime airplanes, he selected the large U.S. manufacturers of steam turbines to begin the turbo-jet development. GE was selected to develop a jet engine for the Army Air Force. Having Roy Shoults on the scene in England may have given GE the edge in starting a new business that was to become tremendous. The Navy selected Westinghouse to build jet engines for use on carriers. Allis-Chalmers Corporation received a study contract from the Navy. Of these three only GE persisted in developing turbine engines for aircraft.

GE's experience with the aircraft industry in the installation of their turbo superchargers in several airplanes was of considerable advantage. Because the turbo-supercharger was analogous to the turbo-jet engine in the appearance of the rotor, GE was a logical choice. On October 1, 1941, a duplicate of the original airworthy Whittle engine was shipped from England to the GE plant in Lynn, Massachusetts, arriving on October 4. Asked to develop an engine similar to the Whittle design, GE produced the I-A, which could generate 1,250 pounds of thrust, as compared to 850 pounds approved rating of the Whittle engine on the first flight in May 1941. Two GE I-A engines were installed in the twin-engine Bell P-59A, which flew in October 1942 only one year after GE had begun work on the project; this was an excellent accomplishment for both GE and Bell.

Two months before the Whittle engine arrived at Lynn, the Army Air Force had asked GE to also study the feasibility of a turbo-prop rather than a turbo-jet because the Navy felt it would be generally more suitable for aircraft operations on the short decks of carriers. The turbo-prop engine development was assigned to the Schenectady GE plant, which had already been working on a turbine engine driving a propeller for a Navy torpedo boat. Although the turbo-prop and the turbo-jet engines were similar, the turbo-prop had extra rows of compressor and turbine blades and a gear box to drive the propeller. It was more difficult to develop than the turbo-jet because it required more refined blading to obtain higher efficiencies. Another design difficulty posed by the turbo-prop was the reduction gear, needed to lower the high turbine speed to propeller speeds. On the initial runs in May 1943, GE's TG-100 turbo-prop engine did not produce enough extra power to drive a propeller. However the experience proved to be very beneficial.

The principal engineers were Glen Warren, who had studied gas turbines in college and had been interested in airplanes and ram jets, and Alan Howard. They both preferred the axial compressor to the centrifugal compressor of the Whittle type of engine because the former had the potential to achieve higher pressures and thereby higher efficiencies. Furthermore, the axial engine had a smaller diameter and thus fitted much better into most airplane installations.

At that time, Warren and Howard received no help from previous airplane design studies, but they probably understood that low frontal area was important because it would cause less drag. The compressor was the major challenge. They became familiar with the literature on axial compressors, including the work of Eastman Jacobs of the NACA, the predecessor of NASA, the compressor work of O'Brien and Folsom of the University of California, and the compressors of the Swiss firm of Brown-Boveri. (Folsom later went on to become president of Rensselaer Polytechnic Institute in Troy, New York.) While the TG-100 engine was a failure, the associated development of the compressor components led to the turbo-jet.

At this stage in the T-100 program it was apparent that the development of a successful turbo-prop engine and its controls would require quite a long time. In contrast, the centrifugal turbo-jets were already being built at GE's plant in Lynn and were being flight tested in the Bell XP-59. Interest at Schenectady

Bell XP-59—First U.S. Jet Airplane
Two GE I-16 engines derived from English Whittle engine. First flight October 1942; 50 built; obsoleted by P-80.

thus shifted to the turbo-jet. In May 1943 the Army Air Force asked GE to study the feasibility of a turbo-jet that would generate 4,000 pounds of thrust, enough to permit a single-engine fighter rather than a twin-engine fighter like the XP-59. In this regard, GE decided to study two engine concepts, continuing with the centrifugal type at Lynn and assigning the axial type to Schenectady. Even as the TG-100 turbo-prop development continued, the GE design team leaders began focusing their attention on a turbo-jet design, designated the TG-180. It must have been a big relief to move beyond the turbo-prop, and furthermore, the absence of the propeller cut the development time of the turbo-jet to a fraction of that of the turbo-prop [Figure 17].

The TG-180 first ran on the test stand in April 1944, 13 months after the start of the program. The first flight test was conducted on March 12, 1946, in a Republic XP-84 fighter. Two and a half months later in May, the TG-180 was also flight tested in an XB-43, a Douglas twin-engine medium range bomber designed specifically as a test bed. Douglas submitted a list of 250 complaints on the TG-180. By March 12, 1947, the engine was fully qualified, in plenty of time for the first flight of the North American XP-86 fighter on October 1, 1947, and on the Boeing XB-47 bomber on December 17. The TG-180 was so reliable by the onset of XB-47 flight testing that engine failures were rare and did not retard the airplane program at all, a remarkable achievement. No piston-engine development ever gave such satisfaction.

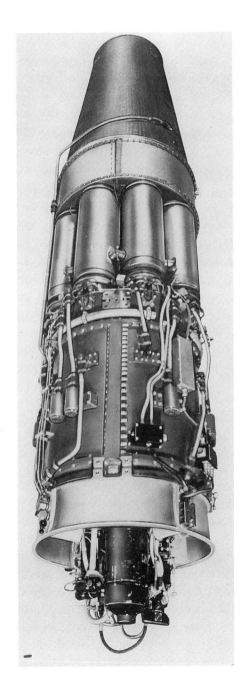

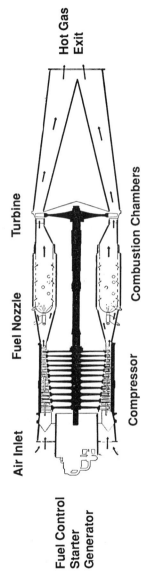

Figure 17—GE TG-180 Jet Engine—4,000 Lbs. Thrust, 1947

Douglas XB-43 Experimental Bomber

Two GE TG-180 engines; first flight May 1946; two built. Served as test bed for engines.

The adaptability of the TG-180 to the pod mount on the XB-47 bomber and its subsequent use in the Korean war on the F-86 fighter put the U.S. ahead of the British in terms of high production of axial-flow turbo-jets. The British had tested an experimental axial engine as early as December 1941, the Royal Aircraft Establishment Metrovic F-2 engine. Initially it produced about 1,700 pounds of thrust. By August 1943 this had been raised to 3,500 pounds. The more powerful version of the F-2 was flown in a twin-engine Gloster Meteor whose nacelles were located close under the wing, similar to the nacelle placement on the Me-262 German fighter. In the meantime, considerable progress on the centrifugal type of turbo-jet was being made in England at Rolls Royce. Consequently, British development of the axial turbo-jet was delayed. It wasn't until 1952 that Rolls Royce Avon built the axial engine for fighters and the deHaviland Comet airliner. The podded wing mount on the XB-47 influenced the U.S. trend towards the axial engine. Additionally, the axial type engine made possible higher thrusts for fighters, causing centrifugal engine development to be dropped. GE was thus established firmly in the airplane engine business.

Pratt & Whitney entered into the turbo-jet engine business about a year behind GE when the Navy asked P&W to build the Rolls Royce Nene centrifugal engine for the Grumman F-9 F-2 straight-wing jet fighter in 1946. Interestingly, the English also helped Russia build the Rolls Royce Nene. It was used in the

Korean war in the MiG-15, a swept-wing fighter that proved to be superior until the appearance of the North American F-86 Sabre swept-wing fighter with the GE TG-180/J47 engine. By the conclusion of the Korean war in 1953, the turbo-jet engine had become standard in fighters, but it was not yet accepted for transports, except for the deHaviland Comet.

9

The Boeing High-Speed Wind Tunnel

EXPERIMENTATION HAS ALWAYS played the major role in airplane development. The first wind tunnel testing was on details such as wing sections to determine their lift and drag, and on other parts like wheels, struts, and engine radiators to determine their drag. Wind tunnel tests of a complete airplane model were often made after the airplane had been flight tested to see if the wind tunnel testing techniques and the balances measuring the forces and moments on the model had been improved sufficiently so that the wind tunnel data agreed with the data from flight. Flight testing results depended largely on the pilot's opinions, as instrumentation in the cockpit was primitive. Recorders for taking data in flight were first attempted in the 1920's. For many years following the Wright Brothers, flight testing was the principal means of checking an idea or discovering something new in the aerodynamics of the complete airplane.

When wind tunnel techniques had progressed so that

complete model airplanes could be tested with some assurance that the results would be meaningful, the designers began building wind tunnel models as soon as their designs became sufficiently defined. The considerable time and cost required to build the first airplane for testing, and the risks on the first flight on a design that departed widely from past experiences, resulted in the building of wind tunnels before flight. The early wind tunnel tests were used mostly to verify the design rather than to find a better one.

At least 30 years were required to develop wind tunnel testing techniques to the point where the data obtained were dependable and complete enough to be a factor in making major design decisions. Up to about 1935 the testing of a model of a new airplane could take only a day or a week of tunnel occupancy. The development of the first large swept-wing airplane, which was started in 1945, required over a year of continual occupancy of a wind tunnel, with the "wind on" day and night, except when the model was being modified or a new version was being installed.

The history of aerodynamic experimentation predated attempts to build flying machines. The early designers soon discovered that they needed data on lift and drag to determine the size and shape of the wings. As early as 1745 experimenters were attempting to measure the lift of wings by mounting models at the outer end of whirling arms, about 25 feet from the pivot point. Power to rotate the arm was applied by dropping a weight connected to a rope and pulleys. The measurement of the lift and drag would have required impossible linkages between the model and a weighing scale located at the pivot. After several revolutions of the whirling arm, a wake would form that reduced the airspeed over the model.

The wind tunnel became possible with the development of small steam engines. The airplane or wing model could then be maintained in a stationary position with a weighing scale to measure lift. In 1871 the first tunnel was built by an Englishman, F. H. Wenham [1824-1908] for the Royal Society. It had a square test section measuring 1 1/2 feet across. There is no record of what was tested in this tunnel. Possibly, Wenham tested the outline of a fish to determine the optimum profile for the lowest drag. The cross-section he drew is surprisingly similar to that of today's streamlined struts. In about 1890 Sir Hiram Maxim, the wealthy inventor of the machine gun, built a wind tunnel with a 3-foot square test section capable of generating airspeeds of 50 mph. It was powered by a small steam engine. He tested many airfoils in this tunnel and he built an unsuccessful steam-powered flying machine that weighed 8,000 pounds. Because he disdained mathematics, it was unlikely that he could have made reasonable performance calculations using his tunnel data. In 1891 a Russian professor, Nikolai E Joukowski [1847-1921] who later became famous in aerodynamic theory, built a tunnel at the University of Moscow.

The Wright Brothers soon found that they could not trust the published data on wing lift and drag, and so in 1901 they built their own wind tunnel. It had a 22-inch square test section and generated airspeeds of up to 35 mph. The fan was driven by a belt from the line shafting that powered the machine tools in their bicycle shop. By that time, electric power was available in Dayton. The Wright's lift and drag measuring instruments were ingenious and accurate. They calculated the airspeed by measuring the wind's force against a flat plate mounted broadside to the airstream in the wind tunnel test section. They calibrated the force versus airspeed on the flat plate by first mounting the flat plate on the handlebars of a bicycle, with a spring scale to measure the force on the flat plate, and using the bicycle speedometer to measure speed, presumably on a calm day. During the design of their flyer, the Wrights measured lift and drag on 200 airfoils. The fact that they were successful on their first attempt at powered flight indicates that they used their airfoil data correctly in making their calculations of sufficient speed for lift-off.

In 1908 an aeronautical wind tunnel laboratory was built for broad research by Alexandre Gustave Eiffel [1832-1923], famed for the Paris tower. Eiffel was a brilliant engineer. He recognized that aviation was quickly becoming a highly technical field. His first wind tunnel was comprised of a round, 4.9-foot diameter test section that could generate airspeeds of 40.3 mph. The tunnel's fan was the same type as that used for ventilation in the Eiffel Tower. His second tunnel, which was operated during WWI, had a 6.6 ft diameter test section and generated airspeeds of 71.6 mph. Eiffel's design of the wind tunnel, as well as the precision balances it contained for measuring the model forces, set an international standard for 15 years. He published extensive data that were bound into a fine volume, published in France in 1910. It was translated into English in 1913 by Jerome Hunsaker [1886-1984], a graduate of the Naval Academy who taught the first course in aeronautics at MIT from 1912 to 1916. Some of the data from Eiffel's tunnels were probably used in designing the French planes flown in WWI. In 1912 a tunnel was built in England at the National Physical Laboratory. It had a 4-foot test section. The airfoils on the British fighters probably were designed using this tunnel to some extent.

The war rapidly advanced European aeronautical design and research, leaving the U.S. so far behind that Congress authorized the formation of the National Advisory Committee for Aeronautics in March 1915. Through the years the NACA produced a large amount of valuable research data that was used extensively by the airplane manufacturers. In 1919 the first NACA wind tunnel was built at Langley Field, Virginia. It had a 5-foot diameter test section and could generate airspeeds of 90 mph. In 1916 MIT had a wind tunnel with a 4-foot square test section that was used in testing the first Boeing airplane. By 1919 the U.S. Army Air Signal Corps had a tunnel at McCook Field, Dayton. The airfoil design for the Piper Cub wing probably came from this tunnel. Soon after WWI the Curtiss Aeroplane Company had a tunnel at Garden City, Long Island, with a 7-foot diameter test section. The fan was driven by a 400-hp Liberty 12-cylinder surplus engine, the type that was used in the deHaviland DH-4 bombers that were built in the U.S. during WWI.

Tremendous encouragement to aeronautical education and wind tunnel testing was brought about by the Daniel Guggenheim Fund for the Promotion of Aeronautics. The Guggenheim fortune was made in mining ventures extending all the way from central Mexico to the Yukon and western Alaska. A portion of the Guggenheim philanthropy was directed towards aviation by Daniel's son Harry. He had become a private pilot while attending Yale. In 1917 he enlisted in the U.S. Navy for flight training. In 1925 Harry began assisting New York University to promote aeronautical education. Out of this effort the Guggenheim Fund was developed. Between 1926 and 1930 grants were made to eight major universities—New York University, Purdue, MIT, Michigan, Cal Tech, Stanford, the University of Washington in Seattle, and Georgia Tech. The fund permitted the construction of buildings for classrooms, laboratories, and wind tunnel test facilities.

The Cal Tech tunnel had a 10-foot diameter test section and was capable of a speed of 200 mph. It was patterned after the tunnels in Germany at Gottingen and Aachen, at the insistence of Theodore von Karman [1881-1963], a pioneer in aerodynamic theory and rockets. The Cal Tech tunnel was outstanding for testing complete airplane models. The test section was sufficiently large and the airspeeds sufficiently high so that the tunnel test data agreed closely with data obtained during actual flight. The University of Washington built a similar sized tunnel in 1937 with state and private funding. Due to their greater size of test sections and speeds, these two tunnels became heavily used by the airplane companies on the West Coast of the U.S., to the point where the data from them became trusted. The nature of the viscous airflow next to the wing surface changes with size and speed. The technical problem of fluid friction was researched on boats as early as 1843, and since 1904 there has been much activity in researching viscous flow on airplanes. The mathematical analysis is still going on. The experimenters in the wind tunnel and the airplane designers have not had much help from the theory.

A technical explanation of viscous flow is beyond the capability of the author, but a simplified explanation may help the reader to understand why the there is a critical size of tunnel above which the airflow more closely simulates that on full-scale airplanes. The air over the wing surface is slowed by friction next to the wing surface, producing a thin layer of slower air below the full speed of the air above. In the first few inches behind the wing leading edge the increase in speed above the surface could resemble that of the sliding of a deck of cards. Further back on the wing the flow next to the surface breaks into turbulent mixing. Thus, on a very small wing much of it could be in the sliding type of flow, while on a larger wing most of the wing would have turbulent mixing in the thin layer of air next to the surface. This turbulent mixing permits the angle of attack to be higher before the flow on the wing upper surface would separate, thus increasing the maximum lift and delaying the airplane stall. By a combination of larger models, turbulent air in the wind tunnel circuit approaching the model, and maybe some artificial roughness on the model leading edge, the sliding flow can be prevented. After considerable testing in the two larger tunnels mentioned above, and with fair agreement of the data from flight testing, confidence in wind tunnel testing was established in the late 1930's.

Shortly before WWII, when aerodynamic knowledge was accelerating, wind tunnel test time was difficult to obtain anywhere in the U.S. and had to be scheduled far in advance. Yet most often the problem to be resolved was of immediate importance to a project. Such a scheduling effort might be likened to reserving a hospital operating room three months before a possible appendix attack. The ideal situation was to involve the airplane designer directly with the tunnel testing so that tunnel data could be quickly incorporated into design improvements on a continuous basis and so that recommendations generated by the test effort did not overlook engineering requirements.

By the late 1930's wind tunnel test time was in such high demand that some of the airplane companies wanted their own tunnels. In 1940 Lockheed built a tunnel having the same test section size and airspeed capability as the University of Washington tunnel. Boeing had just started to copy Lockheed's tunnel design when von Karman intervened. He was a high-speed enthusiast and recommended to Eddie Allen, the head of Boeing flight test and aerodynamics, that their tunnel should be designed for very high airspeeds, close to the velocity of sound.

The logic behind this recommendation was not apparent in August 1941, given the type of airplanes Boeing was designing. The B-29 tests that had been conducted in the fairly new NACA 8-foot wind tunnel at Langley Field demonstrated that the B-29 wing did not reach the speed above which the drag rose rapidly. At the time, there was very little high-speed data on full-sized, complete airplanes. The preliminary design studies being conducted at Boeing did not yet anticipate a "jet age," and so the idea of a high-speed wind tunnel seemed unsupportable. The jet engine work in England was still highly classified and known only to a very few in the U.S. Dr. von Karman may have known about the jet engine through General Hap Arnold, who had visited England in the spring of 1941 to review its development. Also, the swept wing, which was soon to open up a higher speed regime, was not yet in the picture. This topic had been discussed in an international meeting in Rome in 1935, but apparently, virtually everyone in U.S. aviation circles had overlooked it.

From the standpoint of Boeing's current business, the added expense of a high-speed wind tunnel could not be justified. However, despite all these factors, Eddie Allen received authorization to go ahead, with an estimate that the project would probably cost a million dollars, about four times the cost of a low-speed tunnel. Such a large outlay of company funds would seem to indicate a careful calculation of risks and benefits. In actuality, the selection of a wind tunnel concept that would generate very high airspeeds was born more from simple enthusiasm rather than a genuine presentiment of the technology to come.

The design was all "in house," rather than being contracted out, as was the custom in the NACA. Therefore, it had to be simple and practical. The author was in charge, with the work being divided with an assistant, H. W. Withington, both fairly recently out of MIT. We knew how to draw and test. The detail drawings for distribution to the builder, the Austin Company, were made by the small group that designed the Boeing wind tunnel models. Delegating such a job of designing, on what turned out to be a tremendous asset, to two relatively junior engineers, would not be considered nowadays.

Because of the newness of high airspeed testing at Boeing, two consultants were engaged, von Karman of Cal Tech and Professor John Markham of MIT. They advised that a simple tunnel that operated at atmospheric pressure would produce aerodynamic high-speed data that would be at least as realistic in interpretation to full airplane scale as a complicated tunnel, such as Cal Tech was then planning. This latter tunnel was to be pressurized at lower speeds, as theory predicted that multiplying the air density in the tunnel was equivalent to multiplying the size of the model, giving full scale data. The fallacy of this tunnel design was that it had to be evacuated at maximum speeds to lower the required fan power and to reduce the tunnel air-cooling load. In the enclosed tunnel air circuit of the Cal Tech design, there had to be a large refrigeration system to take out the energy added by the fan. The evacuation in the Cal Tech tunnel reduced the effective scale of the model at high speeds, and thus at high speeds it simulated a lower scale than the atmospheric Boeing tunnel. The principal problem of the future was deemed to be at high speeds. The two Boeing consultants guided us to a simpler and yet superior design.

The wind tunnel design sought to ensure convenience and simplicity in terms of the test procedures that would be implemented. The design aimed for a smooth, uniform airflow in the test section with an enclosed air circuit to save the momentum of the air. This acted like a "flywheel," with only 10 percent of the energy going through the test section being added each time the air went around, so as to minimize the cost of the high-power equipment. The general arrangement was based on Boeing's experiences in the high production wind tunnel testing of the B-29. The air circuit and the fan were developed by extensive testing of a 1/20th scale model. Like the University of Washington tunnel, it had a rectangular test section 12 feet wide by 8 feet high, and a flat floor with a turntable for testing directional stability. The round test section at Cal Tech did not permit a turntable and was awkward in which to work.

The wind tunnel balances that measured the forces and moments about the airplane center of gravity were distinctly ahead, and used many ideas from the University of Washington's tunnel balances, designed by Professor Fred Eastman, and from the MIT balances, designed by Professor John Markham. The object was to minimize the flow interference of the model supports that extended up from the floor of the tunnel. Also it was desired to have the data printed out on a wide sheet of paper in final form that did not require any computations to access the beneficial or adverse effects of the last change to the model. The object in much of the testing was to determine which way to proceed in reducing the drag, so as to decide on the next quick change to the model. High accuracy data production and quick advice to the airplane designers were the main objectives.

Unlike the NACA tunnels, the walls of Boeing's tunnel structure were constructed of reinforced concrete rather than steel plate, to avoid coming up against the wartime priorities

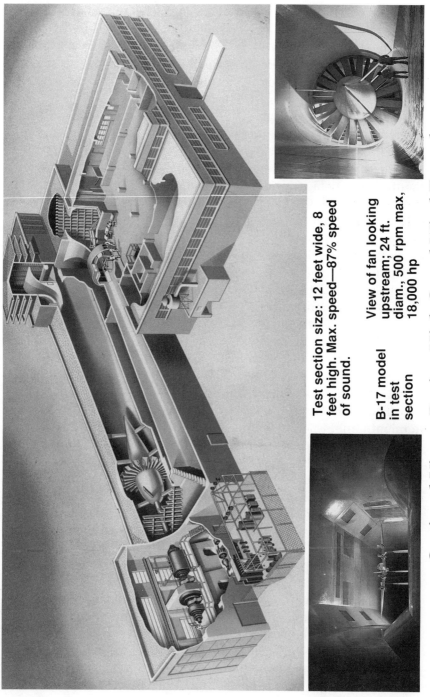

Test section size: 12 feet wide, 8 feet high. Max. speed—87% speed of sound.

B-17 model in test section

View of fan looking upstream; 24 ft. diam., 500 rpm max, 18,000 hp

Sectional View—Boeing High-Speed Wind Tunnel

that had been placed on this particular commodity for shipbuilding. President Roosevelt had banned the shipment of scrap iron to Japan on September 26, 1940. The Bethlehem Steel Company plant in Seattle melted the scrap into reinforcing bars for the concrete construction, and this was still available at the time the tunnel was built. The recently completed Grand Coulee Dam was ample assurance that there would be enough electric power to run the wind tunnel's 18,000 hp motor.

In terms of the future development of jet technology, the timing of the wind tunnel go-ahead in August 1941 was ideal, although no one knew it at the time. Two years previously, in the summer of 1938, funds at Boeing were tight, and on Wednesdays there were often rumors in the drafting room that the bosses might not be able to meet the payroll and issue checks on Friday. But by the summer of 1941, B-17 production had reached a fever pitch of activity and revenues were high. The top bosses were so busy planning the expansion of the plant for the B-17 production that they probably gave little thought to the high-speed wind tunnel after giving the go-ahead.

The Austin Company, who had built most of the Boeing plant in Seattle, was contracted to build the wind tunnel. By the time of the Japanese attack on Pearl Harbor, the Austin Company had finished the design and had already started construction of the concrete structure, the major part where outside help was needed. Westinghouse built the main electric power system and fan shaft. Dynamatic Corporation of Milwaukee built the variable-speed coupling between the motor and the fan. The balances were built in the Boeing machine shops. If the construction had been delayed even a little, it might have been postponed indefinitely or canceled outright, but since the momentum of the project was already established, it was easier to let it continue.

The tunnel became operational in February 1944 and was fully checked out by the end of the war, in time for the start the XB-47 swept-wing bomber. The tunnel had cost three quarters of a million dollars, about 25 percent less than the original estimate, but still a very significant sum in the minds of those that had lived through the lean years in the airplane industry. During the postwar years, Boeing was uniquely fortunate among U.S. airplane manufacturers in having at its disposal the uninterrupted use of a high-speed wind tunnel, at a time when technical innovations were badly needed. The cost of operating the tunnel in a postwar period was given little thought at the time of construction. As it turned out, this did not become a problem, as an enormous amount of new business was generated with the help of the tunnel.

10

The Swept Wing

In 1935 THE POSSIBILITY that sweepback could be used to increase the speed capability of the wing was disclosed publicly for the first time in Rome at the Fifth Volta Congress of High Speed Flight. This international meeting was organized by General Arturo Crocco, the director of scientific research for the Italian Air Force, and it was attended by leading aerodynamicists from around the world. Dr. Adolph Busemann, a professor in Germany, presented a long and highly mathematical paper dealing with the effects of sweepback on airflow at supersonic speeds, but his paper did not have suggestions on applications. At dinner that evening General Crocco made a sketch on the back of the menu depicting an airplane with a sweptback wing and sweptback propeller blades. He gently chided Dr. Busemann for being too conservative in not actively advocating the application of sweepback to aircraft design. For several years there was no follow-up research on sweepback. During the war, fighter speeds had not yet approached the speed of sound, which marks a critical point where the forces acting on an airfoil change radically. Although some knowledge in the area of high-speed aerodynamics was available by this time, it was not enough to motivate a new wing design, principally because the jet engine had not yet appeared. For example, the existence of a rapid rise in drag at sonic speeds was already known from testing propellers and studying the aerodynamic forces acting on the fast moving tips. Other tests had measured the drag forces acting on projectiles in very small supersonic wind tunnels. However, this knowledge was not seen as applicable to the wings of the relatively slow aircraft then on the drawing boards.

The fundamental theory of the swept wing is surprisingly simple. On the upper surface of a swept wing the airspeed can be resolved into two legs of a right triangle, one parallel to the wing span (see "A" in Figure 18) and one perpendicular to the wing leading edge ("B" in Figure 18). The latter is the effective component that produces the negative pressures on the wing's upper surface that results in lift. The airspeed component (A) parallel to the wing span has no effect.

Imagine a plane in flight with wings whose sweep can be varied with a touch of a control. Assume there is excess thrust available from the jet engines. In level flight the wings are first set in the forward, unswept position. The plane is being flown just below the speed where the airflow on the wing's upper surface, which is always faster than flight speed, is very near the speed of sound. At slightly higher speeds the upper air flow will start to separate and the plane will approach what is sometimes called a "high-speed stall." Imagine that the pilot then activates a control to start sweeping the wing back. At the same time the thrust is increased so as to keep the component (B) perpendicular to the wing's leading edge, the same as when the wing was unswept, in order to maintain the required lift. The negative pressures on the wing's upper surface have remained constant during this operation, as has the lift. The airplane is now traveling faster and is still below the high-speed stall. Because of the extra thrust the plane can now climb to a higher cruise altitude where the thinner air allows a return to the earlier level of fuel consumption. Sweepback is that simple. The airflow on the wing upper surface changes with speed, and is so complicated that the theoreticians have not been able do much in reducing the drag rise at the "sonic barrier" [Figure 19]. Progress has been dependent on wind tunnel testing.

In 1939 Dr. Albert Betz and his associate Ludweig at Gottingen University performed the first wind tunnel test to evaluate the benefits of sweepback in delaying the rise in drag that occurs at high speeds. By this time design studies of the

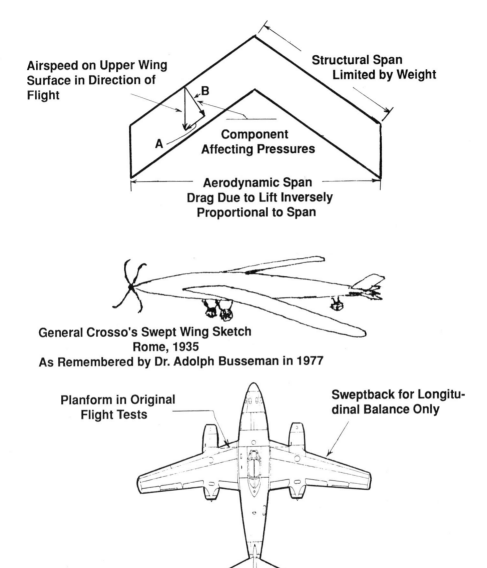

Airspeed on Upper Wing
Surface in Direction of
Flight

Structural Span
Limited by Weight

B

Component
Affecting Pressures

A

Aerodynamic Span
Drag Due to Lift Inversely
Proportional to Span

General Crosso's Swept Wing Sketch
Rome, 1935
As Remembered by Dr. Adolph Busseman in 1977

Planform in Original
Flight Tests

Sweptback for Longitu-
dinal Balance Only

Messerschmitt 262

Figure 18—Inspiration for Sweepback

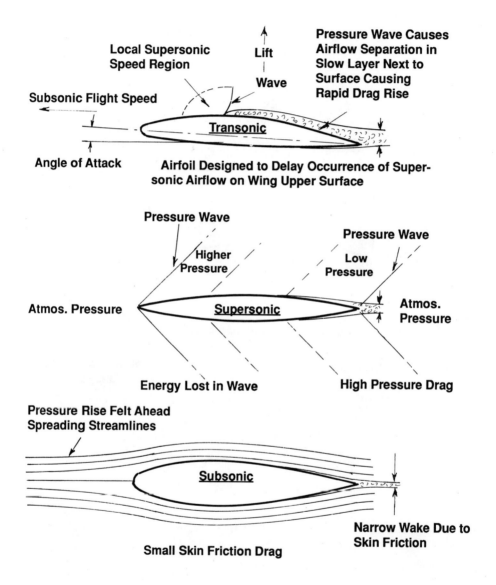

Figure 19—Transonic Drag Rise

Messerschmitt 262 jet fighter were underway. The 262 wing was slightly swept in order to obtain satisfactory longitudinal balance, given that the engine nacelles were hung aft under the wing rather than forward as in conventional fighters. Initially, the portion of the 262 wing that was inboard of the nacelles was straight, having no sweep whatsoever in relation to the fuselage. Early flight tests showed, however, that this portion of the wing exhibited a premature flow separation at high speeds. Consequently, the design was changed and this portion of the wing was swept as well. A Messerschmitt engineer named Puffert had learned of the benefits of sweepback from Betz, and he may have been behind the change. Apparently Busemann's paper in Rome had not previously alerted the Messerschmitt designers about sweepback. Several jet airplanes with swept wings were soon started as a result of Betz's wind tunnel tests. But the German efforts were not known in the U.S. until the end of the war.

In late 1944 when it was anticipated that Germany would soon surrender, General Hap Arnold asked Dr. von Karman to select a group of experts to examine the German research accomplishments on site in Germany as soon as the military front lines permitted. Von Karman's team was called "The Scientific Advisory Group." Its mission was to investigate all areas of German aeronautics and weaponry, including aerodynamics, rocketry, radar, nuclear weapons and electronics. Among its members were many nationally known technical experts. Most of them came from government service and from educational institutions. Among the few who had experience in aerodynamics was George Schairer, head of aerodynamics at Boeing. Dr. von Karman had been associated closely with Schairer during the design of the Boeing high-speed wind tunnel and probably felt he was as up to date as anyone with respect to airplane design, and would thus make a good addition to the team.

There was some objection to including an individual from industry, as this might give certain companies competitive advantages. If the objectors had stopped to think, they would have realized that if this were a valid objection, it would have been because such an individual would have hardware experience that would make it more likely that he, rather than the academic and military types, would be the one to spot an exceptional technical development. And clearly, an exciting discovery that answered some worrisome technical problem had the potential not only to enrich academic theory, but also to stimulate parallel development activity in American industry. There were other survey groups formed by the Navy and the Army Air Force that did include a larger number of representatives from industry. To one who stayed at home, the U.S. government's plans to investigate the achievements of German technology sounded like a big Easter egg hunt.

It had become known that the Germans were engaged in advance developments. In 1939 British Intelligence learned from Norway about long-range German rocket developments, and in 1943 the rocket development center at Peenemunde on the Baltic coast was photographed from the air and bombed by the British. The V-2 ballistic rockets that were developed at Peenemunde started attacking London in September 1944. The Messerschmitt Me-262 jet fighter started operating against U.S. piston engine fighters in October 1944, clearly indicating that Germany was ahead in some aeronautical developments.

Before leaving for Germany in April 1945, Schairer had seen Robert Jones, an aerodynamicist at the NACA at Langley Field. Jones had fairly recently prepared a report on wing sweepback, but the editorial committee had rejected his report for publication as being too farfetched. No NACA wind tunnel tests had been made, but Schairer was thus alerted to the implications of sweep. When the investigative team entered Germany soon after the allied troops had secured the country, von Karman knew where to go for aerodynamic data before it might be destroyed, since he had studied and worked at the German universities.

In fact, some of his old acquaintances were still around, among them Professor Prandtl, a pioneer in theoretical aerodynamics. Schairer and von Karman visited Prandtl at the University in Gottingen, in central Germany. The roof of Prandtl's home had been blown off by the bombing, and his research had come to a halt. There was little friendship between von Karman and Prandtl because Prandtl had in effect worked for Hitler. When Prandtl asked if there was research he could do for the U.S. after the war, von Karman replied, " You will work for anybody, just like a prostitute." In Germany during the data seeking mission, Schairer also encountered another German professor, Heinz Peters, who had taught at MIT shortly before the war. Obviously, Peters had bet on the wrong country.

However, the most interesting data on sweepback's application to airplane design came from German industry rather than academia. The Junkers Company had conducted swept-wing tests in a high-speed wind tunnel with a relatively small test section that was only 1 meter square. The team obtained considerable data on an experimental Junkers four-engine bomber, the model 287. Its wing was swept forward by 25 degrees rather than being swept back, probably because of concerns about wing tip stalling and loss of aileron control at high lifts, which might have been aggravated by sweepback, but prevented by sweepforward. The German wind tunnel data clearly showed the benefits of sweep in permitting higher speeds. The photographs of the Junkers 287 that the team obtained showed that two of the four engine nacelles were located forward on the body, while the remaining two were located very far aft on the wing, probably in order to avoid airflow interference with the wing. Obviously the Junkers' engineers had conducted extensive wind tunnel tests. Despite the advanced features of the general configuration, however, the experimental 287 had a fixed landing gear and was to be flown only at low speeds. The end of the war had cut off further development.

Just before the war ended, Messerschmitt had been in the process of designing a successor to the Me-262. It had 45 degrees of sweepback and was almost ready for flight testing when Germany surrendered. The engines were located close to the body just behind the wing, instead of being located on the wing as on the 262, thus avoiding a loss in speed due to nacelle-wing airflow interference. The Arado Company had built a twin-engine bomber, designated the model 234, which had straight wings and whose engine nacelles were located immediately under the wing similar to the Me-262. Arado was well aware of the nacelle interference problem; their wind tunnel tests varied the fore and aft locations. The Me-262 and the Arado are on display at the Air Space Museum in Washington, DC.

The ability of the Germans to perform this advanced

development under wartime conditions is truly amazing. The allied bombing was mostly directed at the airplane production plants, which were dispersed. The Junkers main office, which may have escaped the bombing, was in Dessau in East Germany, on the Elbe River southwest of Berlin. The experimental 287 may have been designed there. The Russians surrounded Berlin in April 1945, and thus Junkers had little time to flight test and manufacture a high-speed airplane. After the Russian victory the Junkers engineers were moved to Russia to continue their work, possibly voluntarily, or maybe with some urging.

The Messerschmitt developmental office was located in Augsburg in southern Germany and the 262 was probably designed there. Messerschmitt also had a bomb-proof developmental center in the mountains at Oberammergau, the site of the famous passion play. The production plant for the Me-109 fighter at Regensburg, northeast of Munich, was effectively bombed by B-17's. Even during the last years of the war when victory must have looked questionable, the German engineers were still engrossed in wind tunnel testing and advanced design. Maybe this activity provided a means of escaping from reality or perhaps it was merely to keep busy.

All the German data that the investigative team gathered were photographed with 35 mm cameras and distributed to U.S. industry. Soon after Schairer came across the data on sweepback, he wrote a letter to Boeing in Seattle, dated May 10, 1945. In the letter he stated that sweepback was a very important discovery. He included a brief calculation he had made of the trade-off between increased airspeed and increased wing weight, assuming a sweep of 29 degrees, that showed there was a lot to be gained from a swept wing. In his letter back to Boeing he gave instructions that copies of his letter should be sent to six aerodynamic leaders in the U.S. industry. He was not sure when the importance of sweepback as he saw it would be distributed through other channels, and in any case, his presence on von Karman's committee required this cooperation. In an attempt to avoid censorship and delay, he mailed it through the Army APO, with CENSORED handwritten on the envelope and his signature underneath.

This was the extent of the knowledge on sweepback in the U.S. at the end of the war. The U.S. response to the German data

Junkers 287 Experimental Jet Bomber

Note swept forward wing, probably to avoid tip stall. Valuable wind tunnel data obtained by U.S. at end of the war. The 287 was taken to Russia along with the Junkers engineers.

was mixed, except in the case of the North American Company, which built the F-86, a fighter that proved itself supreme in Korea. Years later, Harrison Storms of North American told Schairer that it was the data from Boeing that had caused them to sweep the wings of their F-86. There was a feeling among some institutional types in the U.S. that when the war was over, the frantic production efforts should give way to a long period of research, in order to "do things logically," as if the tremendous technical progress that had been made during the war could have been better achieved without pressure. As a result, research on sweepback was not widely undertaken, except by Boeing on the XB-47 and by North American on the F-86. The Korean War turned this attitude around. The engineers in industry were desperate to develop new and better products. Russia promptly used sweepback in the MiG-15 jet fighter that appeared in 1947 and which was supreme in the Korean War until the F-86 became operational.

Part III

The Long-Range Swept-Wing Airplane

11

The Jet Bomber

BY THE TIME OF PEARL HARBOR most of the engineers in the airplane industry were engaged in an intense effort to enhance existing designs already in production in order to maintain vital wartime supplies of combat ready aircraft. However, some conceptual designers were assigned to study new, untried concepts. Likewise the Army Air Force at Wright Field had a few visionary officers who were looking for more effective types of airplanes. The Air Force started work on jet fighters in the spring of 1941 following General Arnold's review of the Whittle jet engine development in England. The first U.S. experimental jet fighter, the Bell XP-59A, flew in October 1942. The idea of applying the jet engine to bombers was soon to emerge.

Initially, the jet engine had been thought of as being useful only in fighters because of its high fuel consumption which resulted in short airplane ranges. However the idea of a "medium-sized jet bomber" was conceived by officers at Wright Field who were in charge of bomber development. Either they were very imaginative or else they just wanted "to get into the act" by proposing such a radical idea. The medium sized bombers used in the war, the North American B-25 and the Martin B-26, had the capability of long ranges at low altitudes and were thus effective in low level attacks on ground installations and on ships. By comparison, the jet airplane achieves its maximum range only at high altitudes, as the jet engine is "leaned-out" in the thin air at altitude, and the drag is less in the thin air. The long-range jet airplane is "at home" at high altitudes. So any mission for a medium jet bomber seemed obscure at the time.

In late 1943 the Army Air Force asked five contractors to study the feasibility of multi-engine jet bombers, all to use the GE TG-180 axial flow jet engine. In May 1946 the first U.S. jet bomber flew—the Douglas XB-43. It had a high wing with two engines that were enclosed within the body. However, the Air Corps desired a four-engine bomber, and so the XB-43 was used only as a means of service testing the GE TG-180 jet engine.

In April 1944 the Air Corps established a preliminary specification for a four engine jet bomber. North American, Convair, and Boeing submitted designs that were all very similar, having thin, straight high span wings with the engines mounted in two twin pods placed close under the wing and outboard from the body about a third of the distance to the wing tip. They looked so much alike that the NACA was able to make a composite wind tunnel model to determine the major aerodynamic characteristics of all three jet bomber designs. After having arrived at a basic configuration, the next most important order of business was to collect high-speed wind tunnel data, as it was anticipated that aerodynamic problems would be discovered. Wind tunnel test time was difficult to obtain, as there were only three suitable high-speed wind tunnels in the U.S. at that time—two of which were located at the NACA laboratories while the third belonged to Boeing. This was during the war, and the NACA tunnels were overloaded with testing to correct design problems found on combat airplanes. The manufacturers, other than Boeing, were very limited in obtaining high-speed testing.

The data from the composite NACA model was sufficiently encouraging so that in the early summer of 1945 the Air Force awarded North American a contract to build three XB-45 prototypes. Similarly, Convair was awarded a contract to build three XB-46's. Martin submitted a six-engine design, the XB-48, and received an order for two. High-speed wind tunnel testing of any alternative configurations that might have been desired by the individual manufacturers was limited. The German wind tunnel data on swept wings was just becoming available. So the

North American B-45 Bomber

Four GE TG-180 engines; first flight March 1947; 142 built. Obsoleted by Boeing B-47.

XB-45 and the XB-46 turned out to be rather ordinary in comparison with the final Boeing XB-47 design, which was delayed and was not a contender at the time of the contract awards to North American and Convair. The XB-47 flew eight months after the first flights of the XB-45 and XB-46.

The Boeing high-speed wind tunnel was in operation when the Air Force issued the jet bomber specification. A model similar to the NACA composite model was first tested in the Boeing tunnel, but the top speed was found to be prematurely limited by the drag of the twin engine pods located on the underside of the wing. A search was then made to find a design that did not have this disadvantage. Therefore, Boeing delayed submitting a prototype design, required for a fly-off competition with North American and Convair. And so Boeing risked having their design studies canceled.

The performance potential with the jet engine resulted in the first encounter of the bomber designers with the problems associated with high-speed aerodynamics, and was possibly the first instance of dependence on the wind tunnel in advancing airplane performance. Heretofore the intuitive designer, using only his drawing board, often produced designs that, with limited development in the wind tunnel, won the air races and the military competitions. Bomber designers had been using high span wings with relatively thick airfoil sections in order to reduce structural weight and to provide maximum volume for fuel in the wing. Higher speeds, on the other hand, required thinner wings to minimize the local air velocity over the wing's upper surface.

When the speed of sound was reached in this area of the airfoil, a rapid rise in drag occurred fairly abruptly when the airplane speed was further increased. This was caused by the airflow separating over the aft part of the airfoil's upper surface. A nacelle located just under the wing further increased the air velocity on the wing's upper surface, requiring either an even thinner wing, or a different configuration altogether [Figure 20]. The early jet fighters avoided this problem by locating the engine behind the pilot, as in the experimental planes that flew with Whittle's and von Ohain's jet engines. After some wind tunnel testing Boeing deviated from the configuration of the NACA composite model by locating the four engines on top of the body, but this turned out to be impractical.

The XB-47 Bomber

The end of the war in August 1945 left an abrupt vacuum in many airplane companies. The B-29 was the last big job at Boeing, and there was nothing left to do except to bring the drawings up to date for filing. The engineers were wondering where they might find work and whether the bosses had anything in mind for the future. B-29 engineers like myself were not much concerned about having to move to new projects, as anything would have been better than the long hours and weekend work on detail drawings we had become accustomed to during the war years. The bosses were more than agreeable to okaying vacations in order to give themselves time to sort things out. I took a two week-vacation in San Francisco.

When I arrived back in Seattle, I was told that I would work in aerodynamics on a new jet bomber, the XB-47, that would feature a radical design change, the swept wing. The program manager was George Martin, who had a strong background in structures. I knew nothing about the Medium Bomber program, jet engines or swept wings. These subjects were classified, with the "need to know" restriction in the distribution of information. This advanced work was far removed from what I had been working on.

For the two years before the end of the war, I had been working in the B-29 engineering group in an old department store building in downtown Seattle. The number of engineers was so large that there was no room in the main Boeing plant for the B-29 paper mill. I had been working on special equipment such as fast-acting bomb doors, radar, cabin pressurization, and numerous gadgets. Since coming to Boeing in 1938, I had had little experience in structural design, and so I was thought of as a gadgeteer. Due to the importance of the B-29 program, the engineers had little contact with those in the main engineering organization at Plant 2 in south Seattle, and so had little idea on what was going on elsewhere in the airplane business.

When I was told that I would be head of a very small aerodynamics group on a high-speed bomber, I wondered why. I was not qualified in high-speed aerodynamics. The only logical connection was the fact that the development of the swept wing would involve a lot of wind tunnel testing and I had done quite a bit of this on the B-29. Also, I was the co-designer of the Boeing high-speed wind tunnel, along with Bob Withington, so I understood its operation. I surmised that the top bosses wanted somebody who did not know enough to argue on the finer technical points and to question whether the XB-47 would be successful or not. At this early time the XB-47 was considered to be an unsure venture, and the livelihood of Boeing would have to come from elsewhere.

The unique position of Boeing among those in the medium bomber competition was in having a high-speed wind tunnel that could be used full time on the XB-47. This changed the whole character of the usual preliminary design process and opened up room for novel ideas concerning the airplane configuration as well as new approaches to researching high-speed airflow. The original XB-47 design, which was like the NACA composite wind tunnel model with a straight wing and engine nacelles tucked close under the wing did not seem to make sense and so the wind tunnel tests with the swept wing began with the engines relocated on top of the body. The Boeing XB-47 had been delayed so long to find an airplane design that would make

**Combined Airflow Would Cause
Higher Velocity on Wing Upper
Surface**

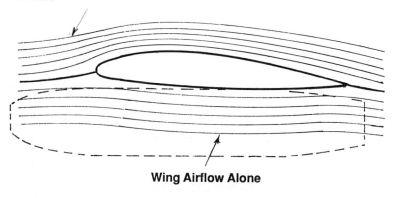

Wing Airflow Alone

The Reason for the Forward Strut-Mounted Pod

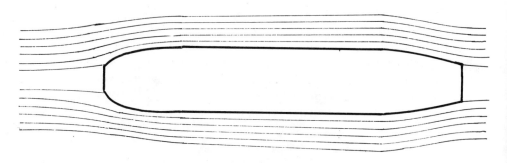

Nacelle Airflow Alone

Figure 20—Nacelle—Wing Interference

better use the capabilities of the jet engine, that it was far behind North American and Convair, who by this time were in the process of drawing their prototypes for manufacture.

Up to this point Boeing's research on the medium jet bomber had been funded on company overhead, as allowed by the Army under an arrangement called "Independent Research and Development." The size of this allowance was proportioned in relation to the company's military business under contract. With this arrangement the research and testing was carried out as Boeing thought best, but with Wright Field being kept abreast of developments. The Air Force's interest in the XB-47 might have ended except for a new idea which came just in time. The swept wing, which was introduced to Boeing in George Schairer's famous letter mailed from Germany in May 1945, provided Boeing with an opening in cooperating with the Air Force at Wright Field, so as to become quite active in the medium bomber competition.

Schairer had included in his letter from Europe on sweepback a short calculation showing that 29 degrees of sweep would allow a higher speed than could be achieved with a straight wing and that the weight of the swept wing would still be reasonable. This calculation indicated that the sweep might be increased even further. Although the German data pointed the way, the testing of sweep at Boeing had to start from scratch. One week after Schairer's famous letter was received, the original straight wing XB-47 model was cut on the center-line in order to test a range of sweep angles, to verify the general effectiveness of sweep, and to obtain data on the amount of sweep needed versus the critical speed at which the drag would rise.

At this early stage the determination of the optimum sweep angle would have required that the whole airplane be rede-signed many times over. This would have taken too much time, but more pertinent, there still was not enough data available to design an airplane with a swept wing. It was sort of a "chicken-and-egg" situation. Regardless of which exact sweep angle turned out to be optimum, in order to get started, an initial standard sweep had to be selected so that work could begin to investigate possible problems that might be brought on by sweep.

Using the preliminary data from the model that had been

Straight Wing, Two
Twin-Engine Nacelles

Straight Wing,
Engines on Body

35-Degree Swept Wing,
Extended Wing Tip,
Six Podded Engines

XB-47 Wind Tunnel Models —1944 to May 1946

sawed in half, a sweep angle of 35 degrees was selected by Victor
Ganzer, a University of Washington graduate who was then
working in the small XB-47 aero group. According to Vic's
calculations, 35 degrees of sweep were required so that the
airflow on the wing's upper surface would not be separated at
the airplane speed resulting from full thrust of the engines.
Enough performance calculations had been made to indicate
that six GE TG-180 engines would be needed to allow such a
large bomber to meet an increased range goal that had been set
by the Boeing project engineer, George Martin. The range of the
XB-47 in the military specification was 2,200 miles, the same as
that of the XB-45 that was then being built by North American.
But George Martin did not think such a short range would sell
a production airplane in the postwar period. This judgment was

to be proven very correct when the concept of intercontinental bomber range became popular.

The GE TG-180 engine could produce 4,000 pounds of thrust and no larger engines were in sight, thus the need for six engines. The sweep angle of 35 degrees that Vic selected became "locked in" during the development process of the XB-47 and was never changed. It was amazing that today's transports have sweep angles very near to this, considering that the original figure of 35 degrees came about with so little hard test data.

The change to a swept-wing configuration had to be coordinated with the Bomber Project Office at Wright Field, which worked closely with the airplane manufacturers. Understandings between the manufacturer and the Project Office had to be good, as otherwise the Air Force's desires would not be satisfied and there might be no business. During this period Boeing was operating under an Air Force study contract, the terms of which were cost plus a fixed fee. An additional stipulation was that the Air Force and Boeing would reach an agreement on technical matters. The Wright Field Project Office was generally receptive to new ideas provided they had confidence in the manufacturer's technical ability. In the case of the XB-47, Wright Field must have been attracted by the potential of Boeing's wind tunnel to accelerate research of a swept-wing bomber. The Project Office was probably looking for something new at the war's end, just as Boeing was.

The swept-wing change was presented to the Project Office by the Vice President of Engineering, Ed Wells, and the head of Preliminary Design, Bob Jewett. The Project Office accepted it as a risky but reasonable venture, based on Ed Wells' say so. Ed had established a solid reputation as the co-designer of the B-17 and as one who would only sell what he believed in. However, the Project Office had to obtain agreement from the other side of the Wright Field organization, the Laboratories, and here the Project Office met resistance. The Labs viewed Boeing's swept-wing bomber as a wild idea, which in actuality it really was. There was no technical data to support such an idea other than the German wind tunnel test results and the operational demonstrations of the Me-262 jet fighters. Possibly, the Labs had not been thoroughly alerted to the extent of the German development efforts in this area, or perhaps they thought that fighters were the only jets suitable for swept-wing development. However, on a second trip to Wright Field Ed Wells was able to convince the Laboratories that the swept-wing XB-47 was a worthwhile project.

Trying to obtain a broad consensus outside of Boeing that a swept-wing jet bomber was a good idea would have slowed down the program or killed it, as there were a lot of would-be experts who would have liked to get into the act and research the individual problems to death rather than to first tackle the airplane as a whole. Attempting to make a thorough analysis on paper beforehand would have resulted in the discovery of only a few of the problems, which could have been so alarming and difficult to resolve on paper as to cause a halt to the program. As it turned out, all of the significant problems were discovered during the course of testing the complete airplane in the wind tunnel and in flight. Changes were introduced and retested with reference to the complete airplane rather than to isolated components. In several instances this tactic resulted in being "painted into a corner," as the preferred solution to a particular problem brought on another problem. Further testing, however, inevitably led to the proper solution in terms of the airplane as a whole.

The Army had been burned many times by manufacturers who promoted questionable ideas and then built a poor airplane at great expense. A lot of experimental airplane failures can be attributed in part to insufficient wind tunnel testing and poorly defined goals. In the case of the XB-47 the design had to be proven as much as possible in the tunnel and on the drawing board before a prototype could be built. The widespread doubt that existed during the early stages of the XB-47 development project proved to be an asset, as the doubters did not want to waste their time on what they had predicted would fail anyway, and so the engineers on the XB-47 were free to pursue various design alternatives without being asked to present lengthy justifications at every step along the way. After the initial flight tests in the spring of 1948 the other entrants in the jet bomber competition were left far behind.

The support for the XB-47 during the period of resolution of the airplane configuration from the Air Force Project Office, particularly from Colonel H.E. "Pete" Warden and from Colonel

Ed Nabel, was outstanding, especially in view of some of the Air Force's previous bad experience with experimental aircraft. They knew very well that there would be problems along the way that they would have to endure while remedies were being found. Without these supporters there might have been no XB-47. The reasons for their support might be explained by the novelty of the swept wing, the intensive wind tunnel testing, the rapid corrective actions in response to their criticisms of the configuration, and the prospects for a revolutionary bomber.

First Wind Tunnel Tests and the Low-Speed Stall

The objective of the first wind tunnel tests of the swept-wing model was to confirm the effectiveness of selected sweep angle in increasing the top speed and then to explore for potential problems, without taking the time to solve each one as it was encountered. Solutions to the major problems required eight months of wind tunnel testing in which every component of the airplane was significantly changed from two to five times. So little was known about the swept wing that accidental improvements on one problem could occur as the design was changed for other reasons. For example, a change in the general configuration to solve an outstanding mechanical problem or to make the layout more practical might bring about an accidental improvement in performance. The engineers had to concentrate on finding solutions using the model at hand, rather than succumbing to panic and starting all over with a clean piece of paper every time there was a problem.

The swept-wing stalling characteristics were of primary concern, as severe rolling and pitching could be dangerous, and if such a major problem was not corrected before the prototype was built, the pilots would most certainly have rejected the plane altogether, preventing its approval for production, as the changes that could be made to an airplane during flight testing were limited. In the first wind tunnel tests an early stall with a severe pitch-up just at the start of the stall was encountered. At first this was thought to be due to stalling at the wing tips, as they were behind the airplane center of gravity, while the forward portion of the swept-back wing was in front of the center of gravity and might be still lifting, thus causing the pitch-up. Some past airplanes with small amounts of wing sweep had the tendency to stall first at the wing tip. The usual remedies for such problems entailed twisting the wing to lower the angle of attack at the wing tip and using higher lift airfoils at the tip. Wing tip stalling could also cause the loss of aileron control and rolling in the stall. However, on the XB-47 model, these strategies had little effect. At this point one could have concluded that the whole idea of a highly swept wing was nearly impossible. There was also concern that the raw wind-tunnel data Boeing was required to send back to Wright Field as each major test series was completed would be so discouraging that a would-be expert outside of the loyal XB-47 Air Force Project Office might judge that the Boeing design for the XB-47 was unworkable and should be canceled.

To further investigate the pitch-up problem, wind tunnel tests were then run with the horizontal tail installed, and then with the tail removed. The results showed that the tail was not contributing any nose down pitching moment in the deep stall, which implied that the tail was caught in a stalled wake of air that trailed behind the wing. The first attempts to remedy this situation involved the relocation of the horizontal tail upwards and downwards along the vertical fin. However, this had little effect because the stalled wake was too thick and encompassed considerable vertical distance.

A simple experiment was then conducted to determine where the stalled air flow from the wing was going. With the tunnel operating at a very low speed, a long pole with a foot-long string attached to its tip was inserted into the airstream to follow a streamline from the wing back to the tail. A streamline is the path that a particle of fluid takes as the air flows over the model. The end of the string was first placed in front of the model and then repositioned at points backwards in the direction the string was pointing towards the tail. It was quickly found that the air flow was separating abruptly at the wing's inboard leading edge [Figure 21]. This resulted in a very thick wake that completely enveloped the horizontal tail.

Sharp leading edges had long been known to cause the stall to start at the leading edge. This is what made the early biplanes

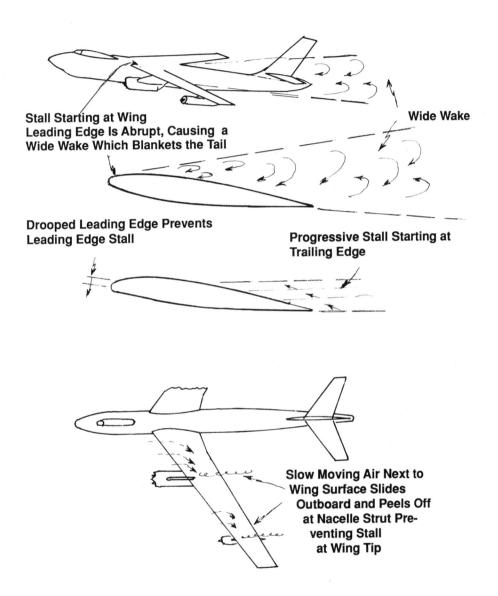

Figure 21—Two Fixes for Pitch-up at Stall

to have sudden stalls with no warning. It was known from wind tunnel tests on airfoils that bending the leading edge down so as to lower the front end of the airfoil's chord line helped prevent stalls from starting at the leading edge. A new wing model was quickly built and tested while Schairer was out of town, as we "crude" aerodynamic types were embarrassed in altering an airfoil section that had been selected as necessary for high-speed performance. As it turned out, the change mostly cured the pitch-up problem, did not affect the top speed, and Schairer thought it was a great idea. With the new wing, the stall started at the wing's trailing edge and progressed forward as the angle of attack was increased. This narrowed the wake so that the tail was in good air, which restored most of the stability and cured the tendency to pitch-up. High-speed wind tunnel tests soon followed. They showed that the redesigned leading edge did not decrease the effective top airspeed. Wind tunnel testing involves a lot of simple tools like the string on the end of the pole.

The airfoil purists might have been offended by the arbitrary change to a theoretically derived airfoil, as at high speeds it was thought desirable to have nearly symmetrical airfoils, so as to spread the wing lift evenly from the leading edge back to the trailing edge, thus minimizing the peak velocities that normally occur at the maximum airfoil thickness. Extreme designs to satisfy ideal lift distribution at high speed might even have the airfoil appearing to be installed upside down from the normal design practice. While drooping the leading edge in the forward region might have decreased high speed, flow separation at the leading edge in the low speed stall could not be tolerated, as the pitch-up could be sudden, and pushing the control stick forward for down elevator might not prevent the airplane from going over on its back.

A little tendency to pitch-up still remained, but this was eliminated several months later when the wing was tested with podded engines suspended out on the wing. At high angles of attack the struts supporting the pods caused the thin layer of slow moving air on the upper surface of the wing to peel off at the struts and trail backward, instead of flowing out along the wing span and piling up at the tip. Thus with the pod struts the full stall would start inboard and near the normal center of wing lift, and would not cause pitching of the airplane in the stall.

Because the pod location was outboard of the tail, this small wake of stalled air did not impinge upon the rear control surfaces. Furthermore, the pods protected the wing tips from the stall. In viewing the airplane from the side (see frontispiece), it can be seen that the wing tip is back, about halfway between the center of lift (which is near the pods) and the tail. Clearly, a loss of lift at the wing tip would cause a pitch-up, making it all the more important to avoid wing tip stalls.

This new wing configuration, with the drooped leading edge and the engine pod placement, had good stalling characteristics, comparable to those of the best straight winged airplanes, and better than a lot of later-on airplanes that had to resort to artificial "stick pushers" that took control from the pilot by pushing the control forward when an electric sensor detected the approach to the stall. This sounds like a dangerous remedy when an airplane would be on final landing approach near the ground and the stick pusher would be activated. The XB-47 was designed before these relaxations were allowed, and it had good stalling characteristics.

This episode illustrates the effectiveness of common sense experimentation in the wind tunnel to solve a problem that would confound anybody attempting to solve the problem by technical analysis on paper. It also illustrates how a late change, in this case, moving the engines from the body to pods on the wing, can clean up a previous problem. A major hurdle had been overcome in the design of the first swept-wing jet bomber.

Podded Engines on the Wing

In 1944 when Boeing began XB-47 wind tunnel tests, the initial design featured conventional straight wings with twin pods located closely underneath each wing. It did not take long to discern that the engine pods greatly reduced the high-speed capability of the relatively thin wing. Furthermore, it was clearly impractical to thin the wing even further as a means of compensating for the pods. The design was then changed to locate the four engines alongside each other on top of the body and slightly forward so as to balance the weight of the aft body [Figure 22]. Although it was obviously unsatisfactory for sev-

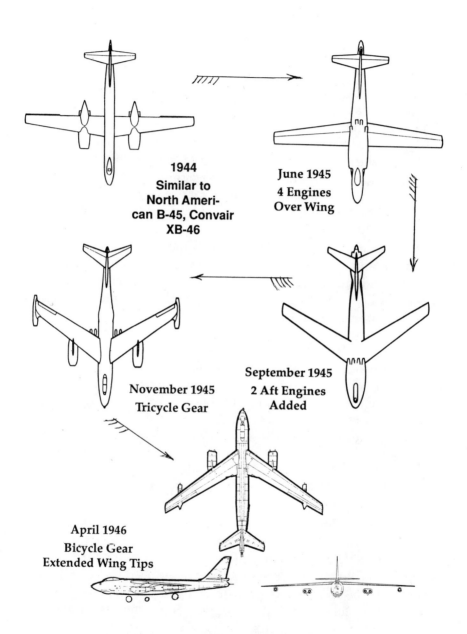

Figure 22—XB-47 Development Models

eral reasons, this engine configuration was retained when the wing was swept. Among the disadvantages presented by such an arrangement were the need for a very wide body, the chronic damage to the top of the body that would occur due to the scrubbing effect of the jet exhaust, the danger of cabin fires in the event of engine damage, and the maintenance problem posed by poor engine access. Yet, no other solution to the engine location problem was envisioned at that time.

Ed Wells and Bob Jewett took the drawings of this configuration back to the Wright Field Project Office and presented it as part of their progress report in October 1945, about a month and a half after the start of the swept-wing design effort. The body location of the engines was soundly rejected and for good reason. A wind tunnel test had been run at Wright Field on a Lockheed P-80 jet fighter with the jet engine running. The P-80 had the engine installed in back of the pilot and the engine tail-pipe extended back inside of the body to the tail. Gunfire damage had been simulated by drilling a .50 caliber-sized hole in an engine burner can. Since the cans operated at high internal pressures, an intensely concentrated flame, similar to that produced by a blowtorch, emanated from the hole. Although this was highly undesirable in the first-single engine fighters and an inherent hazard when the jet engine was placed in the body behind the pilot, it was considered to be intolerable in a bomber, based on the recent experiences in the bombing of Germany, where hundreds of B-17's and B-24's had been lost due to fire. The Project Office insisted that the engines be mounted out on the wing as on all past bombers.

On the way back to Seattle Ed Wells and Bob Jewett sketched various alternate engine locations on the back of envelopes. They understood the aerodynamic problem posed by nacelles tucked up under the wing, and so they suspended the nacelles on struts, experimenting with both engine forward and engine aft configurations with respect to the chord line of the wing. They suspected that the forward location might be better, as the mass of the engines forward of the wing elastic center was in the direction favorable in avoiding wing flutter, which was a concern on the wing which was long and thin and therefore somewhat flexible.

Back in Seattle there was some dismay at what appeared

to be a radical idea. The new engine location, it was thought, might cause too much drag and too great an increase in the weight of the engine installation. However, the rejection by Wright Field of the body-mounted engines was so firm that the new idea had to be explored. The Germans, particularly Arado, had tested small fore and aft locations of nacelles tucked up under the wing, which had shown some effect in reducing engine-wing flow interference.

A versatile wind tunnel model of the XB-47 was then built to explore all locations, practical or not, to determine the effect that nacelle location had upon the point where drag rose to critical levels in relation to increasingly high air speeds. It was found that if the nacelle was situated low enough so that the jet exhaust missed the flaps' trailing edge when the flaps were in the full down position, and forward enough so that the tailpipe exit was below the leading edge of the wing, there was no unfavorable flow interference, and the wing was performing like the pods were absent.

Once the designers had drawn this configuration, those who were uneasy about it like myself soon got used to it, almost trying to act like we had invented it. The weight of the strut mounting was surprisingly small. With the engines located out under the wing, the bending moment at the wing's root was decreased and therefore the wing's weight was actually reduced. The wind tunnel tests showed that the drag increment of the pods was low, as they were slim and smooth and the strut supporting the nacelle from the wing had thin airfoil sections. If an airplane's surface was smooth, having good component intersections, then the friction drag would be proportional to the total "wetted area" of the airplane's exterior. The removal of the engines from the top of the body permitted the fuselage to be slimmed considerably. This reduction in the total wetted area of the body offset the added area of the pods.

The possibility of low skin friction drag on smooth surfaces had been verified long before by both theoretical work and experimentation. There had been a long standing prejudice that nacelles had high drag. This was due to the radial engines being rough, with their cowl flaps, exhausts, and numerous air scoops. We on the XB-47 project at Boeing found that jet pods could have very low drag characteristics. Others in the airplane industry

B-47 Engine Pods—An "arbitrary" Air Force requirement

were late in finding this out, and persisted in burying the engines within the wing.

We soon became accustomed to the looks of the configuration and were greatly relieved finally to have found a practical location for the engines. To achieve the desired long range, the size of the airplane had grown so that six 4,000 pound thrust engines were required. Twin engine pods were located under each wing at about a third of the wing span. The remaining two engines were mounted singly, one under each wing tip. The idea came from the Lockheed P-80 fighter, which featured streamlined fuel tanks at the wing tips (these had been found to have low drag).

Bicycle Landing Gear

The design of important details such as the landing gear remained to be resolved. The gear could not be retracted into the thin wing or inside the slim pods. The conventional tricycle arrangement was preferred because of its directional stability on the ground, but retraction into the body aft of the bomb bay would necessitate a considerable bulge in the otherwise slim body. The regular landing gear designer at Boeing was bypassed, as it was felt he would take one look at the XB-47 configuration and pronounce that a landing gear retracted in the aft body behind the long bomb bay would be a mechanical impossibility. A mechanism was then designed by Dick Nelson (the wartime B-17 project engineer back on the drawing board) to give sufficient spacing between the gears for lateral stability on the ground. The mechanism had some weird and undesirable mechanisms. It was dubbed the "crippled chicken" gear.

At that time, the XB-47 was the most interesting thing going on at Boeing and jobs were scarce. Some of the top engineering talent was available to the XB-47 project to design the parts and components like the landing gear due to the collapse of airplane manufacturing at the end of the war.

By this time the Project Office at Wright Field was sufficiently encouraged by the progress of the wind tunnel tests and by the development of the general configuration that they made an additional requirement that the bomb bay be large enough for the atom bomb. The other jet bombers, the North American XB-45 and the Convair XB-46, were being built and had small bomb bays for conventional bombs. At that time the A bombs were very large compared to conventional bombs and quite a bit larger than the so-called "suitcase" A bombs that were developed later. The Project Office suggested a "bicycle" gear that permitted a longer bomb bay than could be accommodated using a tricycle gear. With the bicycle gear the atom bomb could be located so that its and the airplane's centers of gravity were nearly the same. Bicycle landing gear had already been flight tested by Wright Field on a surplus Martin B-26, the twin-engine medium-sized bomber that had served in the European theater during the war. This plane had been dubbed "The Middle River Stump Jumper," the nickname having been derived from the location of the Martin plant near Baltimore. The bicycle gear permitted a clean slim body on the XB-47. All spaces could be efficiently utilized for the bomb load and the fuel tanks [Figure 23].

But a new and obvious problem was introduced by the bicycle gear. The rear gear was located far behind the center of gravity, thus shortening the distance between the gear, which acts as a fulcrum, and the tail, where a down force is applied by the elevators in order to rotate the nose upward for take-off. With such a short distance to the fulcrum, the elevators would have to generate even more force to rotate the nose. But they were incapable of providing the additional force that would be

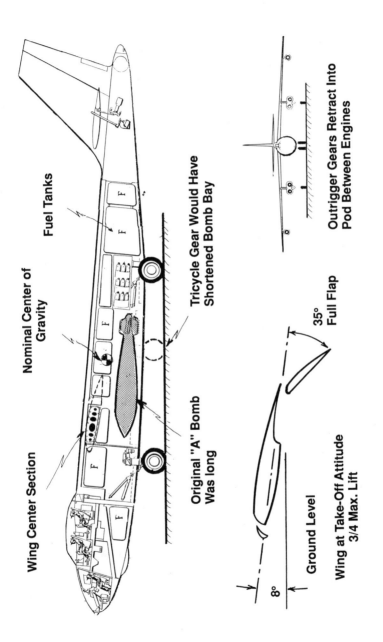

Figure 23—Bicycle Landing Gear

necessary. Therefore, the plane's attitude on the ground had to provide sufficient lift to initiate take-off. To achieve this, the wing's angle of attack with respect to the ground had to be high enough so that, combined with a high lift flap, sufficient lift for take-off would be available. Additionally, the high lift flap had to have low drag characteristics, so as not to impede climb-out of what would inevitably be a heavily loaded airplane.

Since none of us working on the XB-47 design had seen the Martin bicycle gear, we felt that the XB-47 version would look horrible. Chuck Davies, the designer who was assigned the task of making the three view drawings, was assigned the job of drawing the bicycle gear version. Chuck was my skiing companion, and so I had to cooperate on what I thought might be a mess. My job was to determine the appropriate angle of attack of the wing while the airplane was on the ground. It had to be high enough to assist the flaps in generating enough lift for take-off without rotation, but low enough to ensure an adequate margin of safety below the stall.

With some trepidation I told Chuck to use 8 degrees between the wing airfoil chord line and the ground, this figure being based on the lifts that had been measured in wind tunnel tests. When I dared to review his layout, I was agreeably surprised. The airplane looked quite reasonable and almost exciting (it has always been my belief that a good airplane should look good as well). As it turned out, during flight testing the take-off presented no problems, and in fact this angle of attack proved to be safer than conventional arrangements as the airplane could not be yanked off the ground until it was ready to climb.

However, flight testing revealed that landings required considerable skill. One interesting aspect of the landing deficiencies of the bicycle gear was that jet airplanes earned a bad reputation generally. Later on when the airlines became interested in the possibility of jet transports, the airline pilots would ask the military pilots about the flying characteristics of jets in general. They received discouraging answers. Jet airplanes were viewed as being only for the most highly trained pilots with the top skills. In the post war transport competition during the middle 1950's some airlines were slow to recognize that a jet transport could look reasonable with a tricycle gear and have good flying qualities. Even at Boeing, the first jet transport illustration presented to the airlines depicted a bicycle landing gear, which furthered this false idea.

The Slender Elastic Airplane

The correction of the stalling problem and the development of the podded engine installation had taken about six months. During this time the general airplane configuration had progressed to where the airplane looked real, so that the optimization of the wing for performance might be timely. The drag would be decreased by increasing the span, and this would increase the range, except for the increase in weight of the wing that was caused by the increase in span. At this point in the design process the wing was realized to be quite flexible in bending, which was due to the airfoil being thinner than we were accustomed to on low-speed airplanes, and it had a high span for long range. To permit the highest speed in what was judged to be a practical airplane, a thin airfoil had been selected, with a maximum thickness of 12 percent of the wing chord. The figures were kept constant from the wing root to the wing tip because the existing theory indicated that at the critical high speed, flow separation would occur first at the wing root.

The stress engineer who had been a party to the original selection of the wing span and sweep, Zeke Grey, found that the wing deflections under flight loads were quite high. He also realized that the wing bending deflection reduced the angle of attack at the tip and therefore the lift at the tip, and also the bending moment at the wing root next to the fuselage would be reduced. This can most easily be visualized by bending a cardboard model of a swept wing while viewing it from the front [Figure 24]. The stress analysis then required a series of computations of the wing bending moments to correct for the decreasing wing tip loads, with each step becoming smaller and smaller to correct for the change of angle of attack at the wing tip. This led to the discovery that the bending loads at the wing root were less than originally estimated. The lower bending moments would in turn permit either thinner skins in the wing's structural box to save weight, or a longer wing span, which would decrease drag, and therefore increase the range.

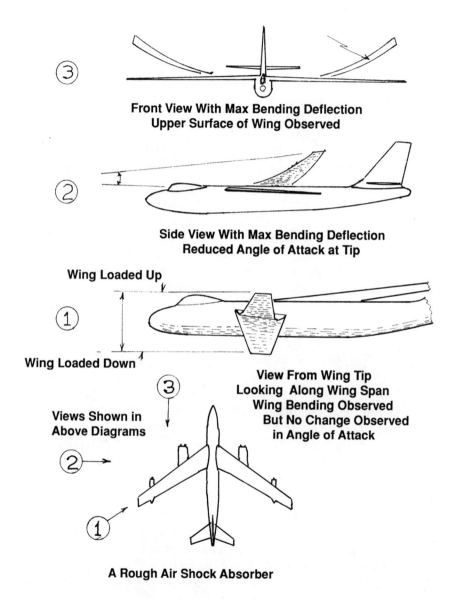

Front View With Max Bending Deflection
Upper Surface of Wing Observed

Side View With Max Bending Deflection
Reduced Angle of Attack at Tip

Wing Loaded Up

Wing Loaded Down

View From Wing Tip
Looking Along Wing Span
Wing Bending Observed
But No Change Observed
in Angle of Attack

Views Shown in
Above Diagrams

A Rough Air Shock Absorber

Figure 24—Inherent Swept-Wing Load Relief

Soon after the war ended, the idea of an "intercontinental bomber" became popular. Since the range of the XB-47 was still considerably less than desired, and its use in the Air Force remained undecided, the wing tip was extended in the simplest manner with an eight-foot extension added to each tip. This saved redoing a lot of the drawings and wind tunnel models. The inboard twin-engine pod and the outboard single-engine pod were left in the same locations with respect to the fuselage. In view of the general lack of knowledge of swept-wing airplanes, a complete reinvestigation of the optimum compromise between sweep, span, and airfoil thickness would not have been warranted. Besides, money and manpower were limited, as was time, for the competing medium-range bombers were already under construction.

The experience gained thus far showed that the original concerns about the weight penalties associated with sweep had been exaggerated, and that high wing spans and long range jet airplanes might be possible, contrary to the early belief that jets were only for fighters. Later on when jet transports were in operation, it was found that a gust would bend the wing tip up enough to appreciably reduce the incremental bending loads on the wing due to the gust (i.e., a shock absorber), thus giving a smoother ride in rough air. This effect is pronounced at maximum speeds, which is the opposite from the case with conventional straight wings, where the faster you fly, the rougher the ride. (If the reader has difficulty in visualizing this, he should have solace in that a lot of would-be technical experts were slow to wake up.) At this stage in the development a lot of enthusiasm was evident because it was thought that all the major problems had been overcome. We found out later after construction had started that the longitudinal stability was affected by the flexibility. Sometimes to be ignorant is to be lucky.

Contract to Build Two Prototypes

At about this time we were becoming confident that we had a practical airplane configuration. Wind tunnel data were plotted in the standardized form, the same for all airplanes, so that they could be compared in numerical terms without reference to the configuration of the particular airplane. An analogy might be like a doctor reviewing the paper work after a thorough physical examination. The XB-47 looked good to those involved with the project; it had low drag and good stability and control. It also looked like a useful high performance military airplane, as distinguished from the small research airplanes being built for the NACA to test advanced technology. Building a useful airplane represented a more meaningful advancement but was little more difficult to accomplish.

A milestone was reached in April 1946, when the design had jelled. This was the result of 10 months of design studies and intensive testing of the swept-wing concept. The Air Force Project Office at Wright Field was sufficiently enthusiastic to offer to buy two prototypes at a fixed price contract of $10 million. Apparently this money was part of a collection of unexpended funds from several cancelled programs which would have reverted to the U.S. Treasury by law if not allocated by June. It was a case of "Take it or leave it." The signing of the contract for the two XB-47 prototypes required that the engineers be prodded into agreeing that they had a workable airplane, even though detail design was the next step and a lot of subsystems remained to be designed. The engineers had to agree that they would not continue researching indefinitely, but would come up with practicable solutions within a given time frame.

Longitudinal Stability With Flexible Wings

By December 1946, 16 months after the change to the swept wing and eight months after the contract signing, the basic structural design was almost complete and the heavy parts of the wing were being made in the shop. Everything seemed to be going well when an apparently fatal defect was suddenly uncovered. The stress expert, Zeke Grey, was making a final analysis of the wing strength when he told my expert, Vic Ganzer, that the bending of the very flexible swept wing at maximum speed caused the center of lift to move inboard, and thereby also forward. This shift was sizable, amounting to the equivalent of a CG shift of 15 percent.

Pilots have always been very aware of the CG in loading an airplane—if the CG was too far back the airplane could be dangerously unstable and if too far forward it could be uncontrollable. The equivalent of a 15 percent shift between high and low speeds could not have been accommodated by a reasonably sized tail on the XB-47. Shifting the CG in flight by transferring fuel between tanks, as occasionally was done later in supersonic airplanes, was so impractical that it was not considered. This problem shocked us, providing as it did an example of our ignorance. Maybe this was the reason why there were skeptics outside of Boeing, possibly evidenced by the XB-47 not being copied. At that time, the XB-47 aerodynamics group was composed of about six engineers.

Just after this shock Vic Ganzer quit to teach at the University of Washington. Times were pretty hectic and higher-ups were keeping a watch on the XB-47, often interjecting conflicting orders. The XB-47 was far from being viewed as the cornerstone of Boeing's future. The "bread and butter" was to be a very long range bomber with a "compound" engine, a combination of piston and turbine engines. Nevertheless, the XB-47 was the most interesting project in sight. After Vic left, I wandered around in a daze trying to think of a solution. I surmised that, while the wing tip would bend up when the airplane was subjected to G forces, thus causing the center of lift to move forward and the airplane to pitch-up, the body must also deflect downward due to the large weight of the aft body. The resulting increase in the angle of attack of the horizontal tail might help counteract the effects of the wing bending.

Without much hope, I walked across the drafting room to Zeke Grey's desk, and asked, "If the airplane weight was evenly supported in the manufacturing jig, what would be the change in the angle of attack of the horizontal tail when the aft body support was removed and the tail was allowed to droop, while the wing center section remained clamped in the jig?"

Zeke replied, "I can't tell you now, but come back after lunch." [Figure 25]

A few hours later Zeke had a number. How he did this in so short a time remains a mystery. As I walked back to my desk, I multiplied Zeke's number with the number representing the horizontal tail's effectiveness in controlling pitch. Within the very small aerodynamics group longitudinal stability and control was my job, so this was easy, and before I was back at my

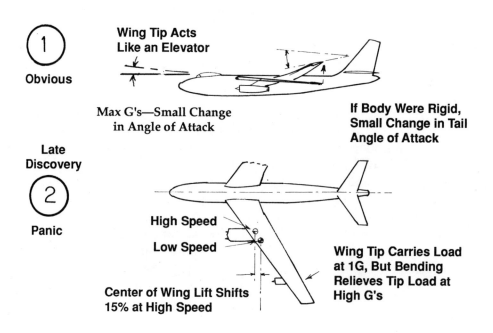

① Obvious

Wing Tip Acts Like an Elevator

Max G's—Small Change in Angle of Attack

If Body Were Rigid, Small Change in Tail Angle of Attack

Late Discovery

② Panic

High Speed

Low Speed

Center of Wing Lift Shifts 15% at High Speed

Wing Tip Carries Load at 1G, But Bending Relieves Tip Load at High G's

Body Bending Offsets Wing Bending—and Design Is Rescued

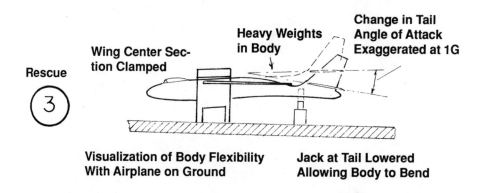

Rescue

③

Wing Center Section Clamped

Heavy Weights in Body

Change in Tail Angle of Attack Exaggerated at 1G

Visualization of Body Flexibility With Airplane on Ground

Jack at Tail Lowered Allowing Body to Bend

Figure 25—High-Speed Stability With Flexible Structure

desk, I realized that the body's downward deflection exactly counteracted the 15 percent shift of the wing's center of lift at high speeds. The emotional relief I felt is hard to describe. Without this unexpected answer, we all would have been looked upon as the stupidest of engineers, as this was exactly the type of problem the theoreticians had been afraid of, and it could have killed the whole project because changing the design at that late stage would have been impossible.

The relationship between the upwardly bending wings and the downward bending body with its rear control surfaces was carefully checked during the first high-speed flight tests. Small increments in speed were made, during which the ratio of elevator angle versus normal acceleration G's was measured. This ratio remained constant when corrected for the increase in elevator effectiveness with speed, showing that the longitudinal stability was maintained up to maximum speed.

After the early XB-47 flight tests showed no signs of trouble, the NACA at the Ames Laboratory in Sunnyvale, California, asked for the data needed to compute the effects of flexibility. This data covered the stiffness of the wing and body structures and the distributions of weight in the wing and body. Some time later a national high-speed conference was held at the Ames Laboratory, where a paper was presented that described this analysis. The conclusion drawn was that the body deflections counteracted the wing deflections. In the discussion following, George Schairer made a comment to the effect that "This did not just happen," inferring that we had designed this to be so. The human mind has a tendency, with time, to rationalize critical achievements. I arrived at the moral, "Don't admit luck, rather, claim superior intelligence."

Flight Controls

To better assure optimum flying qualities and to protect against unknowns in high-speed flight, the XB-47 flight controls departed from past designs. The acceptance of such a radical airplane for a production contract would depend heavily on pilot opinion. Ideally the control forces should be low and within the pilot's capability, but sufficiently high to restrain him from imposing destructive G forces on the airplane. The forces also should have a smooth and increasing force gradient from center. If the pilot liked the controls and was confident that the airplane was stable so it could be flown "hands-off," he would be less concerned about the seemingly weird airplane behind him. To a considerable extent the success of the XB-47 was due to innovations in the flight controls [Figure 26].

Pilots could control the early small airplanes by applying muscle power to the stick and rudder pedals that were attached to a simple cable system running from the cockpit to a control surface. As airplanes became larger, the control forces were kept within the pilot's capability by "aerodynamically balanced" elevators, rudders, and ailerons. This was accomplished by locating the hinge line part way back, between the leading and trailing edges. As airplanes became larger still, and when more balancing was attempted, overbalancing could occur at high elevator angles when the leading edge balance would project out into the airstream. The forces on the pilot's controls would have a reverse direction tending to cause higher elevator angles, like severe "oversteering" would be on a car, rather than the normal control centering forces. The elevator on the B-29 could overbalance in an extreme dive recovery, maybe causing the pilot to overcontrol in the recovery pull up and to exceed the G rating of the wing strength.

Near the speed of sound overbalancing could be more severe, and therefore, the XB-47 was fitted with a unique internal aerodynamic balance that overcame the problem of the conventional, exposed leading edge balances. This internal balance was composed of pivoted plates. The deflection of the control surface would cause a rise in air pressure at the gap between the control and the fixed forward surface when the surface was deflected. This pressure would act on the pivoted plates. An added advantage was that the exterior surfaces on the XB-47 control surfaces were smooth, thus reducing drag.

The hydraulics and control mechanisms engineer, Ed Pfafman, and I decided to use hydraulic servos in the control system with "artificial" control forces that were optimum, rather than the natural forces from the pressures on the control surfaces. This was to avoid undesirable forces that might occur when high-speed pressure waves struck the control surfaces. The only previous experience with hydraulic servo controls at

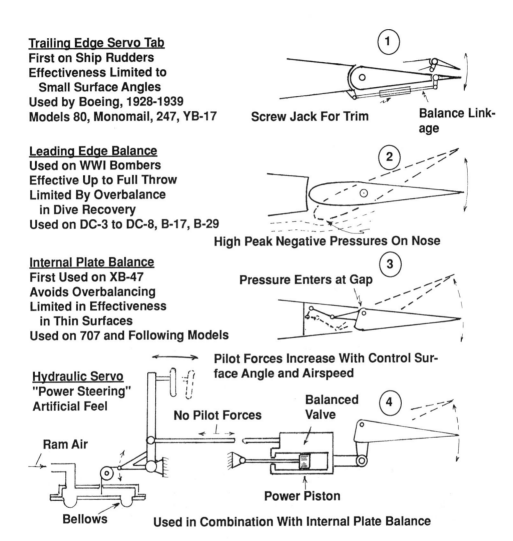

Trailing Edge Servo Tab
First on Ship Rudders
Effectiveness Limited to
  Small Surface Angles
Used by Boeing, 1928-1939
Models 80, Monomail, 247, YB-17   **Screw Jack For Trim**   **Balance Link-
                                                                                          age**

Leading Edge Balance
Used on WWI Bombers
Effective Up to Full Throw
Limited By Overbalance
  in Dive Recovery
Used on DC-3 to DC-8, B-17, B-29
High Peak Negative Pressures On Nose

Internal Plate Balance
First Used on XB-47   **Pressure Enters at Gap**
Avoids Overbalancing
Limited in Effectiveness
  in Thin Surfaces
Used on 707 and Following Models

**Pilot Forces Increase With Control Sur-
face Angle and Airspeed**

Hydraulic Servo
"Power Steering"   **Balanced
Artificial Feel**   **No Pilot Forces**   **Valve**

Ram Air

Bellows   **Used in Combination With Internal Plate Balance**

Power Piston

Pilot Needed Assistance With Increase in Size and
Speed of Airplanes, Desiring Smooth Increase in Force
to Full Throw With Good Centering and No Dead Spots

Figure 26—Control Surface Balancing and Hydraulic Servos

Boeing was on the 307 rudder, which was installed after the accident on the first airplane in 1939. With regards to hydraulic flight controls, Lockheed had accumulated the most experience in this specialty as a consequence of work that was done on the Constellation four engine piston transport, designed before the war, and on the Lockheed P-80 jet that flew at the end of the war. Lockheed used a "weighing" linkage in the control mechanism operated by the pilot. With this linkage the pilot felt a fixed fraction of the natural aerodynamic forces on the control surfaces.

The power steering and powered brakes in automobiles operate on this same principle. While this system gave an acceptable level of forces, it could be "jerky" due to friction and stretch in the long cable system leading to the cockpit. To avoid this characteristic, the pilot's control on the XB-47 was connected directly to a small valve that in turn controlled the hydraulic power piston, the latter resembling an ordinary hydraulic jack. No force was required to move the valve. In order to simulate a more natural feel, any pressure applied by the pilot to the control was automatically opposed by a bellows inflated with ram air pressure, which he effectively squeezed when the control was moved from the trim position. This "artificial feel" caused the muscular force required to operate the cockpit control to increase as airplane speed increased, thus preventing the pilot from overstressing the airplane structure and yet allowing the control to re-center itself when the pilot reduced manual pressure. The hydraulic servos gave a smooth feel without a dead spot near neutral.

The reliability of hydraulic servos was heavily dependent on the pressure supply system which proved in the flight tests to be unreliable in the XB-47. The pressure was supplied by individual pumps driven by an electric motor located at each aileron and in the tail to power the elevator and rudder. The XB-47 had a manual backup system intended for emergencies. This backup system made use of the internal aerodynamic balances and servo-tabs on the trailing edges of the control surfaces. During flight tests, it was found that the elevator might be out of trim when reverting to manual control. Although the XB-47 was provided with the means to re-trim manually, the time required to do so could be critical in an emergency situation. The

XB-47 represented one point on what was a very steep learning curve. (The safety problem with hydraulics is still with us today.)

Detail Design and Manufacture

Because of the highly experimental nature of the XB-47 project as well as the necessity of keeping costs as low as possible to remain within the parameters of the fixed price contract, enhancements to the drawing system and to manufacturing tooling were minimal. Once mass production became imminent, a comprehensive redrawing and retooling effort would be required. It was expected that a fairly extensive redrawing effort would be necessary anyway, to integrate the numerous modifications that no doubt would be identified during flight testing. Two prototypes were to be built so that the flight testing could be continued uninterrupted if one prototype crashed before sufficient data had been accumulated, a situation which had occurred when the 299 crashed at Wright Field in 1935.

It was desired that flight testing begin as soon as possible, to quickly expose any hidden defects as well as to explore opportunities. Thus, short cuts in drawing and manufacturing procedures were numerous. In a typical scenario, the eager head of manufacturing, Bud Hurst, would ask the engineering liaison engineer, Bill Ramsden, to secure some early drawing prints, as yet unfinished, presumably for planning purposes. Bill would look over a drafting board and ask the engineer to let him borrow his drawing of the unfinished design during lunch time so he could make a print. Looking over the drawing with Bill, Bud would ask him if he thought it likely that changes between the early print and the finished drawing would be significant. The two of them might then agree that the print was sufficiently complete to make the part. Later, when the final drawings were released, there were comparatively few parts that had to be reworked and a lot of time was thus saved. (This would have been a configuration control nightmare in production.) This type of maneuver was probably common in the aircraft industry and was made famous by the late Kelly Johnson in the Lockheed "Skunk Works" (see Chapter 6).

The manufacture of parts was done with the minimum of

tooling. Some of the tools were made of wood. Parts were "trimmed to fit" on the prototype airplanes. Although the parts were of high quality, with smooth exterior surfaces, they were not sufficiently accurate to be interchangeable, as would have been necessary for mass production. The manufacturing center for the XB-47 was in the old original Boeing Plant I, where the prototypes of the B-17, B-29, and all the early airplanes had also been built. The XB-47 body was barged from Plant 1 a mile up the Duwamish River for final assembly at Plant 2, which had been built for the wartime production. The high bay buildings that would accommodate fully assembled airplanes were across the highway from Boeing Field. In September 1947, 17 months after the contract to build the prototypes was signed, the first XB-47 prototype was rolled outside the hanger and across the highway to the airport for fueling, engine runs, and final system checks. This time frame compares with the 11 months that were required to roll out the 299.

Flight Testing

Pilot familiarization for first flight was limited to running the engines and conducting functional tests of the controls in the tandem cockpit under the bubble canopy. The runway was too short for a high-speed ground run to check the effectiveness of the controls, and much too short for a quick hop to get the feel of the bicycle landing gear. Therefore, the first high-speed ground run had to lead to a successful take-off. The first flight was made on December 17, 1947, with Bob Robbins as the pilot and Scott Osler as the copilot. Even though every imaginable happenstance had been analyzed, it is difficult to adequately describe the level of anxiety that existed among the engineers who were witnessing the first take-off of what was a radically new design. The principle concerns were the reliability of the engines and the adequacy of the flight controls. The trim settings and the required pilot control inputs had been pre-dicted. With the bicycle landing gear there was not much required of the pilots up to lift-off other than pushing the engine thrust levers forward and guiding the airplane down the run-way.

As it turned out, the lift-off speed and the distance to

unstick correlated closely with the engineers' calculations. As expected, the climb-out was steep due to the light weight of the aircraft. The flaps were supposed to be retracted slowly using one of two electric motors. However, they would not come up initially. Each flap motor was connected to a differential gear, much like that on the rear wheels of an automobile. When only one motor was being operated, there was a "no-back" device to block the idle motor from being driven backwards, and this device malfunctioned. The pilots then retracted the flaps using both motors. To those of us on the ground who had worked on the project, the first XB-47 lift-off was a very tense, dramatic event. The emotions of the test pilots must have been intense, but as usual with this breed, they were positively controlled so as not to interfere with their observations and actions in controlling the airplane, which were calmly related afterwards.

The first landing was made at the Moses Lake airfield across the Cascades in the middle of the vast sagebrush area in eastern Washington, about 120 nautical miles from Seattle. This had been a large, wartime training airfield, and it featured a hangar, a control tower, and wooden barrack buildings, all of which were empty except for one that housed an Air Corps captain who acted as the caretaker. The captain had a play-thing, a small diesel locomotive that had been used in wartime to bring materials from the town of Moses Lake to the base, on a spur from the main line. With our arrival he had an excuse to use the locomotive.

Moses Lake was to be used for all XB-47 flight testing. It was an ideal facility for this purpose, partly because it was distant from Seattle and therefore subject to minimal interference from other air operations and also from kibitzers. Yet it was close enough to enable overnight trucking of parts and supplies. The test crew of pilots and two or three engineers, including myself, quickly became enthusiastic about the advantages of jet airplanes, particularly because the XB-47 could fly regularly without the reliability problems associated with piston-engine installations. There was still some feeling of caution with regard to the TG-180 engine, although we were confident in its basic reliability because of its previous use on the F-86. In any event, if a failure occurred, we knew that a jet engine easily could be changed overnight, compared to the two or three days that would have been required to change a piston engine and propeller.

Considerable progress was made during the testing in the spring of 1948, and no major problems surfaced. The airplane's low speed characteristics and its high-speed longitudinal stability proved to be satisfactory. At Moses Lake we had first-hand evidence to back up our enthusiasm, but our optimism about the XB-47 being the production airplane that would displace the piston-engine bombers had not spread back to Seattle. Even with the good flight results so far, George Schairer, the instigator of the swept wing at Boeing, astounded me with the statement, "You can play with your experimental airplane but the bread and butter of Boeing is the B-54." This was a stretched B-29 with a compound engine comprised of a Pratt & Whitney 28-cylinder engine and a gas turbine that was driven by the exhaust gases. One can easily imagine the many mechanical complications and maintenance problems associated with such an arrangement. However the B-54 would have been close to achieving the ultimate in fuel efficiency, making it a truly intercontinental bomber, whereas it took a lot of enthusiasm to imagine the XB-47 ever fulfilling this role. It never quite did, but the technology that it uncovered led to the B-52 with intercontinental capability.

The first test flights were directed at insuring the safety of the airplane. Stability and control were checked with small increments in speed. Stall approaches revealed good lateral control and no pitch-up tendencies. There were some precautionary engine changes made due to restrictions on total operating time. The engine fuel controls occasionally had to be replaced. Otherwise there were few mechanical problems. Hours in the air were being accumulated at a good rate. There was practically no publicity, nor outsiders inquiring on how we were doing. Quite possibly, our competitors within the industry had already written off the Boeing XB-47 as being doomed to failure.

Dutch Roll

By this time the pilots had become accustomed to the airplane and so were less intent on closely controlling its attitude. On one flight Bob Robbins looked down at the flight plan for an interval of maybe a minute. When he looked up, he saw that the airplane had deviated from straight and level flight and was in a slight bank. After having corrected this several times, he allowed the airplane to fly freely without any control and observed that it was making a continual series of S turns, the amplitude of each slightly greater than the previous. This type of oscillation in airplanes had been encountered as early as 1913, and had been named "Dutch Roll" by Jerome Hunsaker, an American pioneer in aerodynamic stability and control. The name was possibly derived from the fact that Dutch ice skaters, as they negotiated the long, narrow canals, typically would roll from the outside edge of one skate to the outside edge of the other skate in a series of linked, S turns [Figure 27].

When Robbins concluded his test flight, he was quite perturbed. I responded that since he had been flying the XB-47 for some time now and had not had any trouble previously, the problem he reported must not be that serious. However, he insisted that it be fixed, citing instrument flying conditions, where such an oscillation would add to the pilot's work load. When I asked him how he had stopped the oscillation, he replied, "With the rudder." I then asked if he had observed whether he had applied opposite rudder at the moment when the rate of turn was maximum, as shown on the pilot's gyro rate of turn indicator, he said, "Yes."

I then phoned the controls engineer in Seattle, Ed Pfafman, and after describing the problem, I asked if he could design a control that would automatically introduce a rudder angle that was proportional to the rate of turn, as shown on the pilot's instrumentation, so as to oppose the oscillation. Ed agreed that this could be done, and promptly asked how much rudder movement would be required. Since we both were instinctively afraid of an electrical failure of such a sensitive gadget, that would rapidly drive the rudder to full travel, I guessed that 5 degrees in each direction would be sufficient to damp out the oscillation. Since the total throw of the rudder was 20 degrees, this would leave ample margin for the pilot to offset such a failure.

Ed then asked if the rudder pedals should move, and I replied, "Preferably not," meaning that the automatic control would be superimposed on any control of the rudder by the pilot

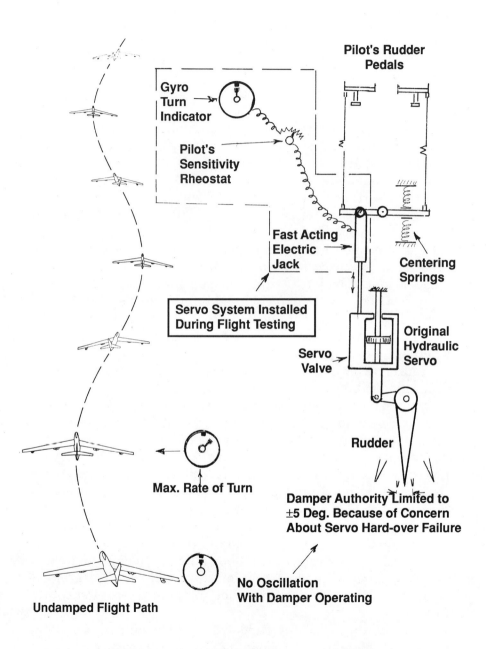

Pilot's Rudder Pedals

Gyro Turn Indicator

Pilot's Sensitivity Rheostat

Fast Acting Electric Jack

Centering Springs

Servo System Installed During Flight Testing

Servo Valve

Original Hydraulic Servo

Rudder

Max. Rate of Turn

Damper Authority Limited to ±5 Deg. Because of Concern About Servo Hard-over Failure

No Oscillation With Damper Operating

Undamped Flight Path

Figure 27—Dutch Roll and Yaw Damping

in making a turn. Ed's last question was what should be the ratio between the rate of turn and the resulting rudder angle that the automatic control would introduce. My reply was," How about a rheostat near the pilot so the pilot could select what he liked?" Within the context of a relatively short telephone conversation, Ed had formulated the basic design of a new and very important invention called the "yaw damper." Ed was as near to a mechanical-electrical genius as I have ever known. His education consisted of a two-year college course at Tri State College in Indiana. There was no advanced degree that would have done him justice. Before coming to Boeing, he had worked at Douglas where he had learned hydraulics.

The hydraulic servo in the rudder control system readily allowed the addition of the yaw damper, since the control valve was sensitive and required no force. The necessary parts arrived at Moses Lake within three weeks and were easily installed in the test airplane. Ed had obtained an electric servo motor and an amplifier that had been used on the B-29 turbo-supercharger waste gate control. He had scavenged both the amplifier and the servo motor from the local junk yard. The Seattle Honeywell representative provided a "rate-of-turn gyro" with an electrical position output and also a transformer to match the gyro to the amplifier. When the gyro was being installed in the airplane, I checked to see that it was not being hooked up backwards. Before it was bolted down to the wing center section, I rotated the gyro to check which way the rudder moved. Hooking it up backwards could be disastrous, possibly driving the airplane to wildly increasing oscillations.

On the first flight the pilots reported that the yaw damper worked perfectly. When I asked where they had set the rheostat sensitivity control, they said they had set it to maximum. With this amount, damping was stopped deadbeat, and yet there was no sluggishness when the pilots disturbed the airplane in yaw. Early in the design of the XB-47 an aero engineer, Paul Higgins, had made a mathematical analysis that showed that the damping of the oscillations was sufficient so that the amplitude would decay. The divergence of the oscillations found in flight was due to small airflow separations occurring at the juncture of the vertical fin and the horizontal stabilizer. Also Dutch roll was accentuated in the thin air at high altitudes. We lacked knowledge of how high the yaw damping should be to satisfy the pilots. In rough air the airplane was being continually disturbed and damping had to be high enough to prevent oscillations and yet not so high as to result in sluggish response to control. This was the same amount of damping as in satisfactory electrical meters in common use.

Outside of the Boeing company, reactions to this fix were interesting. Sometime later Dr. Hunsaker at MIT chided me on having used a mechanical or "artificial" solution to achieve stability rather than an aerodynamic solution. As an early mathematical practitioner of aerodynamic stability analysis, his was the purist point of view. While the Honeywell local representative was very helpful, the home office backed off because they saw the hazards of such a gadget. As a result they lost an opportunity in the auto-pilot business. In the competition for the production airplane contract following the XB-47 success, a Douglas salesman claimed that Boeing did not know how to design airplanes and thus could not avoid the oscillation problem solely by aerodynamic design. This tactic backfired, as Wright Field viewed the yaw damper as a desirable new feature. This was the first application of "artificial" stability control using a servo system. Ed and I each got $50 for a patent that the Air Force owned. Every modern jet airplane has a yaw damper.

Drag Tests

For reasons of safety, the early XB-47 flight tests were restricted with respect to speed and special maneuvers so that the project team could learn as much as possible about normal operations with minimum risk. After considerable testing had been accomplished without uncovering anything critical, it was appropriate to begin performance measurements, as range was the key to the usefulness of the XB-47. There was considerable doubt concerning the portion of the drag that was caused by skin friction and turbulence. The enthusiasts working on the XB-47 felt it would have much lower drag for its size than the current piston engine airplanes. Small smooth wind tunnel models tended to have lower drag than that measured in flight on the full-scale piston-engine airplanes because the drag of radial engines with cooling air exiting from cowl flaps and air scoops for oil coolers could not be adequately represented on the wind tunnel models. The XB-47 pods were smooth and free of scoops and exhaust stacks sticking out in the breeze.

Because of the flight testing of conventional piston-engine airplanes had shown higher drags that could not be accounted for from the wind tunnel, an empirical drag per square foot of surface of the airplane was generally assumed throughout the airplane industry, and this was considerably higher than that from wind tunnel models. The theory on skin friction, which had been developed starting in 1904, said that skin friction per unit area decreased with size, so that the drag of the XB-47 should be even lower than on the wind tunnel model. But you might be considered inexperienced if you believed that. This unbelief was to become a major factor in the paper competition for the bomber production contract that followed the XB-47 flight testing.

The most positive method of determining airplane performance was to measure the speed by timing the distance traveled between two points and the fuel consumed during the flight. But in order to prepare general performance charts, the engineers needed to know the airplane's drag at each weight and speed. To calculate the drag forces occurring in flight both the thrust of the engines and the accurate airspeed had to be measured.

The airspeed is determined by the difference between the ram pressure in a forward facing hole and the static atmospheric pressure far away from the influences of the airplane. The pilot's airspeed meter relies on a hole for the static pressure, usually on the side of the fuselage, that was determined to be the most accurate location from wind tunnel tests, but this is subject to error, as this pressure varies all over the airplane. (On small general aviation airplanes the manufacturers can cheat by locating the hole so that the airspeed meter reads high.) To accurately measure the static pressure in flight testing, a streamlined weight with a calibrated static probe was trailed on a long tube behind and below the fuselage. The Air Force went further by using a fighter pacer to fly in close formation with the test bomber. The pacer was calibrated by flying at a very low level where the pacer is timed as it passes over a measured course. The early pacer fighters had straight wings and could not keep up with the XB-47 at the higher speeds. Chuck Yeager was one of the Air Force pacer pilots.

The second measurement necessary for drag analysis was engine thrust. This was quite involved and inaccurate with the old piston engines and propellers, with errors introduced by settings of rpm, manifold pressure, mixture, plus the errors from propeller efficiency charts, yielding maybe a cumulative error of 5 percent. Measuring the thrust of the jet engine was a lot more straightforward; the measurement of the test stand forces was accurate because these forces were directly related to tailpipe pressures.

In preparation for the flight tests at Moses Lake, the engineer doing the performance work, Ken Holtby, computed the engine rpm required at each speed so that we would have a quick estimate of the associated drag. This computation was based on a conservative drag estimate that was OK'd by Schairer. Of particular interest was the amount of drag occurring near maximum speeds, as on a jet airplane the maximum range is also near this speed. The tests were simple. At each increment in rpm a level run was maintained, allowing enough time for the airplane to accelerate and stabilize on speed.

Once the pilots had transmitted by radio to those of us in the Moses Lake control tower all the speeds and the corresponding engine rpm's, Ken quickly realized that the drag was about 15 percent lower than the accepted estimate, a very pleasant surprise. I phoned the results back to Seattle, and from that time on company interest in the XB-47 really picked up. These low drag results were not broadcast for the benefit of the competition.

Air Corps Flight Tests

Following the company tests, the Air Force was to fly the XB-47 to determine its military operational suitability and to the limits of the specified operational envelope, in terms of performance, stability and control, bad characteristics. Major Guy Townsend, the Air Force test pilot, was from Wright Field. He had considerable combat experience in B-17's in the South Pacific during the early part of WWII, and in B-29's flying from the Marianas to bomb Japan. The copilot was Captain Jack Ridley. Jack was a test pilot from Muroc, named Edwards Air Force Base. Jack was of considerable help to Chuck Yeager

XB-47 Experimental Test Pilots, December 1947-1948

Left to right: Capt. Jack Ridley, XB-47 Co-Pilot; Capt. Chuck Yeager, P-84 Pacer Pilot; Maj. Guy Townsend, XB-47 Pilot; Bob Robbins, Pilot; Scott Osler, Co-Pilot. Crew on first flight—Robbins & Osler.

when Chuck flew the X-1 rocket research airplane through the speed of sound. Jack was killed riding in the back end of a transport when it hit a mountain in Japan, an incredible fate for a test pilot.

During the course of this testing several design defects were discovered. The most obvious deficiency in operational suitability was in making landings with precision in stopping distance. The ability to make corrections to the glide path was poor. The drag of the airplane was inherently low because of the high span slender wing. The flaps were designed to have low drag in order to facilitate taking off with a maximum load. The placement of the bicycle landing gear necessitated full flaps on take-off. But what was useful and beneficial to take-off was detrimental to landing when high drag was preferred to steepen the descent without increasing speed. On approach the glide angle was fairly flat even with the added drag of the landing gear. The engines required a long time to accelerate to high thrust from idle rpm, as the engine fuel control would increase the fuel flow only slowly to protect the engine compressor from surging, when the thrust momentarily quits with a loud bang. Correcting for a low approach by adding thrust was therefore slow. Carrying extra airspeed was not advisable, as the airplane would be nose down and the front gear would touch first, causing a bounce back up into the air. Once on the runway the brakes could not be applied until there was some weight on the wheels. The air drag on the runway was low, and therefore the distance before heavy braking could be applied was long.

After a few landings Major Townsend suggested deploying a parachute at touchdown. The Air Force had used parachutes in emergencies to slow down B-17's, by deploying a personal chute out the side gunner's window. Wright Field quickly sent for the German inventor of the ribbon chute, Professor Theodore Kanake, who was one of the German scientists brought to the U.S. shortly after the war. The ribbon chute was designed to be strong at very high speeds. A neat installation was quickly designed in Seattle and installed at Moses Lake. This arrangement became standard on the production airplanes. The chute did not drag on the runway while in motion due to the ground effect and the engine blast. The Air Force later added another small chute that was deployed on approach so that higher engine rpm could be maintained. This unorthodox means of inducing drag saved the XB-47 program, for attempts to train operational pilots without the chutes would have resulted in severe problems.

I got to know Professor Kanake a little bit while we were together at Moses Lake. He was amazed at Major Townsend putting up with living in the tar paper barracks at the old base and eating at a pool-hall-restaurant in the town of Moses Lake, at that time little more than a wide place in the road. The professor said that the German test pilots would insist on plush accommodations. The professor was in charge of an Air Force captain and was being led around resembling a dog on a leash. When I apologized for this treatment, he cast this off lightly, saying that the military was the same all over the world.

1. Chute deployed on approach

2. Chute open

3. Leveled out

4. Touch-down—chute clear of runway

XB-47 Drag Chute Landing Sequence—Moses Lake, 1948

From this experience a lot was learned about landing a jet airplane. The reason why it had been easy to land previous airplanes that relied on piston engines and propellers was that the propeller with a closed throttle produced high drag, enabling a steeper glide path. The piston engine was quick to accelerate, and the blast of the slipstream on the flaps added high lift, both of which helped the pilot correct for a low and slow approach.

The Martin airplane on which the bicycle landing gear was first tested was a B-26, a propeller airplane. It had been my job to anticipate this problem, but although I had made an analysis, it did not allow for operational variations. Sometimes enthusiasm reduces the worrying. In this case my ignorance was fortunate because at that time there were no readily available alternatives to address the landing problem, and the program might have died on the vine. Although the parachute saved the day, at the start of the program no one would have bet money on such an unorthodox solution.

Later, other methods were perfected to make the jet transport more practical to land. Among the features that would one day find themselves on modern jetliners were better engines, thrust reversers, tricycle landing gears and spoiler lateral controls that could be raised to induce drag and to dump lift, thereby putting more weight on the wheels to facilitate braking.

Lateral Control at High Speeds

One of the first problems encountered during the Air Force testing was a lack of lateral control at high speeds. The XB-47 had been designed to have a large amount of control at low speeds because swept wings have a large rolling moment when encountering cross winds on take-offs and landings. The upwind wing is more broadside to the relative wind and therefore has higher lift. In addition to a conventional aileron, the outboard half of the flap on the XB-47 was hydraulically actuated to decrease its angle when the adjacent aileron was up. This flap never stalled, even when the wing was stalled, giving positive control in the stall, but the real problem was at high speeds, when the flexibility of the wing decreased aileron control.

At very low speeds the aileron could be moved to full travel without significant effect in distorting the wing. But at maximum dive speeds small structural distortions can have large effects. The forces imposed by the aileron caused twisting and bending deflections of the wing to such an extent that an appreciable part of the lift added by the aileron's deflection was cancelled by the outer wing's decreased angle of attack. Some loss in control at high speeds had been calculated by Paul Higgins in the small XB-47 aerodynamics group, but the problem was aggravated by slippage in the wing box structure. During manufacture, the final panel on the bottom of the wing box was screwed on in order to close the box. The rest of the box had been riveted and was tight.

The ease with which the box was twisted can be visualized by the ease with which a grocery store cardboard box can be twisted with the lid removed [Figure 28]. While the screws were as tight as possible, there had to be enough hole clearance to permit turning the screws with the screwdriver, which left a little play.

When the pilot put the wheel over to roll the airplane, the lower panel would slip, causing a twist in the wing, and when the pilot returned to level flight, the box did not slip back into place due to friction in the joint, and the control wheel would then be off center. (This problem has been avoided on modern transports by securing the final panel of the wing box with tapered blind fasteners that pull tight.)

Even though this reduction in lateral control at high speeds could be tolerated in military operations, Major Townsend suggested a positive fix by using wing spoilers in addition to the ailerons. He had had experience with spoilers on the Convair XB-46, a straight-winged medium jet bomber which flew seven months before the XB-47. Spoilers could be conveniently located on the XB-47, just inboard of the aileron. The spoilers were hinged at their forward edge and were attached to the wing rear spar. This was a more forward location on the wing than the aileron and therefore would cause less twisting of the wing, and because they were located at mid span, the spoilers would cause little bending of the wing. The spoiler installation was flight tested on the XB-47 in a follow-on program. Although they worked, they were not considered necessary for the production model B-47. Spoilers were to become standard on future large

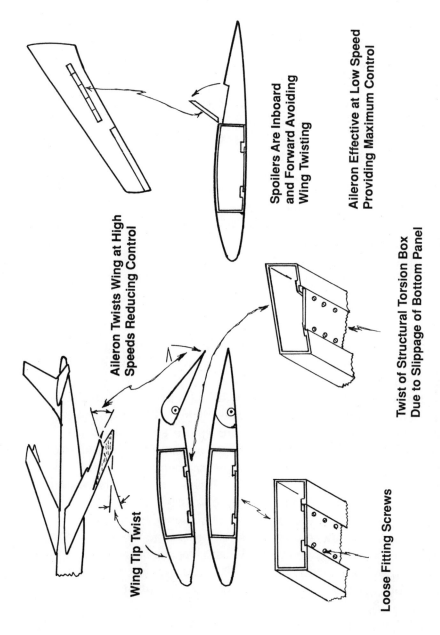

Aileron Twists Wing at High
Speeds Reducing Control

Wing Tip Twist

Spoilers Are Inboard
and Forward Avoiding
Wing Twisting

Aileron Effective at Low Speed
Providing Maximum Control

Twist of Structural Torsion Box
Due to Slippage of Bottom Panel

Loose Fitting Screws

Figure 28—Lateral Control—the Reason for Adding Spoilers

swept-wing airplanes. It could be said that pilots are never satisfied with the total amount of lateral control.

The XB-47 flight test program was most successful because the design had not been "frozen" to the point that the team was prevented from making changes and exploring new ideas. In fact, a flight test program that did not discover desirable changes could be viewed as being unsuccessful.

As an aircraft that was designed for a military mission, but which allowed experimentation, the XB-47 prototype advanced the state of the art to an extent not possible were it mandated that flight testing be conducted using only a production airplane, with its concomitant, large investments in tooling and a production line jammed with additional airplanes, all waiting for confirmation that not much had to be changed. Since the unknowns at the time were considerable, starting the XB-47 program off by building a prototype saved both time and money.

The flight test program was marred by one fatality. Scott Osler, the copilot on the first take-off and flying all during the company testing, had become the pilot in the front seat on the follow-on testing. The cockpit canopy became unlatched and came off, due to a poor design that was soon fixed. The XB-47 was landed safely by the copilot.

It is usually this type of small detail, rather than the major technical concerns that have received so much attention, that cause most accidents. This was the case on the 299 accident in 1935 that killed the Boeing chief pilot, Les Tower, and the Air Corps chief pilot, Major Hill, and in the XB-29 accident in 1943 that killed Eddie Allen—all highly skilled and experienced pilots. A list of the test pilots that were killed by something that was later easily fixed would be very long.

The Production Sale

The Air Force flight testing was nearing completion at Moses Lake when we were alerted by Colonel Pete Warden that he would try to get General K. B. Wolfe to stop by Moses Lake in his B-17 on his way back to Wright Field. General Wolfe was head of bomber production at Wright Field and was in Seattle to review the progress on the forthcoming B-54 piston bomber.

Colonel Warden suggested that if Major Townsend could

take him for a flight he would be impressed when he saw the airspeed meter wind up rapidly, as never seen on a piston-engine airplane. General Wolfe had been in command of the first B-29's that bombed Japan, flying out of China and supplied over the hump from India. He was experienced in conventional airplanes, but he had not yet had a ride in a jet. The only jets then flying were single seat fighters and the other bombers currently being tested, the North American XB-45, and the Convair XB-46.

Colonel Warden was successful in getting General Wolfe to stop by, presumably to just to take a look. When the general arrived, the XB-47 was parked outside ready for flight. After a walk around the airplane Major Townsend asked if he would like a short ride. When he accepted, he was helped into the copilot's seat in the rear under the canopy, with Captain Ridley crouching in the aisle near him to explain what was going on. The flight was comprised of a climb up to altitude for a level speed run. Major Townsend then flew a low pass by the tower, followed by a steep climb. The company bosses had flown over for the event, including the president, Bill Allen, executive vice president and chief salesman, Wellwood Beall, and XB-47 project engineer, George Martin.

After the flight they were all standing out in front of the airplane. General Wolfe was visibly elated and asked Major Townsend if he considered the airplane to be operational. When Townsend answered, "Yes," General Wolfe almost immediately responded that the Air Force would buy it and that it would be built "as is" in Wichita. General Wolfe thus revolutionized strategic bombing, after only a 20-minute ride. The Boeing bosses were probably astounded, as there had been no sales effort on the XB-47, and they had been pushing the B-54 piston-engine bomber. The bosses had to quickly switch their attentions to the B-47. Just what exact role the B-47 was to play was not mentioned.

High-Speed Pitch-Up

During the Air Force flight tests the pilots became well aware of a pitch-up at maximum speed. This had shown up in the wind tunnel tests. It had been determined that the pitch-up

**Purchase of B-47 Production After General Wolfe's Ride—
Moses Lake, July 1948**

**Left to right: Maj. Gen. K.B. Wolfe, Chief of Procurement; Wellwood
Beall, Ex-V.P.; Capt. Jack Ridley, Co-Pilot; George Martin, Proj. Eng.;
Gen. Joe McNarney, Com. Air Mat. Com.; Maj. Guy Townsend, Pilot;
William Allen, President**

was caused by a high-speed stall occurring outboard on the wing, and therefore aft of the center of gravity. When the speed of the XB-47 reached about 83 percent of the speed of sound, the local airspeed in this small region on the wing's upper surface was at the speed of sound. This air did not slow down normally towards the trailing edge, but separated instead, causing a loss of lift in this aft area and a consequent pitch-up of the nose. When encountering this pitch-up, the pilot had to push forward on the control wheel and reduce the thrust to slow down.

In a record speed flight across the U.S. in February 1949, Colonel Russ Schleeh encountered this situation frequently. While this was not dangerous, it was nevertheless quite irritating. It was also contrary to the Air Force standards on acceptable flying qualities.

After production was assured, I visited Wright Field to help clear the airplane specification with the technical experts in the Aircraft Laboratory, as required by the production contract. I explained the pitch-up problem to one of the Wright Field experts, Mel Shorr. I claimed that it was an inherent problem but not serious operationally, and I summarized the considerable research that had been done on the fundamentals of this airflow problem. When Mel refused to allow any exceptions to the Air Force requirement, I made a capricious remark, saying that maybe he should buy a different airplane. This was a once-in-a-lifetime chance to play the wise guy, for I knew the B-47 had been solidly sold. The representative from the Air Force Project office, Rube Stanley, had to contain himself from giggling.

As it soon turned out, I was wrong. An easy fix had been discovered by two United Aircraft engineers, Bruynes and Taylor, who had cured a flow separation problem on the diffuser of their wind tunnel in East Hartford, with a discovery they called "vortex generators." They published their data in 1947. Their invention consisted of a series of short lifting vanes that mixed the fast moving air with the slow moving air next to the surface [Figure 29].

The NACA flight tested vortex generators on a straight winged jet fighter, the Lockheed F-94. The vortex generators were effective in delaying flow separation, but in a subsequent flight test using the swept-wing F-86 fighter, the vortex generators did not function, probably because they had been placed incorrectly along the airfoil's curve, at the wrong angle of attack. A Boeing wind tunnel engineer, Jim Osborne, had learned of the United data, and so alerted an engineer in my small aero group. Bob Brown charged ahead with a design application for the XB-47. The difficulty was to pick the right-sized vanes and to locate them very precisely, on the wing's upper surface just forward of the point where airflow separation would otherwise begin. There was a lot of skepticism about the effectiveness of the vortex generators. I had just told the Air Force that the problem could not be solved. George Schairer said vortex generators "wouldn't work," but then caught himself and said, "Test it anyway."

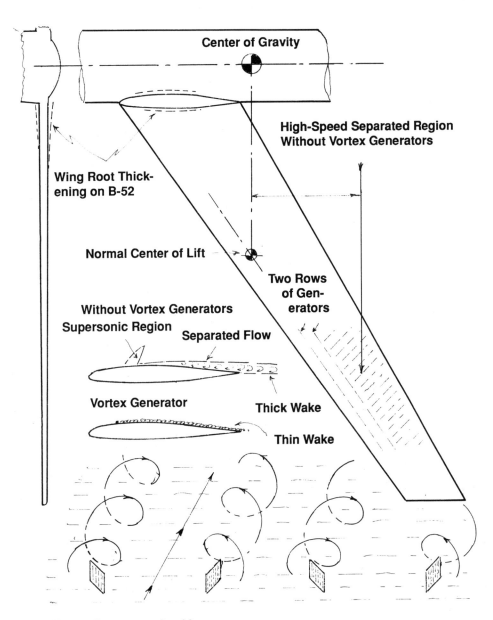

Center of Gravity

High-Speed Separated Region
Without Vortex Generators

Wing Root Thick-
ening on B-52

Normal Center of Lift

Two Rows
of Gen-
erators

Without Vortex Generators
Supersonic Region   Separated Flow

Vortex Generator   Thick Wake

Thin Wake

Vortex Generators Looking
Downstream—Half-Size

Figure 29—Pitch-up Cured by Vortex Generators

Bob placed two rows of vortex generators on the wing's upper surface outboard on the wing span and at the fore and aft location within the wing span where flow occurred and just ahead of the region where flow separation occurred. The determination of the best angle of attack of the many short vanes also was an open question. A test on the XB-47 wind tunnel model was unsuccessful due to the very small scale of the generators. Bob's first and only design was quickly installed on the XB-47 prototype, and it worked perfectly.

Vortex generators are so useful in correcting local flow separations that they can now be found on almost every modern airplane. A row of vortex generators was installed on the 707 just forward of the inboard aileron to prevent it from shaking at high-speed cruise. This violated the sensibilities of a famous American Airline engineer, Bill Littlewood. He thought the engineers should design the wing properly without having to use a crutch. Despite this attitude, the use of vortex generators came to be widely recognized as an essential part of high-speed aerodynamics. In fact, a technical book that was published in England on airflow contained an entire chapter devoted to explaining the design of vortex generators.

B-47 Planning

The XB-47 was so successful that it was decided to produce it without any major changes to the general configuration, although enough was known by that time for an even better bomber to be built. But this would have added years of delay. Near the end of the XB-47 testing I asked the GE field engineer stationed in Seattle about larger engines suitable for a four-engine version of the B-47. He told me that the production version of the GE TG-180 was near the theoretical limit in jet engine thrusts. This reply was not surprising, as a field engineer had a tough job, and still does. The factory may not have told him much about new research, or maybe the factory didn't have much to tell.

Ideally a field engineer should have the technical ability to appreciate what might be going on at the airplane company in terms of existing design work and to anticipate possible future trends. He should be able maintain this broad perspective while being more or less continually harassed by the airplane engineers regarding ongoing engine problems. He should prevail on the doubters at the home office that what he saw at the airplane factory was actually so. Being newly associated with the airplane business, GE depended on the Air Force for guidance. The company did not realize the extent of the revolutions in airplane design and was thus slow to take advantage of its pioneering position.

The production B-47's were generally the same as the XB prototypes, but they featured a great deal of additional equipment. The gross weight was increased from 125,000 to 200,000 pounds, increasing the maximum range to approach intercontinental mission capability—with the aid of in-flight refueling . However, the maximum range still fell far short of the range requirement established by the B-36. The start of the Korean War in June1950 gave the B-47 production a big boost, and Colonel Warden said that as a result, far too many were built. Between them, Boeing, Douglas, and Lockheed built over 1,600 B-47's. The Korean War gave the big boost to production.

The J-47 engine was the production version of the GE TG-180 engine and was also ordered in larger quantities than the B-47 to provide for spares, as an airplane might go through several sets of engines during its operational lifetime. The provisioning for engine spares that was selected in a meeting at Wright Field that I attended was based on only 85 hours allowed between engine changes, which seemed extremely short in view of the favorable experiences on the XB-47 flight testing. This number was based on an official cautious maintenance procedure to best insure the safety of experimental airplanes. This required that a complete engine be changed, even if it could have been fixed while still on the airplane. An officer from March Field, an early F-86 base, stated that the cause of most engine problems was the fuel control, a small unit that could be replaced within an hour. However the spares procurement types would not risk being caught short during the Korean war. GE was present at the meeting and did not object to having their engine so badly maligned. The government ended up with a warehouse full of obsolete engines.

The XB-47 flight test program was so successful that it had outpaced the development of military equipment such as the bombing system, the radar, and armament. Some in the Air Force who were unfamiliar with the exploratory nature of the XB-47 program felt that the airplane should have been delayed so that everything could have been coordinated to reach fruition at the same time, even to the extent of skipping the prototype phase and moving directly into production, thus saving the cost of the prototypes.

Several lessons might be learned from the unique XB-47 experience, obviously debatable, one being to the effect that "The high cost of installing the ever evolving military equipment indicated that airplanes should be designed on the premise that they would outlast several generations of equipment. Provisions for 'plug in' installations would minimize the cost of equipment changes while keeping the airplane up to date."

Thick Wing Root Discovery

A major discovery in the design of swept wings was made during the last wind tunnel tests on the XB-47, but by this time the wing was already being built and so no change was possible. At the end of the war there was a false theory that air flow over the swept wing would separate first at high speeds in the region next to the body, indicating that the airfoil there should be thin.

Thus the XB-47 was designed with a constant airfoil shape from root to tip, producing a conical wing shape, where the heavy upper and lower wing plates could be simply formed in the shop between three long rolls, a common tool in any sheet metal shop. However, late tests on the XB-47 showed that the first separation occurred outboard on the wing, indicating that the inner wing could have been greatly thickened. This would have provided greater beam depth so that the structure could have been lighter and so there could have been a larger volume for internal fuel in the wing.

The wind tunnel test technique used to locate the first flow separation simply involved the use of ram pressure tubes as commonly used in airspeed meters to measure the vertical width of the air wake flowing behind the wing's trailing edge all along the span. By employing this technique to pinpoint flow separation along the entire span, a completely new wing could have been designed whose thickness varied in accordance with the measurements, thus optimizing air flow from the root to the tip, as well as providing space for fuel tanks. This technique was not applied to the wings of the XB-47. As a consequence, the XB-47 wing could not carry fuel, as it was much too thin. However, the YB-52, which rolled out in March 1952, utilized this technique to great advantage and had a wing that could hold 60 percent of the total fuel due to the greater thickness of the airfoil near the root. Wright Field put this innovation in the category of a "breakthrough."

An amusing note on this subject concerns the British. They used wing root thickening to house the jet engines in their transports and bombers, leaving less volume in the wing for fuel. When they desired greater range, they hung external fuel tanks out on the wings. The British had a general knowledge of the XB-47, but they did not investigate the finer points of the design such as the engine pods.

Sir George Edwards, the head of Vickers, a major British company, visited Moses Lake during the Air Corps flight testing and was briefed by Major Townsend while examining the XB-47. However, the discovery during flight test of the low drag characteristics of the podded engine arrangement was too valuable to broadcast outside the company. The British designers were probably as concerned as we were about the potential for interference drag between the pods and the wing. The pods on the XB-47 were generally regarded by outsiders as being the result of an arbitrary Air Force decision that we were stuck with. Years later, at a technical meeting in England, Schairer made a remark that the British had "installed the engines inside and the fuel tanks outside for better maintenance!"

Given the significant discoveries that had been made in the wind tunnel and in flight testing during the XB-47 development, the design of this pioneering swept-wing bomber could have been greatly improved, as it had already lagged behind the quickly advancing state of the art before the first production model left the shop floor. But rather than backtracking on the XB-47, the decision was made to apply this knowledge to an entirely new and much larger bomber, the B-52, powered by the Pratt & Whitney J-57 engine.

The B-52 Bomber

During the spring of 1948 when the XB-47 flight tests were underway, RAND (a think tank formed out of Douglas) issued a report that said, in effect, that the XB-47 should have been designed as a turbo-prop, in order to attain intercontinental range. This report was authored by Thomas Jones, later head of Northrup. Such a conclusion was logical based on the jet engines then in sight and on the well-known skin friction drag characteristics of conventional piston-engine airplanes. To appease the turbo-prop proponents, a B-47 was modified by replacing the inboard twin pods with turbo-props. As a result of the prop's slipstream flowing over the top of the swept wing, this modification, called the B-47D, exhibited terrible low-speed stalling characteristics. The Boeing test pilot, Ray McPherson, said it was the worst airplane he had ever flown.

As a result of RAND's report, which recommended a turbo-prop bomber the size of the B-47, the Air Force held a competition for a swept-wing bomber to be powered by four turbo-props. RAND had been assigned the job of evaluating the entries. They asked Boeing for the XB-47 flight test results relating to drag, and they sent a former Douglas aerodynamics expert, Gene Root, to Seattle to investigate. Schairer refused to furnish the data, as it appeared that, via RAND, Douglas might be in a position to obtain the Boeing data for themselves. RAND then sent another employee, Schairer's brother Bob. The Boeing response was still "No."

Aided by their experiences with the XB-47, Boeing won the paper competition with a preliminary design for the XB-55 turbo-prop. However, the production of the B-47 was then underway, and the development of the jet engine-propeller combination for the XB-55 was some time off. Despite the RAND recommendations, Colonel Warden hated propellers and requested Boeing to study a jet version of the XB-55, which would be powered by the Westinghouse J-40 jet engine that was soon to be available.

About the time the XB-47 was being flight tested, the Air Force asked for design studies on a large intercontinental bomber. Based on the RAND report, turbo-props rather than jets were presumed to be necessary. A long-range mission would require a bomber of great size, and consequently the engines would have to be very powerful. This in turn would require large diameter counter rotating dual propellers Such an arrangement went far beyond the state of the art at that time, since the design of the engine-propeller gear box and shafting would have to overcome severe mechanical problems. The proposed engine was a Curtiss-Wright turbo-prop with multi-staged centrifugal compressors, which would be nothing less than a monstrosity. Other manufacturers of gas turbine engines had gone over to axial compressor designs.

There was much concern that development of the propellers would be impossible, or at the very least cause a long delay. An important aspect of the design would have to address the complicated issue of propeller feathering during engine out conditions. Failures in this regard had already resulted in ditchings of Boeing Stratocruisers in the Pacific. Until a reliable, large turbo-prop engine and propeller could be proven in flight, attempting to build such an airplane would have been very unwise.

In October 1948 the performance of the XB-52 turbo-prop was up for review at Wright Field. The XB-52 performance engineer, Vaughn Blumenthal, handed the latest document to Colonel Warden. When he opened it and saw that the XB-52 was still being planned as a turbo-prop, he promptly slapped it shut and asked, "How about a jet?" Colonel Warden had obtained some data on a jet version that had been generated by one of the German engineers who had been brought to Wright Field shortly after the war and who was working for him at the time. Woldemar Voight had been head of Messerschmitt preliminary design during the development of the Me-262 jet fighter. Being such an old hand, he had accumulated so much technical knowledge and knew so many short cuts that he could outline an airplane design almost on the fly, without having to refer to a pile of books. He must have indicated to Colonel Warden that a change from prop to jet was feasible.

This decision in the Bomber Project Office at Wright Field was probably unilateral, as Voight probably had been converted to jets by the Me-262 experience, while Colonel Warden had an instinctive enthusiasm for jets and a hatred for props. Colonel Warden told Blumenthal that he was going to the Pentagon in a week for a decision, implying that if he left without a jet version, the XB-52 program might be cancelled. Convair was competing with the B-60, a swept-wing version of the B-36. But this was an absurd attempt to match an all new design.

The reconfiguration of the XB-52 as a jet had to be accomplished in Dayton, as there was insufficient time to return to Seattle. Fortunately at Wright Field at that same time a review of the jet version of the XB-55 was also underway. The simplest way to convert the XB-52 to a jet version was to discard most of the turbo-prop version and draw a greatly enlarged XB-55, in which both the wing area and the number of engines were doubled.

Besides Blumenthal, other Boeing personnel who were available to work on the redesign were George Schairer, aerodynamicist, Ed Wells, vice president of engineering, and Bob Withington, the XB-55 performance engineer. It took a week for them to put together a document that included estimates of weight, drag, and performance, plus a three-view drawing and an inboard profile [Figure 30]. Ed Wells made the drawings and Schairer carved a wooden model out of balsa. It was to use the forthcoming Pratt & Whitney J-57 jet engine, which was to produce more thrust than the Westinghouse J-40, which had been proposed for the XB-55. However, the J-57 might not be available in time for the first XB-52 prototype, possibly necessitating the use of the J-40 on the first test XB-52 airplane. Colonel Warden took the 1/2-inch thick document they produced during the week in the hotel room in Dayton back to the Pentagon. Today, it would take a panel truck to transport the required paper work. Colonel Warden was able to sell the idea to the higher ups in the Pentagon, in some undisclosed negotiations.

The method of engine selection for the XB-52 was quite contrary to past practice, whereby an engine had to be proven on the test stand before it could be considered as a candidate to power a new airplane design. In October 1948 the J-57 jet engine could have been classified as a "paper engine," except that the compressor, the most critical component, had to some extent been developed in the Pratt & Whitney "Willgoos Lab" in East Hartford, the Lab being named after the Pratt & Whitney engineer that conceived it. The J-57 compressor had to be tested

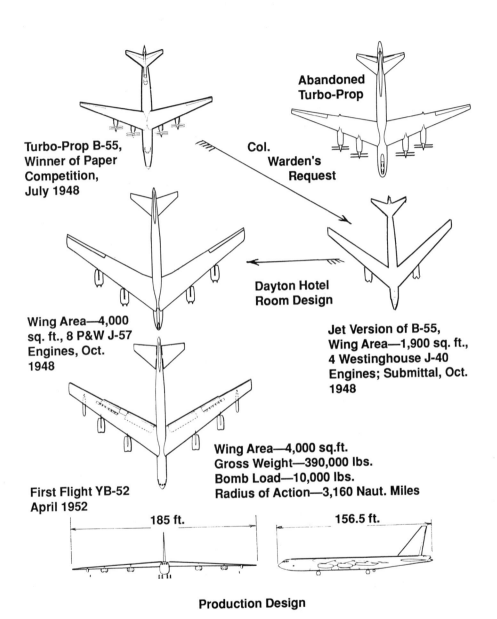

Abandoned
Turbo-Prop

Turbo-Prop B-55,
Winner of Paper
Competition,
July 1948

Col.
Warden's
Request

Dayton Hotel
Room Design

Wing Area—4,000
sq. ft., 8 P&W J-57
Engines, Oct.
1948

Jet Version of B-55,
Wing Area—1,900 sq. ft.,
4 Westinghouse J-40
Engines; Submittal, Oct.
1948

Wing Area—4,000 sq.ft.
Gross Weight—390,000 lbs.
Bomb Load—10,000 lbs.
Radius of Action—3,160 Naut. Miles

First Flight YB-52
April 1952

185 ft.   156.5 ft.

Production Design

Figure 30—Last XB-52 Development Models

separately from the turbine that normally drives it in the completed engine, and this required a tremendous amount of power. The Willgoos Lab had a high powered drive that had been assembled using steam boilers and a steam turbine that were salvaged from Navy warships being scrapped in Philadelphia after the war. By 1947, this test facility had become operational, allowing a year in which to develop the J-57 compressor before the XB-52 decision was made. This lab was to jet engine development what the Boeing high-speed wind tunnel was to airplane development.

The decision to use the J-57 jet engine on the B-52 was based largely on tests of the compressor. The data was shown to George Schairer by Perry Pratt, a Pratt & Whitney engineer in charge of the compressor development, no relation to the Pratt of Pratt & Whitney. Schairer probably examined the data on airflow capacity, compression pressure, turbine temperature, and the efficiency. From these figures the thrust and fuel consumption could be calculated. On January 21, 1950, the completed J-57 engine ran on the test stand, 15 months after the XB-52 go-ahead decision, which normally would not have been possible without a running engine on the test stand. It was first tested in flight while slung under the bomb bay of a B-50 bomber. Its first application was on the XB-52.

The J-57 powered both the 707 and the DC-8 and therefore is of lasting historical interest. It had two compressors in series, the second compressor turning at a higher rpm than the first in order to obtain high compression and high efficiency, in terms of power in and compressed air out. This general idea dates back to the 1920's, but the J-57 may have been the first application to a production airplane. Compressor blades act like airplane wings, inasmuch as a higher airspeed generates higher lift, and in the case of a compressor higher pressure as well. The design limit on the tip speed of the compressor blades was near the speed of sound, just as on a propeller. As it progressed through the stages of the compressor, the air was compressed, which raised the air temperature. This in turn increased the speed of sound. Thus the second compressor could run at an even higher rpm. This second compressor was driven by a tubular shaft, with a second shaft inside to drive the first compressor up forward. Pratt & Whitney's successful development of a reli-

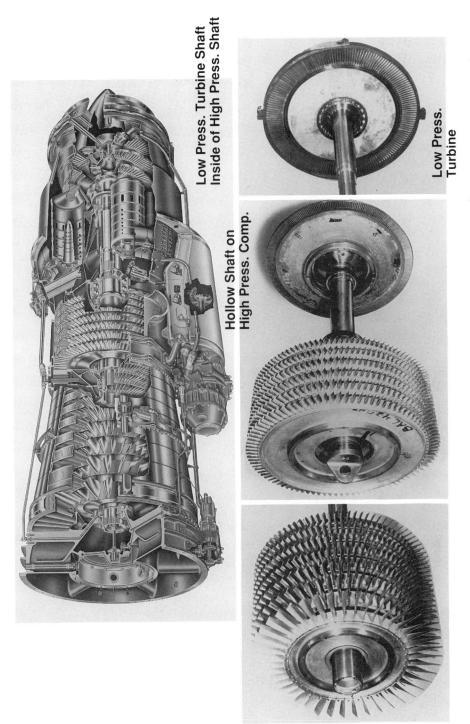

Low Press. Turbine Shaft
Inside of High Press. Shaft

Hollow Shaft on
High Press. Comp.

Low Press.
Turbine

J-57 Jet engine with low and high compressors separated.

able, new jet engine in time for the first flight of the XB-52 in April 1952 was a very significant achievement.

Colonel Warden's ability to obtain Pentagon approval for the B-52 program with such meager data on the airplane and engine, although puzzling, was truly a mark of genius. Colonel Warden had a big hand in revolutionizing the Air Force. The Air Force was very anxious to get a high performance intercontinental bomber to replace the B-36, which was very complicated and hard to maintain. The B-36 was prominent in the controversy between the Air Force and the Navy concerning roles and missions, and this may have been a factor in the Air Force acceptance of the XB-52 program, though the supporting data was sparse. The success of the B-47 and the full time use of the Boeing high-speed wind tunnel to optimize the B-52 design may have been factors in the Air Force decision. Nowhere else in the aircraft industry could they obtain this experience in long range jet airplanes combined with a high-speed wind tunnel that could be used full time.

In order to meet the extreme range requirement, the empty weight of the B-52 had to be kept to a minimum, necessitating a highly refined structural design and considerable machining. The thick, aluminum plates in the wing box and the large fittings in the airplane were machine tapered all over. This was well before the advent of numerically controlled machine tools. The early B-52's forgings for bulkhead and landing gear parts were machined using pattern-following machine tools that had been developed by Keller of Chrysler in the manufacture of automobiles to contour dies to press fenders and other sheet metal parts. Using these now outdated methods, the weight of the waste chips removed in the machining process on the B-52 could be several times that of the finished part.

The flight tests of the XB-52 demonstrated that the drag was 11 percent below that originally quoted. During the flight tests the basic J-57 engine gave no trouble except for the fuel control, which likewise had been a problem on the XB-47. If a jet engine would run at all, it would run almost indefinitely. The jet engine was damaged more by the heating up and cooling down that occurred when starting and stopping. Unlike piston engines, the life of a jet engine was determined by the expansion and creeping of the hot parts rather than friction wear, reminiscent of the creaking of a parlor stove when it is lit.

XB-47 Low-Speed Model in the Boeing Tunnel

XB-47 and XB-52 "wind-on" time exceeded 2,000 hours from 1945 to 1950.

The B-52 was designed for maximum weight savings, although the very narrow chords on the elevator and rudder carried these measures to something of an extreme. Longitudinal trim was achieved by means of an adjustable stabilizer instead of elevator trim tabs. While the B-52 controls proved to be operational, the flight testing of the B-52 showed that commercial transports would need more conventional control surfaces. The aerodynamic efficiency of the B-52 was probably the highest in any large airplane. The principal advancements demonstrated by the XB-52 were the thickened wing root and the performance and reliability of the J-57 engine.

Neither the XB-47 nor the XB-52 could be viewed as being entirely satisfactory, in that the state of the art was advancing rapidly, so that by the time of the first flights there were changes that would have made them better. But the knowledge obtained from their developments was of inimitable value. The remarkable characteristic of these two developmental programs was the cooperation between the manufacturer and the Air Force. The Air Force Project Office and their test pilots could and did make major contributions to the design. Without competition the developments were open for examination and for receiving suggestions. To one who participated during much of this, the modern competitions between military contractors, as reported in the media, sound like closed in-house developments that end up in "liars contests," with the designs being frozen for production before the performance objectives have been realized.

12

The Dash-80 Prototype

AT BOEING, the data and experience accumulated during five years of concentrated high-speed wind tunnel and flight testing of the B-47, from 1945 to 1949, fostered the idea of a commercial jet transport among the more enthusiastic engineers. Although the B-47 had numerous faults, the enthusiasts knew these could be eliminated. A very preliminary study of jet transport configurations was begun shortly after the XB-47 flight tests had indicated the possibility of a long range jet. However the rapid advancements being discovered during the development of the XB-52 indicated that the design of a transport should be delayed. One of the early ideas on transport configurations showed a bicycle landing gear, but this design was quite misleading.

About the same time this enthusiasm for a transport was being generated at Boeing, the world's first commercial jet transport, the deHaviland Comet, was flown. The Comet was built at Hatfield, near London, where many famous airplanes were born. Following the first flight in July 1949, demonstration flights were made in Europe during 1950. A second jet transport, the Avro of Canada Model C-102 flew in August, 1949.

Early Boeing concept of jet transport, 1949. Note bicycle gear and twin-engine pod like B-47.

Both transports were designed for shorter routes and were ahead of their time during a period of rapid development in the state of the art in aerodynamics and engines. But the U.S. airlines took little notice. The Comet generated a moderate amount of interest at Boeing, but the experiences with the B-47 and later with the B-52 indicated that it would be practical to build an airliner whose performance was much higher than that of the Comet. A brief history of the Comet is related in the chapter that follows.

When the wind tunnel testing and development of the XB-52 had shown great technical progress, it became apparent that the B-52 would go into production and that a military jet tanker to refuel the B-52 would have considerable business potential. This provided the motivation towards building the Dash-80 transport prototype. After the war, air-to-air refueling had become a standard feature of the intercontinental bombing mission. The first application was the refueling of the B-50 piston-engine bomber with the KC-97 piston-engine tanker. Later, the KC-97 was used to refuel the B-47 jet bomber. But the performance difference between the two types of aircraft was too great for efficient refueling. The KC-97 had to dive near the end of the transfer of fuel in order to keep in position ahead of the B-47, which was struggling to maintain sufficient speed above the stall as its maximum weight was approached. In 1954 when the B-52's first entered service, refueling was dependent

DeHaviland Comet
The world's first jet airliner, August 1949. Passenger service to Johannesburg, August 1952. Note the engines in the wing root and the fuel tank on the wing.

on the KC-97. The refueling rendezvous had to be accomplished at about 15,000 feet, and often in the weather. It was projected that a four-engine jet tanker design could transfer twice the volume of fuel at 30,000 feet of altitude above most of the bad weather.

In a decision to build a jet transport prototype, a military version was considered to be essential because it was doubtful that orders for a commercial jet transport would be sufficient to cover all start-up costs. A great many ideas had to be explored on the drawing board in order to accomplish the conversion from the jet bomber configurations of the B-47 and B-52, which had high wings and bicycle landing gears, to the low-wing configuration and tricycle landing gears that had become standard in transports. It was logical to design such a jet tanker to use J-57 engines so that it would be compatible with the B-52 in terms of engine maintenance and spare parts supply. The prototype was therefore optimized around the J-57 engine. This in turn determined the size of the wing. The resulting tanker would be large enough to completely fill the B-52's fuel tanks at the desired rendezvous point.

With the exception of the body, many major components could be the same between a military tanker and a commercial transport. Planning the tanker and commercial transport as a joint project would better assure sufficient financial support to justify a thorough evaluation of the many options being studied during the preliminary design phase. Due to the novelty of the various designs depicted in the preliminary layout drawings, and the departure from the previous bomber configurations, the need for a prototype was clear. This would permit a second design to incorporate the considerable improvements that would no doubt be discovered during construction and flight testing.

The cost of the prototype was estimated to be $16 million. However, a considerable part of this cost could be charged to the government as "Independent Research and Development." The size of this allowance was proportioned in relation to the company's military business under contract. The reason for this allowance was that the military contracts were cost-plus-fixed-fee, where the fee was based on the estimate at the start. This fee was so small as to be insufficient for a company to have much chance of survival in a business that was heavily dependent on research, and the government recognized the need for the "IR and D" on the part of the contractor. The cost of the prototype to Boeing was maybe only $3 million. Since in this case the "Independent Research and Development" was directed towards a military product, the jet tanker, the government later realized a tremendous bargain.

The building of the Dash-80 prototype was authorized on April 22, 1952. The first airplane to be flight tested was to be a true prototype, a one-of-a-kind model rather than the first production line model. It was to be used strictly for developmental purposes to demonstrate its suitability for bomber refueling and airline operations. No amount of brochures and drawings would have convinced the U.S. airlines to buy a transport that looked so strange in comparison to the piston-engine transports they were operating.

Tooling for the prototype would be minimal, as it was possible that extensive changes would be made to finalize the production model, which in turn would require new drawings and new tools. The experiences with the prototype probably lowered production costs by a considerable amount by reducing the number of changes during the start of the mass production. As it turned out, the cost of the prototype amounted to much less than 1/20th of the total investment in the engineering and tooling on the tanker and the commercial transport. The government got a bargain in its implied investment in the KC-135, as the tanker was named on purchase. As a result of being preceded by a prototype, the production tankers required very few changes to correct deficiencies. The design permitted a later change to more efficient engines. The KC-135 still is a very useful airplane 35 years after it was conceived.

Over 30 configurations were studied before arriving at the design that became the Dash-80 prototype. With so many drawings and so much test data, the most logical configuration soon became obvious. There was no need to resort to poorly supported, off-the-cuff decisions from a "chief designer," as may have been the case on the Boeing 247 airliner of 1934 and the deHaviland Comet. Some of the worst airplane designs have resulted from committees who had little data upon which to base decisions. But although a top level committee might not be helpful in making engineering decisions, when the data were adequate, it was most helpful in sales and in providing support for a prototype construction.

In a low-wing transport, the internal layout of wires and cables was much simpler than that of high-wing bombers. The cable control runs to the engines and control surfaces were located under the floor and had fewer bends and pulleys. One pleasant surprise was that the tricycle landing gear could be pivoted sideways on the aft side of the wing rear spar. It retracted into the body just behind the wing center section box, a neat arrangement [Figure 31]. Tricycle gears have to be located close enough behind the airplane's center of gravity so that on take-off the elevator can raise the nose while the the wheels are still in contact with the runway. But the gears have to be located far enough back so that during loading on the ground the airplane would not tilt so that the aft body would hit the ground as the nose rose. In airplanes with a lesser wing sweep such as the Comet, the landing gear had to be pivoted forward of the wing rear spar, so that a hole had to be cut in the wing's structural box in order to house the landing gear in the retracted position. This was a very undesirable solution because it compromised the structural strength of this very important area. In addition, it prevented the use of this prime space for carrying fuel.

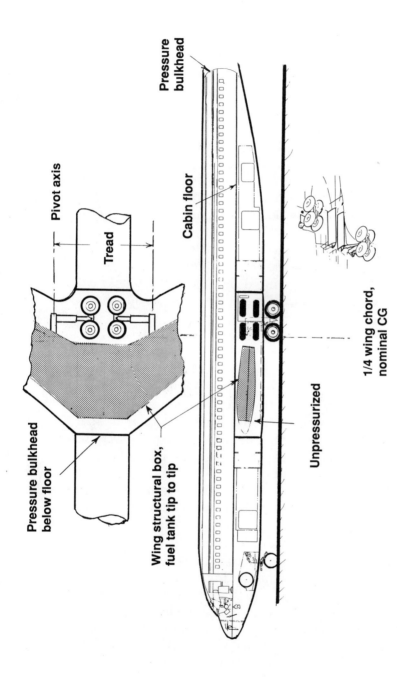

High wing sweep avoids gear retraction into wing.

Figure 31—Landing Gear Retraction With Swept Wing

Dash-80 right-hand landing gear retracted into body behind wing center section. Doors left open.

To enhance passenger comfort, the Dash-80 body was designed to maintain modern pressurization in which sea level pressure is maintained to 22,500 feet of altitude, an improvement over the lower pressurization of previous airplanes. To hold this higher pressure and still keep structural weight to a minimum, the upper and lower body lobes were designed as segments of circles which were mated at the cabin floor. There was a little flattening of the circles at the crease in the side of the body at the floor line. The upper deck was to be used for cargo, while the lower deck accommodated fuel tanks for the refueling of the B-52. The double lobe concept had originated in 1938 with the wartime Curtiss C-46 twin-engine transport. A double lobe body also had been used on the Boeing Stratocruiser piston-engine transport.

In the first layouts of the Dash-80 the four engines were located in double pods, as on the B-52. However, it was soon decided that four separate single pods would be safer in case of an engine burst or fire. An additional advantage was that the single pod provided better access to the engine for purposes of service and inspection. Later on, the choice of the single pod proved fortunate in another respect as well, in that it allowed for the use of the larger fan engines, which became available somewhat unexpectedly.

The design of the Dash-80 flight controls posed a difficult challenge. A lot had been learned from the B-47 and the B-52, on which many new ideas had been tested. The controls in neither airplane were entirely satisfactory for commercial operations. However, from these experiences an outstanding lateral control was designed for the Dash-80. The combination of wing upper surface spoilers and a small aileron behind the inboard nacelle resulted in good lateral control at high speeds, avoiding the decrease in effectiveness of the outer aileron, as had occurred on the B-47. Landings in high cross winds and gusty conditions were facilitated by the combination of spoilers with both the inboard and outboard ailerons. This provided very high lateral control at low speeds. The outboard aileron was locked in neutral except when the flaps were down, as its effectiveness would be low at high speeds [Figure 32].

In order to counter extreme turbulence, particularly at low speeds near the runway, wide chord elevators were used like those on the B-47, instead of the narrow chord control surfaces that were used on the B-52. Longitudinal trimming was accomplished with an adjustable stabilizer, as on the B-52. Trimming with the stabilizer was much more effective than with trailing edge tabs, which had been universally used on larger airplanes since 1930. After the war, the use of trim tabs was soon abandoned on the first jet fighters because they lose their effectiveness when the airplane is flying near the speed of sound. Even a commercial transport might need the higher effectiveness of stabilizer trimming to recover from a dive, an unusual situation, but one that happened on the 707. In the past, the use of adjustable stabilizers had been discontinued because they contributed to accidents on account of their poor mechanical design.

But the design of the Dash-80 stabilizer was much improved over its predecessors. It was operated by an electric motor, which was controlled by two independent side-by-side

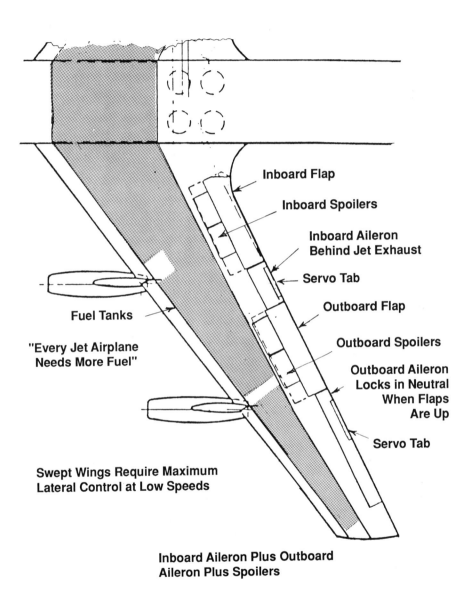

Inboard Flap

Inboard Spoilers

Inboard Aileron
Behind Jet Exhaust

Servo Tab

Outboard Flap

Outboard Spoilers

Outboard Aileron
Locks in Neutral
When Flaps
Are Up

Servo Tab

Fuel Tanks

"Every Jet Airplane
Needs More Fuel"

Swept Wings Require Maximum
Lateral Control at Low Speeds

Inboard Aileron Plus Outboard
Aileron Plus Spoilers

Figure 32—Wing Controls and Fuel Tanks

momentary rocker type switches operated by the pilot's thumb on the control wheel. One switch turned on the power and the other controlled the direction of the motor. Both switches had to be pressed at the same time so as to avoid a runaway control that otherwise could result from an electrical failure. The stabilizer could also be manually trimmed by turning a large wheel on the cockpit aisle stand.

A major decision on the Dash-80 was to forego the use of servo-hydraulic powered controls in favor of manually operated controls that utilized aerodynamic balancing. A few years later this decision was questioned by pilots who had become used to the improved feel that is made possible by hydraulic controls. Pilots are inclined to overlook the possibility of failure in a new system when that system makes flying easier under normal conditions, that is, until they have experienced an emergency. At the time the Dash-80 was being designed, it was believed that the internal leading edge aerodynamic balances and trailing edge servo tabs, as used on the B-47 emergency system, would produce reasonable control forces. It was decided that the commercial airliner would be more reliable without the added complication of hydraulics. Also, the southern California manufacturers had discovered that, for safety's sake, dual hydraulic systems were necessary in fighters. However, Boeing had no experience with dual hydraulics and so was reluctant to increase even further the magnitude of complexity.

While the Dash-80 elevator and aileron controls proved generally satisfactory without hydraulic servos, the Dash-80 rudder should have had a hydraulic power servo and a yaw damper, as on the B-47 (these were added later on the 707). Lessons from the past are too easily forgotten. The 1939 accident of the 307 Stratoliner, mentioned previously in Chapter 4, and the XB-47 dutch roll, unfortunately had been forgotten by many, including myself. The original manual rudder required hazardous flight training to simulate engine failures, and the risks from this training should have been minimized by the use of a power hydraulic servo which is similar to power steering in automobiles. This mechanism allows the pilot to maintain full control of the rudder even in the event of a complete power failure, enabling him to avoid the yawing that might lead to a tail spin.

The moral here is that when flight testing exposes a hazardous condition or a system where a mechanical or an electrical failure would be critical, to the greatest extent possible the condition should be eliminated by redesign, rather than by insertion of a note in the emergency section of the pilot's handbook, to the effect, "Don't do this . . . !"

The Dash-80 was rolled out in May 1954, exposed to public view for the first time. Once outside the factory, it was fueled and the engines were run. The favorable experience with the P&W J-57 engine on the B-52 shortened the period for ground testing on the Dash-80. The first problem was encountered during a taxi test to check the brakes. A main landing gear failed, causing the wing and nacelles to drop onto the runway. The landing gear design did not allow for structural deflections caused by the braking loads. A prying action between parts of the mechanism caused a main supporting member to fail. Also, the steel in a landing gear fitting was brittle, causing it to snap. Consequently, the first flight was delayed until July 15, 1954.

A second near disaster held up the program for a short period when the brakes got too hot and failed on a landing, due to an insufficient oil volume capacity in a part that is equivalent to the master cylinder in automobile brakes. Cars and airplanes are alike with respect to brake problems. The pilot, Tex Johnston, steered the plane over into the dirt to slow it down, which broke off the nose gear. The design flaw was easily fixed and this was the last of most of the mechanical problems.

Once the early flights of the Dash-80 had demonstrated good flying characteristics and the overall configuration had been judged to be highly successful, a major decision had to be made regarding the amount of tooling that could be warranted for production. The market for commercial jet transports was still difficult to predict, although the use of jet transports had been demonstrated for over two years by the Comet, which had been in service between London and Johannesburg.

The question of the financing the production was relieved by the sale of the KC-135 tanker to the Air Force, which had been impressed by early flights of the Dash-80 during which its capability to effectively refuel the B-52 was demonstrated by the B-52 maintaining a flight position directly behind and below the Dash-80 simulating the tanker. The Air Force pilots were probably elated by the improvements apparent in the Dash-80 as compared to the B-47 and B-52, both of which were difficult to fly.

While the Dash-80 was being built, the government made no commitment to buy the military tanker version, although the Air Force Strategic Air Command was thoroughly convinced that they needed a jet tanker. The KC-135 was sold to General Curtis LeMay, the head of the Strategic Air Command, by Wellwood Beall, the executive vice president of Boeing. However, General LeMay was reticent about asking for a jet tanker until he had acquired five wings of B-52's. Had he asked for a jet tanker at the same time as the B-52's, Congress might have reduced the number of B-52's. He knew that a tanker that would fulfill his needs was under development, and so he waited until the need for the tanker was obvious before petitioning Congress. Wright Field then conducted a competition for a jet tanker. This was a year and a half after the public announcement of the Dash-80 project. Wright Field selected Lockheed as the winner of the paper competition, at about the time of the first flight of the Dash-80. The earlier deliveries of the KC-135 and the flight demonstrations were convincing. General LeMay told Wright Field, "You can go ahead with your winner, but in the meantime buy me some of these." General LeMay's delay in asking for tankers was to Boeing's advantage. The Lockheed tanker was never built.

Another factor in the Air Force decision was the fact that the Lockheed tanker design was similar to their L-193 transport proposal, in that the engines were located on the aft body, and were therefore subject to the same criticism that had caused the engines on the XB-47 to be moved from the body to pods on the wing.

The tanker sale warranted investment in the heavy wartime type of high production tooling for the KC-135. The same jigs for the wing and tail would also be used for the 707. The bodies were different, requiring different jigs. In 1956 when the wing jigs were filled with KC-135 parts ready to be riveted together, the chief designer of the deHaviland Comet, R.E. Bishop, visited the Renton factory. After viewing the jigs, he asked the Boeing chief engineer, Maynard Pennell, "How many 707 orders do you have?" Maynard answered, "87," which was

Outboard Aileron

Spoilers Up

Vortex Generators

Control Tab
Inboard Aileron

Flaps Down

Lateral Controls on Dash-80 and 707.

Dash-80—Early flight.

Dash-80 on landing. Note gap in flaps for inboard aileron.

supposed to be the financial breakeven point. Bishop then said, "Why, you can build all those 707 wings with these jigs in a year." Maynard replied, "That's right." Bishop then asked "What are you going to do then?" Maynard replied, "I don't know."

The moral here is that there was not much point in starting a major project without planning for success by tooling for volume production. In other words, the tooling was so expensive to accomplish that, orders or no orders, it had to be predicated on high volumes. As it turned out, sales volumes were not a problem, and during the years that followed, the tooling had to

Dash-80 simulating refueling B-52.

be multiplied even further to meet the increasing market demand for 707's. Production had reached 916 units by 1982, and was followed by small production of military versions, like the AWACS 707's used in the recent Gulf War to detect enemy activities and to control air operations.

Boeing and the Air Force had an agreement to share tooling costs between the KC-135 and the 707. After the 707 production had greatly expanded, there was talk that the government had

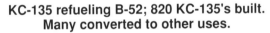

**KC-135 refueling B-52; 820 KC-135's built.
Many converted to other uses.**

picked up the best of that deal, in what may have amounted to a payment to the government for each 707 part fabricated by tools that were common between the 707 and the KC-135. The numerous military adaptations of the 707 and the 707 VIP transports have proven essential in defense and governmental operations. The Dash-80 prototype provided good insurance against being on the wrong track or being left out in a period of technological advances.

13

The Commercial Transport Competition

WHEN THE END of the war brought the production of military piston-engine airplanes to a halt, commercial aviation was the principal hope for substantial postwar business. Yet airline travel during the war had been quite limited in comparison to what would come later. From 1936 to 1945 the twin-engine Douglas DC-3 was the principal commercial airliner. Cruising at a speed of 190 mph it could carry 21 passengers. During the war the Douglas C-54 four-engine military transport was flown all over the world and thus prepared the way for international air routes. The long range land planes displaced the less efficient flying boats. During the war new airports were built around the world to ferry bombers and fighters and to accommodate the C-54's that were flying military personnel overseas and bringing back wounded. The C-54 carried 44 to 60 passengers and had a range of 3,000 miles and a cruising speed of 220 mph. The English language was the standard in airways communications during the war. After the war it became the international standard, somewhat to the dismay of the French.

After the war surplus C-54's became the peacetime DC-4

227

and were sold to the airlines. This started the rapid expansion in postwar travel. The DC-4 was superseded when Douglas produced a greatly upgraded version, the DC-6, which had larger engines (the Pratt & Whitney 2800), a pressurized cabin, and a lengthened body to accommodate more passengers. The DC-6 was followed by the DC-6B, which had a further extension of the body to add passengers. The DC-6 and 6B were adopted worldwide by the airlines, which was to a considerable extent due to the high reliability of the engine. The British and French did not have engines with comparable reputations. The British also lost out by attempting to modify war-time bombers into passenger transports. These did not have tricycle landing gears like the DC-6 and could not compete for other reasons. Lockheed increased production of the four-engine Constellation transport in quantity for the airlines. Boeing adapted the B-29 four-engine bomber for use as a commercial transport, the Stratocruiser, by designing a double lobe, pressurized widened body, and installing larger engines. In making the transition from war to peace, Douglas was in the most advantageous position because of the large use of the C-54 during the war and the quick upgrading to the DC-6. During this postwar period, Douglas was mostly occupied in the expansion of its commercial business based on its existing product line, although the company was doing some advanced research on jet transports.

Shortly after the war all of the airplane manufacturers were gaining experience with experimental jet airplanes through military contracts. Most companies had a small preliminary design group that was apart from the engineers working on production projects. In 1947 Richard Shevell of Douglas gave a paper at the Institute of Aeronautical Sciences entitled "Operational Aerodynamics of Jet Transports." Possibly, this marked the start of the DC-8. The head of Preliminary Design at Lockheed, Willis Hawkins, had been working on a jet transport design, the model L-193, which featured four engines located behind the wing and low on the aft body. In January 1950 Hawkins visited Pan American, United and American Airlines in an attempt to generate interest.

At that time the development of turbine engines was advancing so rapidly that there was no consensus on the best type of engine for a turbine transport. Jet engines were being developed for military applications and turbo-prop engines lagged far behind in the U.S., being much more difficult to develop than the jet. Those engineers in the U.S. that might have preferred the turbo-prop for its theoretical higher efficiency had little data on a U.S. engine for design purposes and little prospect of a running engine, although the Allison Division of General Motors was working on their 501 turbo-prop engine. It was test flown in the Convair twin-engine CV-580 in December 1950. The lack of strong U.S. military support for turbo-prop engines and the extended developmental time for the combination of a turbine engine with a propeller and a gearbox left the Allison 501 far behind the jet. This engine powered the four-engine Lockheed C-130 cargo plane that flew in August 1954 and the Electra airliner that American Airlines and Northwest ordered in 1955. In England the situation was quite the opposite. The Rolls Royce Dart turbo prop first ran in 1946 and in July 1948 it flew in the four-engine Vickers Viscount airliner that became widely used throughout the world.

In the spring of 1949, when Boeing's B-52 design had been changed by Colonel Warden to incorporate a Pratt & Whitney jet instead of a Wright turbo-prop "paper engine" that posed many mechanical problems, Pratt & Whitney was still looking toward the turbo-prop as the engine of choice for commercial transports, although they did not have a suitable candidate. One of the Pratt & Whitney engineers showed me their T-34 turbo-prop engine in a P&W test stand in East Hartford and said that this, rather than the jet, was to be the commercial transport engine of the future, even though Pratt & Whitney already was well along in the development of their J-57 jet engine for the B-52. At Boeing it was a matter of getting on with a real engine, and the T-34 turbo-prop was too far behind in development as a proven reliable engine to be realistically considered in a commercial transport. It had about twice the power that would have been needed to convert the existing four-engine piston transports to turbo-prop transports, and so it was unsuitable for use by the airlines in that time period. In 1953 it was qualified for use in the very large Douglas C-133 transport, eight months after the start of the Dash-80 program. Pratt & Whitney had little feel for the design studies of airliners going on in the U.S. They were lucky that the J-57 was a good fit for the 707-sized transport.

Douglas obtained early jet experience in designing and testing the first medium-size jet bomber, the two-engine XB-43. It flew for the first time in May 1946 a year and a half before the XB-47. The XB-43 was used to test the GE TG180 engine. Douglas submitted a list of 250 complaints on the engine. Such a high number as this might well be expected in the early stages of development, although it could have been viewed as evidence that the development of jet airplanes had a long way to go before a successful transport could be produced. But by the time XB-47 flight testing was begun in 1948, the TG180 had been improved to where it gave little trouble, at least compared to the contemporary piston engines. At Boeing, during the early experiences with the Pratt & Whitney J-57 on the B-52, doubts concerning the reliability of jet engines were mostly eliminated. Two years later, Douglas became familiar with the J-57 on the Douglas A3D twin-engine bomber and the F4D fighter. But Douglas was late in recognizing the progress that had been made on jet engines, and the fact that the engine would no longer impede the development of the jet transport. By this time the Dash-80 was already flying and Boeing had a head start.

The principal impediment to the timely development of a jet transport at Douglas was the DC-7 program because it absorbed engineering and financial resources during the time when the Boeing Dash-80 prototype was being designed and built. The DC-7 was the result of considerable pressure that had been placed on Donald Douglas, Sr. by C.R. Smith of American Airlines in late 1951. By that time American Airlines had been operating the Douglas DC-6B for eight months. The DC-6B used the most reliable piston engine, the Pratt & Whitney R2800. As an airliner it was immediately successful, and through the years it would prove to be the best piston engine transport ever built. One would have thought American would have left well enough alone. But no, C.R. wanted Douglas to increase cruising speeds by replacing the P&W 2800 engine with the new and more powerful Wright 3350 compound engine. American would then be in a position to compete with TWA's new version of the Lockheed Constellation which used this same new engine. C.R. Smith had done a similar kind of arm twisting to get the DC-3 started, and it would have been hard for Douglas to turn down a customer who had been so helpful in the past [Figure 33].

	Boeing	Douglas	Lockheed
1951	XB-47 1st Flight Dec. 1947	DC-6 Production DC-8 Studies DC-7 Project Start	L-193 Jet Trans. Studies, Visits to Airlines ⊢Competition Winner C-130, 4 Eng. Turbo-Prop
1952	⟋YB-52 1st Flight ⟍Dash-80 Project Start ⟍Dash-80 Public Announcement	Comet Service London-Johannesburg	Constellation Production ↑ ↓
1953		⊢DC-7 1st Flight	
	USAF Tanker Paper Competition		
1954	⊢Dash-80 Roll-out ⊢Dash-80 1st Flight ⟍KC-135 Initial Order ⊢Dash-80 Demo to PAA		Tanker Competition Winner Engines on Aft Body
1955	⊢KC-135 Large Order ⊢PAA 707—120 Order ⊢AA 707—120 Order	⊢DC-8 Announced ⟋PAA DC-8 Order ⊢United ⊢DC-7C 1st Flight	⊢AA Order Electra L-188, Turbo-Prop
1956	⊢KC-135 1st Flight		⟋Constellation 1649,1st Flight, Piston Trans.
1957	⊢KC-135 1st Delivery ⊢707 1st Flight		⟋Electra L-188 1st Flight
1958	 ⊢PAA 707 1st Ops	⊢DC-8 1st Flight	
1959	⊢AA 707 Transcont. Service	 ⊢DC-8 1st Ops	⊢Eastern Electra Service

Figure 33—Competition Timing

In late 1951 a decision at Douglas to forego the DC-7 in favor of a jet transport would have been quite difficult. Douglas would have had to convince C.R. to stay with the DC-6 until the jet transport could be developed. But the Douglas preliminary design unit probably did not yet have available sufficient design studies or wind tunnel test data on jet transports. Thus, no case could be made. Even at Boeing, which had the flight experiences with the B-47 to draw upon, there was not sufficient material to convince an airline that the jet transport was near and that further development of piston transports would be unwise. What made the difference for Boeing was the wind tunnel. While at least a few engineers at Douglas felt that the jet age was imminent, without the full time use of a high-speed wind tunnel they could not convince their management to proceed towards building a prototype. Douglas had to share the Cal Tech Coop high-speed wind tunnel with three other companies. This tunnel did not come into operation until well after the war. It was quite complicated and suffered from many operational problems.

The extent to which Douglas lagged behind Boeing in wind tunnel testing was revealed in a lecture given in London in 1951 by Arthur Raymond, the Douglas vice president of engineering. The lecture was entitled "The Well Tempered Airplane," and it covered the general history of the DC-3 through the DC-6. In his lecture Raymond stated that ". . . the wind tunnel tends to become a checking device rather than one for the collection of design information . . . the temptation is to wait and see whether the aircraft exhibits these characteristics in flight." In contrast, the wind-tunnel data on the Boeing XB-47 was accepted implicitly and was used promptly in design.

Within a year after the decision to build the DC-7, the dominance of Douglas in transports must have appeared questionable to the Douglas engineers who were involved in preliminary design. The Douglas chief engineer, Ed Burton, repeatedly urged Donald Douglas, Sr. to build a jet transport prototype. However, he was not successful in making a case for a prototype, even though Arthur Raymond had predicted in June 1952 that the jet transport would appear on the commercial airways within five years. At that time, in the early 1950's, Douglas was producing piston transports at such a high rate that the future looked good to top management. They were overconfident in their assessment that they could change to jet transports without an early prototype. Such a prototype would have reduced the time required to produce the DC-8. The slowness of the DC-8 program prevented Douglas from matching Boeing's delivery dates of the 707, and this proved to be a crucial factor in the initial competition to sell jet transports to the airlines.

At Boeing the decision to take a radical approach was comparatively easy, as competing programs within Boeing were winding down. The last Stratocruiser had been delivered in 1950, ending Boeing's commercial business for the time being. In 1951 Boeing lost a military competition for a four-engine turbo-prop cargo plane to Lockheed, which would produce the C-130, a cargo transport that was popular for many years worldwide and is still extensively in use. At least 1,700 C-130's were built. If Boeing had won this competition, the energies needed to build the Dash-80 might have been diverted and absorbed by such a large turbo-prop program. Another factor working in Boeing's favor was the fact that engineering on the XB-52 was winding down, freeing up a significant amount of engineering capacity that could then be redirected to design the Dash-80. The jet bomber business had generated a lot of enthusiasm within Boeing, and so management was open to the idea of a commercial jet transport, especially since it appeared to be the one remaining opportunity.

On September 8, 1952, Boeing made a public announcement that a jet transport project was underway. This announcement was made five months after the start of detail design. Boeing had made no attempt to sell the Dash-80 idea earlier to the airlines, as this would have disclosed too much. While the airline representatives stationed in Seattle were probably aware of the size of the effort, they paid little attention, partly because they were involved in correcting problems on the Stratocruiser. In any case, the airlines were unlikely to take seriously the idea of a commercial jet because some of those in the military had been advising the airlines that jets had many problems which made them unsuitable for airline operations. Furthermore, it would have made for poor public relations if Boeing were to tell the airlines at this early stage that their entire fleet might be obsolete within the foreseeable future.

Lockheed C-130, Hercules Turbo-prop Cargo Transport

Lockheed won competition over Boeing, August 1951. Lockheed built Electra transport with Allison engines, delivered to airlines December 1957.

Two months after the Dash-80 public announcement the vice president of engineering at American Airlines, Bill Littlewood, gave the "16th Wright Brothers Lecture," entitled "Technical Trends in Air Transportation," a prestigious event in Washington, DC, that was well attended. His presentation reviewed the piston-propeller era with all its problems and made a modest extension of this well seasoned concept into the future. He emphasized the catastrophic effects of propeller blade failures. He mentioned the Comet jet transport, seemingly without enthusiasm, and did not even allude to the Dash-80 program that had been started five months before. Littlewood indicated the possible introduction of the jet by 1960 but added a caveat by outlining all of the possible jet problems he had heard about but with which he had no experience. He included a chart of engine overhaul times that predicted that by the year 1960 jet engines might be capable of achieving 1,000 hours before they had to be removed from the airplane for overhaul. He was way off the mark, for by 1960 jet engines actually could be operated for 4,000 hours before their removal was required only as a safety precaution, not wear-out. Later, this number was raised to 13,000 hours on some engines. Littlewood made no mention of the P&W J-57 jet engine, which was to power the Dash-80.

The lack of curiosity in America concerning the Dash-80

and the J-57 was perhaps due to the airline industry's desire to quietly consolidate their efforts before upsetting the "apple cart" by hitting the market with a radical new product. Pratt & Whitney evidently had not been actively marketing their J-57. (Incidentally, this was an aid to Boeing in keeping Douglas wary of jet engines.) By the time of Littlewood's lecture the J-57 had been in operation on the YB-52 for seven months. During flight testing each of the eight engines had accumulated nearly 100 hours of operation, with virtually trouble-free service except for the engine fuel control, a small replaceable unit that required further development. The great reliability of the J-57 as compared to previous jet engines was not generally known by the airlines, and thus they failed to recognize the true potential of the jet transport at this time. Without a jet transport demonstrator, old-time airline engineers like Littlewood, who had spent years working out problems on many propeller driven transports, were hard to convince that a new era was dawning.

The published version of Littlewood's lecture was followed by comments from the industry. The Boeing chief engineer, Maynard Pennell, wrote that the solution to the problems Littlewood had outlined was the elimination of the propeller. Maynard also briefly stated that many of the problems Littlewood had mentioned had already been overcome, thus inferring that the Dash-80 program was sound.

Secrecy was maintained on the Dash-80 configuration during the design and construction phases. However, if Boeing's competitors had been doing their homework they could have surmised that the Dash-80 was planned around the J-57 engine, and from this they could have determined its size and general characteristics. They also could have analyzed the vulnerability of their current business and the advisability of building competitive prototypes to head off Boeing. Even if their prototypes had been a little late, the airlines would have waited until they had seen everything before placing their orders. It might not have been difficult for Douglas to get most all of the airline orders even with a second rate prototype, since there would have been time to make changes before production started.

While the lack of enthusiasm for the jet transport was widespread in the U.S., Pan American was one airline that was alert to the possibility that the jet age might be forthcoming. In

May 1952 British Overseas Airline inaugurated service between London and Johannesburg with the deHaviland Comet. This plane seated only 36 passengers and had to fly the trip in stages of no more than 1,500 miles, due principally to the low-thrust deHaviland "Ghost" engines. Although its range was short of what was needed for trans-Atlantic service, on October 20, 1952, Pan Am announced an order for three Comets. This purchase order was at the initiative of Juan Trippe, the famous founder and ruler of Pan Am. He placed the order without advice from his engineering experts. Trippe was a leader in buying the latest long range transports.

In an effort to maintain a position of pre-eminence within the industry, Pan Am had been the first airline to buy every new model of commercial transport aircraft, including the Douglas DC-6, the Lockheed Constellation, and the Boeing Stratocruiser. The question of how the airline could operate with such a wide mix of aircraft models and makes did not seem to bother Trippe. Shortly before ordering the Comets, Trippe had offered to buy jet airliners from the U.S. manufacturers, but he had received no responses.

Two months after the Comet order three Pan Am technical experts visited deHaviland. One of these was Captain Scott Flower, who had flown the Pan Am large flying boats before the war and who later managed engineering matters concerning piloting and operations. The other two were John Borger and Bob Blake, MIT aeronautical engineering graduates who were in charge of performance evaluations of new airplanes at Pan Am. The Pan Am team disliked the location of the engines on the Comet, which were buried inside the wing root, nor did they like the plane's small size, as the larger models were always preferred for Pan Am's long, over-ocean flights. They asked the design director of deHaviland, R.E. Bishop, how deHaviland could justify the use of such thin sheet metal skins on the Comet's body, skins which were in fact thinner than those used on the Douglas DC-6B. The logic behind their question was that the Comet would have to sustain the higher cabin differential pressures that are characteristic of jets because they operate at high altitudes. Bishop replied, "Because we know how."

Bishop's confidence was based on tests in which the Comet body had been immersed in a water tank and subjected to twice the flight operating differential pressure. For safety reasons, the tests had been conducted using water pressure rather than air pressure, since a failure of the body when using air pressure might have resulted in an explosion. However, the Pan Am team's concerns proved to be valid, for after only two years of service two Comets were lost in the Mediterranean. The crashes were attributed to cabin bursts that were caused by metal fatigue. From this experience it became obvious that a one-time pressure proof test was not a substitute for a high cycle fatigue test. Boeing conducted a water tank test on the KC-135, but then switched to high cycle fatigue testing. More was to be learned from the Comet.

DeHaviland deserves considerable credit for starting the jet transport age. DeHaviland was a pioneer in the design of jet airplanes. The design of the Vampire single engine jet fighter was started in 1941 and its successful first flight in September 1943 generated considerable interest in the possibility of a jet transport. DeHaviland's layout of a four-engine airliner was sufficiently complete by March 1945 to warrant a wind tunnel test at the Royal Aircraft Establishment at Farnborough. Detail design of the Comet was begun in October 1946.

At the time the Comet design was started, air travel was still considered to be somewhat of a luxury. It was thought that jet transports would require very high fares and that at most, they might be operated on premium routes only. The Comet program started out with 16 orders at a price based on a breakeven point of 50 planes. While the need for a prototype was considered, the go-ahead was made to start off with production airplanes; the first airplane off the line would be used for flight testing. Because of the small number of orders, the tooling for the Comet was minimal, reverting somewhat to prewar methods that required considerable skills in hand work.

The deHaviland designers were out in front and on their own, without the benefit of competing ideas to widen their analysis. They probably were handicapped in not being able to do extensive wind tunnel testing, which realistically would be needed to advance to a radically new design. As an example, preliminary design of the Boeing XB-47, which was taking place during this same time period, required nine months of concentrated wind tunnel testing before detail design could be started.

Without the guiding influence of a comprehensive wind tunnel test effort, the design of the Comet remained unnecessarily conservative, especially with respect to the low wing sweep angle of 20 degrees. At that time there were no published data on swept wings in the U.S. and possibly none in England. Three British military heavy bombers were under development, all of which featured the same engine location as that used on the Comet. The engines were buried in the wing root because this seemed to be the logical place to minimize drag. The XB-47 engine pods were not displayed to the public view until over a year after the start of the Comet design, but even then there was no general acceptance of pods until the Dash-80 flights were begun seven years later.

On July 27, 1949, the Comet made its first flight, 34 months after start of the design. This compares to 26 months for the Dash-80, which was less on account of the shortcuts that are made possible by a prototype program. The fortunes of the Comet were reminiscent of the competition between the Boeing 247 and the Douglas DC-2. It seems that the first model of a new generation of aircraft is always too small while the second has the advantage of bigger engines and more advanced technology. DeHaviland was probably influenced towards an early start and a conservative design by the Brabazon Committee, a British government organization that was intended to coordinate the British airlines and manufacturers so as to gain an early lead in the postwar air transportation market. In 1946 when the Comet program was being started, the general consensus among the U.S. airlines regarding the feasibility of a commercial jet transport probably was that it should be delayed indefinitely.

Soon after the war, several manufacturers in England were working on turbo-prop transports, probably thinking that jets would not have long range capability and that in any case they would not be economical to operate. The British were far ahead of the United States in turbo-prop development, and they were looking for an opportunity to displace the Douglas DC-7 and the Lockheed Constellation in trans-Atlantic operations. In July 1950 turbo-prop service was started on the shorter runs in England and Europe with the Vickers Vicount, which had four Rolls Royce Dart engines. A larger turbo-prop, the Bristol Britannia, with four Proteus engines, was chosen to compete with the U.S. on over-ocean runs. The Britannia was put into service in July 1955, the same time as Pan Am placed its first order for the 707.

The sales argument for the Britannia was that it was more economical than jets because it used less fuel. However, the passenger appeal of the jet transport would prove to be decisive. Scott Flower of Pan Am asked a discerning question, "What is more economical about flying an empty airplane?" This was the first time that the final customer, the passenger, would be involved in a choice between competing technologies. The passenger's choice was between buying a lower cost ticket for a slower, rougher ride at maximum fuel efficiency or maybe buying a more expensive ticket for the less fuel efficient but much faster, smoother ride that could be had at higher altitudes with the jet engine. Up to that time improvements in both speed and fuel efficiency had been achieved in each new generation of propeller driven airplanes. But fuel isn't the only cost factor that affects airplane ticket prices. Factors that favored the jet over the turbo-prop were higher speed and simpler engine maintenance. Although an airline generates revenues per passenger mile, an airline incurs much of its costs per flying hour. This means that the fewer hours it takes to get the passengers from point A to point B, the greater the revenues in proportion to costs, despite higher fuel expenditures.

It is somewhat ironic that the English pioneer in turbine engines, Sir Frank Whittle, had been in favor of jets from the start. Just after the end of the war he made a grand lecture tour, with a stop in Seattle. At the end of his slide presentation he answered a question about the role of the turbo-prop by saying, "It was an unnecessary intermediate step." At the same lecture he showed a diagram of a fan-jet engine. Fifteen years later, in 1960 during a visit to Rolls Royce I asked the chief engineer, "What has happened to Whittle?" His answer to me was, "He has passed the time of his usefulness." Rolls Royce had just developed the Tyne turbo-prop engine for the four-engine Vickers Vanguard. Little did they realize that Whittle's early prognostications were about to come true, which would render their latest achievement obsolete.

During the early Dash-80 flight testing, about 1955, the head of Rolls Royce, Lord Hives, visited Seattle, in part so that he could see the Dash-80. After walking around the Dash-80, Lord Hives remarked to his guide, George Schairer, "This is the end." Schairer asked, "The end of what?" Lord Hives replied, "The end of British aviation." He realized that the turbo-prop had been the wrong choice. At that time the full potential of the jet transport was hard to imagine. The British should not have given up so early after their first try with the Comet, because it was a good start.

The Comet's short range and poor accident record may have been misinterpreted as a judgment against all jets in general. In any case, the negative, prevailing view towards commercial jets was changed upon the Dash-80's public display and first demonstration flights. As soon as the principal bugs in the Dash-80 were eliminated, flight demonstrations were commenced on October 2, 1954, with Pan Am purchasing executives, Kaufman and Gledhill, on board. This was the 27th test flight. From then on demonstrations were numerous.

When an airline visitor happened to be a pilot, he would be directed to sit in either pilot's seat, depending on his recent flying experience, and would be asked to fly the Dash-80 on the first take-off. The Boeing pilot would give instructions on when to rotate and would insure that the climb was steep enough to stay under the flap placard speed until the flaps were up. At light gross weights the climb-out was impressive, particularly to the airline executive pilots, most of whom did not know what to expect having had no experience in jets. At a few hundred feet of altitude the Boeing pilot might cut an engine, and then another. The demonstration would then continue with all engines in a climb to cruise altitude, a few turns, and then a descent and a landing with a little help from the Boeing pilot. The airline pilot would be very much elated, as it was his first exposure to high altitude cruise above the weather. He would have noted the lack of vibration, the low cockpit noise, and the ease of control. This was a sales opportunity never again to be equaled on account of the dramatic nature of the transition from piston engines and propellers to jets. The Boeing chief pilot, Tex Johnston, was a master at that kind of demonstration.

Lockheed seemed unsure of the future, and instead of developing a jet, they elected to stretch the piston-engine Constellation. This effort resulted in the model 1649, which flew for the first time in October 1956, a full year after the Pan Am 707 order and two years after Boeing had started demonstrating the Dash-80 to the world's airlines. Lockheed seemed to have given up on jet transports, going on to produce the turbo-prop Electra. Lockheed was a house divided at the top, with Kelly Johnson, the Lockheed designer of high performance radical airplanes, on the side of the jet.

By the time of the demonstrations of the Dash-80 to the airlines, the J-57 engine, had accumulated considerable service time on the XB-52 bomber. It was virtually trouble-free, and it generated the necessary confidence within Boeing to sell the commercial jet transport to the airlines with assurance. Apparently, as late as 1955 Pratt & Whitney still had not formed a solid opinion as to the future direction of the transport business. The Pratt & Whitney sales manager, T.E. Tillinghast, visited Seattle during the early tests of the Dash-80. When delivery dates for engines for production airliners were discussed, he said that his company needed more time to develop the J-57 to achieve the safety level needed for commercial operations.

During this same time period, the Pratt & Whitney Wasp Major 4360 engine with 28 cylinders and 56 spark plugs was in operation powering the Boeing Stratocruiser. It was giving considerable trouble, and the rear bank of cylinders was running too hot, thus limiting the power output of the engine. It was pointed out to Tillinghast that the J-57 was already much safer than the 4360 with the Hamilton Standard propeller. This was not hard to prove, as two Stratocruisers had to ditch in the Pacific or land on a small island on account of engine failures and the failure of the propeller to feather. In an effort to convince him further, he was invited into the Dash-80 cockpit for a demonstration flight. This was a paradoxical case where an enthusiastic customer was trying to convince a skeptical seller that he was offering a quality product. Tillinghast no doubt found the experience to be a pleasure compared to the usual burden of troubles associated with the 4360 in the Stratocruiser.

Because of the overwhelming success of the DC-6, Douglas enjoyed a very favorable relationship with the airlines at this time. The engine in this airplane was quite reliable, due in part to various improvements that had been made during their long wartime use. Some airlines took the position that they would make the transition from pistons only after Douglas had come out with a jet. Otto Kirchner, a long time engineer with American Airlines, told his sons in Boeing engineering that Douglas could do anything Boeing could do, the B-47 and B-52 experiences notwithstanding. During this period the sales of the piston-engine transports were quite good and Douglas held 70 percent of the large transport business. The airlines were soured on Boeing because of the Stratocruiser and the Pratt &Whitney 4360 engine, which had never delivered the anticipated level of power or reliability.

Initially, the 707 was designed around the Pratt and Whitney J-57 engine, as necessitated by its alternate role as the KC-135 military tanker. Instead of designing for the J-57, Douglas offered a larger airplane which would use a forthcoming P&W engine, the J-75. Intended for fighter applications, this engine was an enlarged version of the J-57. Pratt and Whitney had started developing it even before the first J-57 production engine had been shipped.

At the time when the Douglas DC-8 was in the design process, the P&W J-75 was restricted to military applications, but Juan Trippe of Pan Am felt that, with his political influence, its release for commercial use by Pan Am could be expedited, thus giving Pan Am a temporary competitive advantage over the other airlines. Douglas accepted Pan Am's request as they knew that the J-75 would be released for commercial operations sooner or later—sooner if an airplane was designed to use it. In order to optimize the DC-8 to be compatible with the J-75, Douglas designed with a large wing area, larger than that of the 707, which was based on the Dash-80 wing. This was a bold and logical move by Douglas. The DC-8 body was wider and longer so as to accommodate six abreast seating. Douglas planned to fit the inaugural DC-8's with the J-57 engine until the J-75 became available. These early DC-8's would thus be underpowered, unable to carry a full load until they were retrofitted with the J-75.

On October 13, 1955, Pan Am ordered 20 707's and 25 DC-8's, issuing an accompanying statement that future orders would be for the larger and more powerful DC-8. The world's airlines that had overseas routes paralleling those of Pan Am quickly realized that they would also have to start operating jets in order to stay competitive. Since TWA would be operating jets across the U.S. as well as across the Atlantic, United and American Airlines would need jets. Just 12 days after Pan Am had placed its order, United bought 30 DC-8's, eschewing the 707 for much the same reasons as Pan Am had. On November 8,1955, C.R. Smith of American placed orders for 30 707's, but only after he had forced Boeing to widen the body. C.R. also wanted to be ahead of United, something that would be possible with the 707 because of its earlier delivery dates.

The assurances that were derived from the Dash-80 flight demonstrations coupled with the opportunity to be first in domestic jet transport operations offset the long standing, close relationship between American and Douglas. The technical arguments concerning the relative merits of the DC-8 versus the 707 were difficult for the airline engineers to comprehend and, in any case, were not the paramount issue as far as C.R. was concerned. American's 707's entered service eight months before United's DC-8's. The American order for 707's was absolutely critical to Boeing's future in the commercial jet transport business, as it provided an endorsement that influenced many other airlines to follow American's lead.

The relationship between the airline and the airplane manufacturers was most interesting during this period of early, critical sales. The head of the airline was certainly a strong character who had no doubt brought his company through difficult times. In many cases he may have been the actual founder. There was no question that he would make the final decision. While listening to his top experts to varying degrees, depending on the airline, the chief executive never forgot that his business represented a huge gamble and that he would have to make the final decision on how to win the bet. This resulted in a rather exclusive attitude on his part, and in order to communicate effectively with their boss, some of his advisors probably had to be mind readers.

The next lower level in the company hierarchy was occupied by the airline management's executive pilot. Though his flying skills were probably rusty, with a little assistance from the Boeing pilot in the co-pilot's seat, the Dash-80 was easy for him to fly. He could concentrate on stick-and-rudder flying because the jet engine had only one control compared to the three or more levers that controlled a piston engine. In a typical flight demonstration scenario, the executive pilot would soon be convinced that his airline's pilots could easily fly the Dash-80, but he would probably suggest that the airplane needed a thrust reverser and some better instruments. Then when he visited Douglas, the airline executive pilot had a good understanding as to what made the Boeing Dash-80 easy to fly. Douglas would try to tell him across the table how they could do the job better, but the fact that he had flown a jet was stuck in his mind, and so a different approach would tend to lack credence no matter how well it was presented.

The third player on the airline's decision-making team was its top engineering group. Their principal job was performance evaluation. The performance of the jet airplane was much easier to measure and calculate than that of piston engines. The engineers were probably delighted to get into something that was more technical and less empirical. The biggest question in their minds concerned the airplane's drag characteristics. To chart drag, Douglas had to depend on wind tunnel data, although it is possible that had acquired some data from B-52 flight tests. One particular airline chief did not have on his staff a group of engineers whom he trusted, so he hired a consultant who then came out with a report that attempted to weigh probabilities. Rather than coming to a clear conclusion, the report contained verbiage such as, "on the one hand . . . and then . . . on the other hand." This consultant erred with respect to the DC-8 drags. The Dash-80 was a hard act to follow.

The width of the body was a major factor in the competition between the 707 and the DC-8. The Dash-80 featured the same body width as the Stratocruiser, 132 inches, which accommodated four abreast seating and a center isle. This width was increased by 12 inches on the KC-135 at the request of the Air Force, in order to allow space for wider cargo loads on the upper deck, the refueling tanks being located in the lower lobe. At the time of the original Pan Am 707 order, the body diameter was 144 inches, the same as that on the KC-135. But the DC-8 had a body diameter of 147 inches to accommodate coach seating of six abreast. This was a factor in the loss of the 707 sale to United. The sale of the 707 to American would also have subsequently been lost, except for the fact that Ed Wells, at a sales meeting in

Oklahoma, acquiesced to American's request for a further increase in body width of 4 1/2 inches. While the DC-8's body width remained at 147 inches, the 707 ended up with a body width of 148 1/2 inches. When this last change was made, the 707 body drawings had been completed and tool manufacturing had been started. Much of this work had to be redone. The body lines at the nose and the tail sections were not affected, as the lines emanating from them could be re-faired into the wider, central tubular section. The company was so hungry for business that engineering and manufacturing made the necessary changes without a slide in the schedule.

In order to remain competitive with the larger DC-8 and thus retain a position in the commercial jet transport business itself, a second, larger 707 model was required. This would entail a longer wing span, and in order to tailor the wing properly, a completely new wing had to be designed. The 707 body was stretched by adding length to the long cylindrical section. Only two months after issuing their ultimatum to Boeing, on December 24, 1955, Pan Am ordered 15 of these larger 707's. Despite the additional workload, it was found that the availability of two 707 model sizes was very beneficial to Boeing, for sales were thus increased, the smaller model being favored for domestic routes. Coordination of the additional paper work and tooling for the larger model was facilitated by the organization of the whole company that had evolved during wartime to cope with the many changes made to the bombers. This, in essence, was the beginning of the model "family" concept that has helped to make the Boeing product line so successful.

At the time of the first jet transport orders, air travel was still considered to be somewhat of a luxury, and so the generous seat arrangement found on the DC-6 and the Stratocruiser was retained; each of the rather large seats was located next to a window, and the seats were spaced far enough apart so they could be reclined to enable some amount of sleep. Initially, the 707 seats were bolted to the floor along the lines of the accepted spacing arrangement, but recognizing the potential for growth in passenger air travel, the airlines soon requested that the seats be secured to the floor on tracks so that seat spacing could be varied. In the early days of commercial jet travel when only a few jets were yet in service but when public demand was already high, seats were sometimes located so close together that altercations broke out between the cramped passengers. There was a story going around in the engineering department that there had been one instance in which a passenger actually had hit the person in front over the head with a wine bottle.

In the past, airline interiors had not been engineered with the same attention to detail as had the structure. To help make the interiors more attractive, Boeing contracted for the services of an industrial designer, Frank Delguidice. He advocated more ambient light inside the passenger cabin and towards this end, suggested the possible use of long windows. In order to preserve the structural integrity of the body, Ed Wells recommended as an alternative doubling the number of existing windows while slightly reducing their size. One window was to be located between every circular body frame, spaced at intervals of 20 inches. This contrasted to past transports, in which the windows had been located between every other frame. With high capacity seat spacing, the new arrangement allowed all passengers in the coach section to have at least a limited view outside. In the rush to catch up to the 707, Douglas neglected this aspect of passenger comfort on the DC-8, retaining instead the original window spacing with the result that some coach passengers had to sit next to a blank wall.

A modular body interior was designed for the 707. It featured a "snap-in" hard wall system with roller window shades, which would sustain more abuse than the older cloth interiors. Today, it is hard to imagine that these wall systems were not always standard in all commercial aircraft. The plastic covering on the hard walls was popular with the airlines because it permitted some amount of individualized decor in terms of patterns and colors. The 707 set the standard for modern transport design, even with respect to the aesthetic features that enhanced passenger comfort and acceptance. Major credit must go to Boeing's interior design group under the direction of Milt Heinaman, with recommendations on aesthetic enhancements from the consultant, Frank Delguidice.

After the initial round of sales activity there remained considerable work to be accomplished on the design of the internal airplane systems. This was a field of major interest to the airlines. Boeing was still engaged in a promotional effort to attract additional customers. Representatives from the first airline customers used Boeing's new airline prospects to create additional leverage in order to secure the changes they desired. They exercised every opportunity to request corrections to what they saw as deficiencies in the systems of their previous airplanes. It was a golden opportunity to get exactly what they wanted, for the intense competition among manufacturers had created a buyer's market for airliners, and Boeing was eager to win over as many customers as possible.

The airlines disliked the conventional method of lighting the pilot's instruments, using spot lights and individual post lights at each instrument. Not only was the resulting light uneven and subject to glare, but the numerous small lights and anchoring attachments tended to clutter up the instrument panel. To satisfy these concerns, the flight deck designers invented a clear plastic sheet, painted black, that could itself be illuminated from within, forming a layer of light. It was placed on top of the instrument panel and beveled around each instrument so as to generate illumination evenly and without glare.

Another customer-directed change related to the electrical power system. This had already been designed and the alternators purchased when Westinghouse came out with an alternator that did not have brushes. At high altitudes the brushes tended to spark and quickly wear out. The airlines became aware of this new innovation and insisted that the brushless alternators be installed. The major systems were of particular concern to the airlines because of maintenance costs as well as revenue losses when the aircraft had to be taken temporarily out of service.

The method of procurement of system components was important to the airlines. In the early days when production runs were small, an airplane manufacturer often had to develop and build the components of an entirely new system, such as the cabin pressurization units on the Stratoliner. For the 707, Boeing elected to develop comprehensive specifications and put the task of manufacturing accessories out for bids. The resulting hardware was then lab tested at Boeing, sometimes with an airline overview. In this way innovations from various manufacturers could be evaluated and competition for new ideas could be encouraged. This method usually yielded technical

248 The Road to the 707

improvements over an in-house manufacturing effort, and indirectly benefited the airlines with regard to the cost of spares.

The procurement of the autopilot for the jet transport opened up a new era in systems integration. In the early days the airline chose the instruments, autopilots, and radios. However, in the case of the autopilot the high speed of the jet made small deflections of the structure very significant in terms of the airplane's dynamic stability. This required a highly technical approach to the autopilot-airplane combination, an approach that could not be left strictly to the autopilot manufacturer and airline customer. With the old, slow piston-engine transports, all the facts that the autopilot manufacturer needed to know about the airplane could be tabulated on a simple form. Boeing did not know how to express the problem of the 707's flexibility to the autopilot manufacturers.

When the Sperry submittal was tested in an autopilot-airplane dynamic computer simulation, directional oscillations resulted involving side-bending of the body. Sperry had come up with a somewhat peculiar design specifically in order to avoid a Bendix patent involving rate gyros. Pan Am had been in favor of Sperry because of past experience with the high quality of their products. As a follow-up to these initial tests however, Sperry sent a salesman to Seattle rather than a technical type who could have participated in further computer simulations.

This lack of mutual understanding was of considerable annoyance to both Pan Am and Boeing. For the DC-8, Douglas accepted the Sperry autopilot as is, although the DC-8 was without an autopilot during its first months of service because of this same dynamic problem. For the 707, Boeing accepted the Bendix autopilot which worked well from the start, although failures from poor solder joints were a problem. More recently, Sperry has featured TV advertisements that depicted Sperry "listening" to the customer, but in this case, their "ears" were blocked and they missed an opportunity to learn something new.

While the first production 707's were rolling out of the factory, an important addition was made to improve the low-speed stall margin. This was in response to a Comet take-off accident in Rome in October 1952. The Comet had settled back down beyond the runway just after unstick. Fortunately, there had been no injuries. The cause of this accident was a higher than normal take-off attitude and a low airspeed, which led to an incipient wing stall that greatly increased drag. Four months later a fatal accident occurred at Karachi because of the same problem. DeHaviland then modified the Comet by lowering the leading edge of the wing airfoil to provide higher lift to increase the stall margin. A contributing factor may have been the design of the engine air inlet, which was located on the leading edge of the Comet wing. At high angles of attack the airflow approached the leading edge with very high up-flow. This may have stalled the lower lip of the inlet and thus starved the engine of air, causing a decrease in thrust.

From an analysis of the Comet accidents, it became clear that an early wing stall could also occur on the 707. The misfortunes of others often yield valuable ideas that should not to be brushed off lightly. Wind tunnel tests on the 707 demonstrated that the wing stalled first just inboard of the outboard engine pod, with the flow separation starting at the leading edge. To cure this, a "leading edge flap" was tested in the wind tunnel. The best angle was found to be near vertical [Figure 34]. This flap guided the airflow around the leading edge more directly, thus delaying the separation. The flap was hinged so that it could be retracted under the leading edge just forward of the front wing spar. It was powered down at the same time as the trailing edge flaps were lowered.

A preliminary flight test was made on the Dash-80 using a fixed flap. The vertical angle looked so odd that the test pilot, Jim Gannett, requested that it first be installed pointing in a more forward direction. But Jim soon found out what the wind tunnel had already proven: that this arrangement was worse than with no flap at all. To test the full effectiveness of the leading edge flap, Boeing Flight Test put a wooden protective skid on the bottom of the after-body, so that the airplane could be rotated until the body scraped the runway. The leading edge flap was effective even at this airplane attitude. In fact, the test results were so impressive that a new requirement was defined by Boeing stating that if the airplane could un-stick, it must be able to climb-out at this high attitude.

By the time the leading edge flap production assembly was ready for installation, some of the 707's were already on the

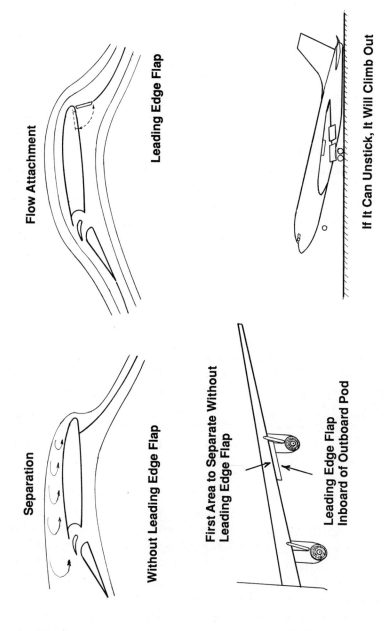

Flow Attachment

Leading Edge Flap

Separation

Without Leading Edge Flap

First Area to Separate Without Leading Edge Flap

Leading Edge Flap Inboard of Outboard Pod

If It Can Unstick, It Will Climb Out

Figure 34—Leading Edge Flap and Maximum Angle Take-Off

Russian Tu-104 Twin-Engine Jet Transport

Photos taken at Vancouver airport during British Columbia Centennial Celebration 1958. Tu-104 entered passenger service in September 1956, two years before PAA 707 service. The Russians were early in many fields but did not have the benefits of competition in the market place.

flight line, where major modifications are always very costly to make. Nevertheless, the flap was installed on all 707's. An early vindication of this effort was demonstrated by a take-off of an American 707 at New York. Several inches of slush on the runway retarded the airplane's acceleration. At the end of the runway there was nothing left for the pilot to do except to pull the control all the way back. The 707 cleared the fence and began a successful climb-out at a very low initial air speed. A prominent engineer at American Airlines, Frank Kolk, said he was sure the leading edge flap had saved the airplane.

All these late changes caused a substantial cost overrun of

about $150 million with respect to the originally established breakeven point of 87 airplanes. This possibly was a factor in the demotion of Bruce Connelly, head of the Transport Division. Years later I expressed my appreciation for his support of this last-minute change, which was made for the sake of safety. Connelly replied simply, "That was my job."

Even after the first 707 delivery, design changes continued to be made, and as a consequence, the cash flow was not favorable until about 400 airplanes had been produced. The many advances that were achieved in the design of the cabin interior and in the airplane systems helped to assure follow-on orders. Douglas was so rushed to keep up that they were often unable to make the necessary changes, and so could not seal off future orders of the 707. The airlines certainly informed the DC-8 engineers about any feature they particularly liked on the 707, and vice versa. But regardless of the fact that the 707 came out ahead in this opening contest between commercial jet transports, the keen competition between Boeing and Douglas at this crucial juncture in the history of aviation resulted in a definitive leap forward into the jet age, leaving behind forever the turbo-prop.

14

The Fan-Jet
Engine

THE DEVELOPMENT of transportation has been paced by progress in the means of propulsion. Any vehicle that moves through a fluid, whether it be a boat moving through water or an airplane moving through air, requires forward thrust to overcome the frictional resistance of the fluid. The size and speed of the vehicle is limited by the amount of thrust that its powerplant can produce. The maximum use of manpower was in the Roman trireme galleys, with 50 oars and two to three men on each oar. The early steamboats had reciprocating engines with up to 5,000 horsepower each. The largest had up to four engines driving screw propellers.

The designers of the largest airplanes with reciprocating engines had to greatly multiply the number of engines due to the limitations in size of the reciprocating engine and the limits of propellers to convert the power to thrust. The very large B-36 bomber of the 1950's featured 10 engines. This was the maximum number of engines that was ever installed on any airplane. Six were reciprocating engines to drive the propellers and four were jet engines which were mounted in twin pods near each wing tip. But adding more and more engines creates new problems. There always has been a desire to minimize the number of engines because they are complicated and costly. The

253

advent of the more powerful turbine engine finally opened the way for larger airplanes with fewer engines.

Forward thrust was thought by many to require having something to "push against," like water in a rowboat. However, when rockets demonstrated thrust in outer space in spite of having nothing to push against, it became clearer to the nontechnical public that thrust can be generated by accelerating a fluid to a high velocity. Although Newton's laws of motion were published in 1687, the concept of propulsion was obscure in the mind of the general public until the advent of modern rocketry provided a graphic, visual example.

The thrust potential of a propeller can be calculated as a function of the aerodynamic lift on the blades. However, it can also be calculated as a function of the acceleration of the air as it goes through the plane of the propeller, which simulates the dynamics of a very large jet. In the jet engines originally conceived by Whittle and von Ohain, all of the air to be accelerated passed through the burner and out a single exit. As was discussed previously, many of the technical types had difficulty swallowing this idea until the jet engine was demonstrated in flight. When the concept was developed further in order to achieve more thrust and less fuel consumption, many who had succeeded in the early jet engine business had a tendency to want to stay with the established design, leaving well enough alone, especially when they were selling a piece of machinery that was working quite wells. The B-52's excellent record of reliability reinforced the desire to stay with a proven jet engine design.

By 1958 a large number of problems had been solved on the 707 and the design appeared to be complete, at least as well as we knew how. The first 707 was scheduled to join Pan Am's fleet in the fall. The engineers were looking forward to a time when they could relax and reflect on their accomplishments. But early in the year it appeared that General Electric was upsetting the apple cart with a radical, new engine development, later to be called the "fan-jet." By adding a large diameter fan to the original jet engine, the total engine thrust could be increased and the fuel consumption reduced. The fan had a larger diameter than the basic jet engine and was enclosed in an annular duct. The fan was driven by the jet engine itself.

To understand the reasoning behind this improvement, one merely has to review Newton's laws. It is more efficient to generate the same amount of thrust by accelerating a larger volume of air to a lower speed instead of vice versa. The propeller is the ultimate mechanism in this regard, but the original idea behind the jet was to avoid the limitations to speed and power imposed by the propeller. Additionally, both the propeller and the reciprocating engine suffered from several mechanical complications. However, it was discovered that the fan-jet provided a practical alternative to the original jet, especially at the subsonic speeds that are typical of the commercial jet transport. With the same sized compressor and burner as the basic jet engine, the fan-jet provided both increased thrust and lower fuel consumption. The reason that the fan-jet had not been used from the start was due to fear of possible trouble in integrating the fan with the existing jet engine. As it turned out, this proved to be a lot easier than originally had been suspected.

Even in 1945, the fan-jet type of engine was not an original idea. On his international lecture tour in 1945, Sir Frank Whittle showed a slide of a fan-jet engine. The first fan-jet engine to be commercially available was the Rolls Royce "Conway." It was installed in the first 707's delivered in 1959 to British Overseas Airways and Lufthansa. It was a very modest application of the fan principle. The volume of air passing through the fan was small, being only 0.3 times the air going through the central, hot section. This was due to the fact that the engine's outside diameter had to be limited so that it could be installed in the wing root of the Vickers "Valiant" bomber. The British airplane designers had not been converted to the pods-on-the-wing concept, and so Rolls Royce had not yet developed the fan-jet beyond the Conway.

Late 1955 at the time of the first 707 sales, the Pratt & Whitney J-57/JT-3 plain jet engine and the Rolls Royce Conway fan-jet were considered standard on the 707. The P&W JT-3 was to be followed by a larger, similar engine, the P&W JT-4, planned for installation on the larger model of the 707 and on the DC-8. During this time period GE had not entered the 707-DC-8 competition. Possibly they believed that the military business would be much more dependable. GE concentrated instead on military engines, except for adapting a military type engine to the Convair 880 airliner that was bought by TWA. The Convair 880 was a four-engine airliner similar to the 707 but smaller. It used the GE CJ805 engine, which was a plain jet that was an adaptation of the military engine used in fighters. Because the Convair 880 was smaller than the 707 and the DC-8, it missed becoming an important factor in the early jet transport market, as this was a time when the total number of jets in operation was still very small while public demand had already increased tremendously. Thus, the largest jets were preferred by the airlines.

The marketing failure of the Convair 880 was to a considerable extent due to Howard Hughes. At that time he was in control of TWA. He insisted on ordering a very large block of the initial 880 production run, but this excluded other airlines that might otherwise have bought the 880 in their rush to fly jet transports. The Convair 880 was a good airplane. In order to reenter the major market, Convair and GE started working together quietly on an engine-airplane combination intended to be revolutionary. Therefore, it was not advertised until it was well along. The new plane was to be named the Convair 990.

The first time that we in the 707 engineering organization heard about the new GE engine was when a young GE engineer showed up at the Boeing plant in Renton with some drawings and performance data. It seemed that GE had finally decided they had better tell the rest of the airplane manufacturers about their new product. The early GE sales approach was naive in not aiming at a broader market from the start, and in not obtaining Boeing's reactions as to the suitability of the installation. GE did not seem to realize that Boeing had originated the pod engine concept and had accumulated a lot of data and experience pertaining to its design. Boeing wind tunnel tests had shown that a restriction of the air flowing over the engine pod and the under the wing could reduce the top speed of the airplane unless the designers had considered this possibility.

The GE engine had a novel design in which an independent turbine-fan unit was located aft in the jet tailpipe, behind the plain jet engine, as used on the Convair CV-880. This design retained the critical, hot units of the original engine while still providing a fan. Presumably, this was the easiest way to incorporate the fan. The fan blades were actually extensions of the turbine blades. Because they were located this far back in the engine where exhaust gas temperatures were lower, the turbine blades retained enough strength to resist the extra centrifugal loads imposed by the fan blade extensions. The amount of air going through the fan was 2.20 times greater than the amount of air going through the hot section. This was a large step beyond the Rolls Royce Conway, where the amount of air going through the fan was only 0.3 times the amount of air going through the hot section. This GE engine was called the "aft-fan," and it looked like a neat idea. The concept had been published in a U.S. textbook in 1949 and was based on an idea that had originated from Dan Hage, a Boeing power-plant engineer [Figure 35].

The GE engine drawing depicted a wing pod mount of the engine, with a large diameter aft-fan enclosed in a short ring cowl that was a part of the aft-fan unit. Since the fan was aft, the ring cowl was located near the wing's leading edge. It was obvious that the ring cowl would block some of the air flow under the wing, and this would increase the airspeed over the top of the wing, which was critical in determining the top speed of the airplane. As a consequence, the attainable top speed would be lowered. In spite of our concerns we tested the 707 wind tunnel model using a model of the GE aft-fan engine which was installed in a pod mount. As expected, the results showed unfavorable drag characteristics. So we put the GE design concept aside, that is until American Airlines became interested in the Convair 990 with the GE aft-fan.

One Sunday morning in January 1958, I was flying back to New York for the annual technical meeting of the Institute of Aeronautical Sciences. With me were three Boeing executives who planned to sign up American Airlines on the 720, a shortened body version of the 707. I was reading the comics when they came to me with an announcement in the Sunday paper on the sale of the Convair 990 to Capital Airlines. In the announcement, Convair claimed lower fuel consumption, longer range and higher speeds. Besides the GE aft-fan, the Convair design featured four long slender bullet shaped bodies extending aft of the wing's trailing edge. These had the aerodynamic effect of a thinner wing, which can obtain higher speeds. This was an idea that had been developed by Dick Whitcomb of the NACA at

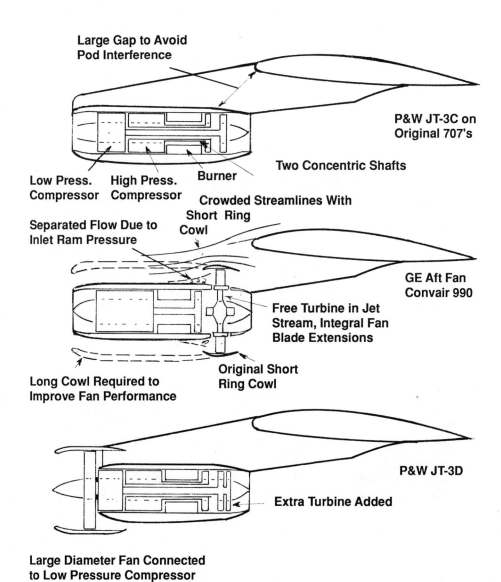

Large Gap to Avoid Pod Interference

P&W JT-3C on Original 707's

Two Concentric Shafts

Low Press. Compressor **High Press. Compressor** **Burner**

Crowded Streamlines With Short Ring Cowl

Separated Flow Due to Inlet Ram Pressure

GE Aft Fan Convair 990

Free Turbine in Jet Stream, Integral Fan Blade Extensions

Long Cowl Required to Improve Fan Performance

Original Short Ring Cowl

P&W JT-3D

Extra Turbine Added

Large Diameter Fan Connected to Low Pressure Compressor

Figure 35—Ducted Fan—Higher Thrust and Better Range

Langley Field, Virginia. We had already tested this addition to the 707 model in the wind tunnel. While the slender bodies did allow an increase in the critical speed beyond which the drag rose abruptly, the added surface "wetted area" of the slender bodies raised the friction drag, which canceled out the advantage. I told the bosses not to worry about the announcement in the Sunday paper, explaining that we had done our homework and that the 990 would not work. I went back to reading the comics.

On Monday morning while I was attending the technical conference, the chief engineer Maynard Pennell summoned me out of a lecture, with orders to get up to the hotel room to meet with Bill Littlewood and Frank Kolk of American Airlines. They were not about to OK their boss in signing up for the Boeing 720. C.R. Smith, the dominant head of American, was concerned that Capital might soon erect a billboard that would be visible to drivers on their way to the New York airport which would read, "FLY FASTER TO CHICAGO WITH CAPITAL." C.R. had a strong sense of the important competitive factors influencing the airline industry.

To answer the speed question, I dreamed up an easily accomplished fix for the 720, although we had no test data to verify anything resembling this. In designing the 707 we had over-thickened the wing root, which reduced the top speed slightly. We could modify the wing's leading edge with a forward extension, or "glove," located inboard from the nacelle, so as to thin this section of the wing. Such an extension would be tapered, starting from the existing wing airfoil at the pod and expanding towards the body so as to increase the sweep angle. Frank Kolk bought this idea but he still wanted a fan engine. We explained the installation faults associated with the GE aft-fan. Another disadvantage of the GE engine with respect to its use on the 720 was the fact that it couldn't produce quite enough thrust to match the airplane's gross weight. However, Frank Kolk was rather experienced in airplane performance calculations and was still very much impressed by the theoretical advantages of large diameter fans as exemplified by the GE engine.

By the time we went to the ballroom for the afternoon cocktail hour, the engine dilemma still had not been resolved.

After getting my first drink I was trailing my boss, Maynard Pennell, when he spotted Art Smith, the vice president of engineering at Pratt & Whitney.

Maynard said to Art, "American wants a fan engine."

Art replied, "That doesn't make any sense."

Maynard answered, "That's not the point—do you want the business or don't you?"

Art answered, "We do."

That is all I can remember of their conversation, as it took me by surprise. This episode showed Maynard's skill in dealing with a problem. Amazingly, by Wednesday night we were told that P&W had available a suitable, large diameter fan which had been developed for a research project. The fan could be located on the front of the J-57/JT-3 engine, and an extra turbine stage would be added to the aft end to drive the fan. This posed no aerodynamic interference problem, as the fan would be far in front of the wing. The fan generated an air flow whose volume was 1.50 times greater than that of the air going through the hot inner section. While this was less than the 2.20 figure in the GE engine, it was still a big step forward since it would increase the thrust and decrease the fuel consumption.

P&W must have had some dissenting engineers who had continued work on the fan engine idea despite its unpopularity at the top of the company, as they were able to supply us with engine performance data within three days of Maynard's conversation with Art. The performance gains of the engine were impressive and it seemed a plausible alternative to those of us in New York, although we had no power plant expert on hand. Since the Boeing bosses had come to New York to sign up American on the 720, and since Convair was also active in trying to sell their 990, it was imperative that the new data describing the 720 with the P&W fan engine be prepared immediately, while we were still in New York.

By the weekend, performance computations were being made in New York with the help of some recruits who were called from Seattle. Within a week, enough performance data and cost estimates had been produced to allow Ed Wells to meet with C.R. Smith. We had prepared a card presentation but this was not used in the meeting between Ed and C.R. We had not yet developed engine installation drawings, but all C.R. wanted was Ed's word that it would work. C.R.'s instincts had motivated the start of the DC-3 program, and he had not lost his ability to quickly recognize a significant advanced development. Ed gave his word that the combination of the 720 and the new fan engine would work. Ed had a very experienced eye for mechanical devices, and he seemed to know intuitively how they would perform in an airplane. Throughout his career at Boeing, which had started in 1930, Ed had collected lots of wins and very few misses. He was the most valuable employee in the company by far. American changed their order for the 720 to include the new P&W fan-jet engine. It seemed amazing that an airline would buy such a seemingly radical change before it had been run on the test stand and demonstrated in flight. Unlike American, United stayed with the plain jet engine on their 720's. With the rapid success of the fan-jet engine, United's 720's became obsolete within a few years and were placed on the used plane market.

American also bought the Convair 990 with the GE aft-fan. It was rumored that the GE president, Cordiner, had pressured C.R. to buy their engine. It seemed to us that American had bet on both horses in a two-horse race, and we were sure to win. The 990 had a limited production run because of maintenance problems on the engine itself and because of the heavy and cumbersome, long, large-diameter cowl, which featured an integral duct that was needed to capture the fan air at the front of the engine. Convair had found this cowl to be necessary in order to obtain uniform, high energy air flow into the aft-fan. This long duct-cowl was so heavy that power was required to raise it so that the basic engine could be inspected.

The slender bullet shaped bodies on the Convair 990 wing, which became known as the "Whitcomb bumps," were intended to increase the airplane's speed. They were designed to carry extra fuel, but when they were full, the resulting weight aft on the wing restricted the speed, as weight aft can cause flutter. Evidently, the Convair engineers had not had the use of a wind tunnel to adequately develop the 990 during the preliminary design phase. The financial types that were running Convair gave up, ending their participation in the commercial jet transport business. If GE had worked early with Boeing to examine the installation problem of the aft-fan engine design, they would have spared themselves a lot of trouble. We at Boeing entertained a whimsical thought that we might have thus saved Convair in the transport business.

In June 1958, five months after the fateful cocktail hour conversation, Pratt and Whitney had ready a J-57/JT-3 engine with the front-mounted fan in a test stand at East Hartford. In order to measure the thrust produced by the fan, the air flowing through the fan was ducted into several, round exit nozzles. Viewing the awkward test rig, it was quite discouraging to attempt to visualize the installation of the fan engine in an actual airplane. However, the Boeing power plant installation engineer, John Morrison, and a talented designer, Alex Vdolek, designed a streamlined pod that made the design look natural. Their design also included an ingenious thrust reverser which was needed for braking on the runway after touchdown.

The long term consequence of the fan engine was that it supplanted the P&W J-75/JT-4 around which the DC-8 and the 707-300 had been designed. Pratt & Whitney had been betting on their JT-4 as the future transport engine. Their salesmen had taken a negative position on the Rolls Royce Conway fan engine, not realizing that it was a very modest application of a good idea. Likewise, Boeing had not been active in thinking about fan engines. It is strange how technological revolutions catch entrenched industries so ill prepared, but with regard to the fan-jet engine, it is also strange that luck seemed to play such a major role for Boeing and Pratt & Whitney. All modern jet engines have very large fans that were derived from this starting point. Many of the early 707's, DC-8's , B-52's, and KC-135's were re-engined to accommodate the fan. With the P&W JT-3D engine, as the fan engine was named, the both larger 707-300 and the DC-8 had nonstop capability across the oceans, even when carrying full loads.

There was a period after the first orders for the large jet transports when sales were slow, and it looked like the market had leveled off. However, the large increase in range allowed by the fan-jet engine was what firmly established the jet transport as the only means for worldwide travel. When the public awoke to the realities of the convenience and comfort of jets, the production of transports expanded greatly, leaving others far behind. The design of a jet transport is problematical because it

707 with Pratt & Whitney JT-3D fan engines, June 1960

requires the integration of a vast number of technologies. To
accomplish this task, a complex but smoothly functioning business and engineering organization must be in place. To start a
jet transport design from scratch and at the same time build up
a satisfactory organization from scratch looks to be almost
impossible.

Conclusion

The modern jet transport can be described as the largest integration of technology into a self sufficient unit. All it needs to fly is a full fuel tank, a small crew, and a long runway. Its economic success depends on performance, low maintenance costs and high passenger appeal. It is unique in that all major sections are highly technical in content, from the wing tips to the nose and the tail. Designing the individual components and fitting them together into a cohesive whole is a long process that cannot be expressed in a formula. Airplane design is a combination of industrial art and technology. Usually the process of resolving the art precedes the application of formulae.

The speed capability of passenger airplanes with piston engines and propellers was increased gradually from 35 mph in 1906 to 350 mph in 1952, when the deHaviland Comet appeared. The jet transport resulted in a quantum jump to nearly 600 mph, and this speed limit has remained nearly constant for the past 40 years despite extensive research whose goal has been to eliminate the sudden rise in drag as the speed of sound is approached, or at least to delay its onset a little bit. The effort to overcome this obstacle has resulted in what appears to be approaching the optimum external shape for commercial jet transports. From this point forward, major improvements in the airframe may be limited to new materials and structural refinements to reduce weight. The competition in engines may yield very significant improvements, extending for some time into the future. However, those who write histories are often wrong when they try to project their experiences into the future, and it might be better to disregard them with respect to what they think will happen and to listen to them only with respect to how to make it happen.

The progress that has been achieved has been due to the unrelenting efforts of engineers, pilots, and airplane operators, all trying to survive in a period when the outcome was unclear. In the middle 1930's, typical engineering departments might have numbered less than 200 employees. Critical responsibilities were delegated to young individuals in a manner that might astound the modern manager. Opportunities for innovation were many. The paths ahead were unmarked and poorly predicted by the analytical tools available at the time. Often it was simply a case where erudite trials and repeated analyses of errors were the only way to test new ground, and the engineer had to be ready to start over at any time. Because monetary prospects were vague, the ranks of management were of necessity composed of airplane enthusiasts, for who else would commit himself to such an apparently impractical career.

After the war the whole picture changed, to the point where younger engineers often looked upon the old-timers as being archaic. However, the old-timers had a great advantage in understanding the airplane as a whole. It was possible for an engineer to have this broad background up until about 1938, when specialization started to bloom. Upon first consideration many problems in design seem to be caused by irresolvable conflicts between two or more technologies. The solution is usually arrived at by logic. In the past, a discussion between several technical specialists on a seemingly difficult problem would often end at an impasse, except when an experienced airplane designer sitting quietly on the sidelines proposed a neat solution. The technical experts might then have looked at each other and said, "Why didn't we think of that?"

A review of the long list of critical decisions that were made in airplane design, from the Wright Brothers to the present time, is very revealing. Some of the best ideas were born of sudden inspirations that an engineer (such as myself) might have had while puzzling over a problem in a warm shower, free of inhibitions and without paper and a slide rule, or while engaged in a conversation during a cocktail hour. The engineer had enough experience and knowledge of airplanes to think while on his feet. Critical decisions during a market competition often required the boss to have the skills and timing of a double play in a baseball game. Not until a computer can be programmed for imagination will this free thinking be bettered. Or, if that appears impossible, maybe the computer can be programmed to ask questions so as to stimulate imagination.

The parochial technical types often try to prove that progress came about because of decisions that seemed quite logical based on past experience rather than on decisions that appeared to be arbitrary at the time. The history of the 707 could be used to prove the opposite.

> The idea of the swept wing by Prof. Adolph Busseman in 1935
> The first jet engines by two students, Whittle and von Ohain, in the 1930's
> The building of the Boeing high-speed wind tunnel in 1942, with no project
> The injection of the German swept-wing data by Schairer in 1945
> The production purchase of the B47 by General Wolfe after a 20-minute ride
> The change of the XB52 to jets from the turbo-prop by Colonel Warden in 1948

It is difficult to describe the excitement and satisfaction felt by the engineers and test pilots who participated in the transition to jets. It was a privilege to have been a party to such a revolution in aviation technology. It was an inspired struggle, fueled by the intense competition between equally skilled organizations. One wishes that the modern engineer could have the same opportunity to explore radically new technologies, to be on the leading edge, so to speak, of an equally dramatic change from the jets we know today. This book is as much a history of engineering as it is a history of aviation.

The same road that started with Leonardo daVinci as he watched birds in an attempt to solve the problem of flight control led to the first demonstrations of flight by the Wright Brothers. The road then proceeded at a more rapid pace to the piston-engine airliner and eventually to the jet transport which has come to dominate long distance travel, changing forever the scale by which millions of ordinary people measure their world. The earliest jet transports, which brought together so many disparate ideas and inventions for the first time, constitute a crucial marker of the advent of the jet age. This was a unique time in history, a turning point when what we take for granted today was thought to be impossible.

Bibliography

Allen, Charles ,E., *The Airline Builders*, Time-Life, The Epic of Flight, 1981

Angelucci, Enzo, *Encyclopedia of Civil Aircraft*, Crown, 1982

Angelucci, Enzo, *Encyclopedia of Military Aircraft*, Military Press, 1983

Beisel, Rex ; MacClain, A.L.; Thomas F.M., "The Cowling and Cooling of Radial Aircraft Engines," *SAE Jour. Transactions,* 1934

Bowers, Peter M., *Boeing Airplanes*, Naval Inst. Press, 1989

Boyne, Walter J., *The Leading Edge*, Stewart, Tabori & Chang, NY, 1986

Boyne, Walter J., *Messerschmitt Me 262*, Smithsonian, 1982

Carter, C.C., *Simple Aerodynamics and the Airplane*, Ronald, NY, 1932

Colllison, Thomas, *Flying Fortress*, Scribner, NY, 1943

Cox, H. Roxbee, "British Aircraft Gas Turbines," *Jour. Aero. Sc.*, Feb. 1936

Dept. of Commerce, Aeronautics Branch, Airworthiness, *Bul. 7A,* 1931-33

Fokker, Anthony, Autobiog. *Flying Dutchman*, Henry Holt, 1931

Foulois, Maj. Gen. Benj. D., *From the Wright Bros. to the Astronauts*, 1968

Gibbons, Floyd, *The Red Knight of Germany*, Doubleday Doren, 1928

Gibbs Smith, Charles H., *Flight Through the Ages,* Crowell, 1974

Gibbs-Smith, Charles H., *The Invention of the Airplane,* Taplinger, NY, 1966

Golley, John, *Whittle,* Smithsonian, 1987

Hallion, R.P., *Legacy of Flight*, Guggenheim Fund, U. of Wash. Press, 1977

Hallion, R.P. *Test Pilots,* Smithsonian Press, Washington, DC, 1988

Heinkel Ernst, Autobiog., *Stormy Life*, E.P. Dutton, NY, 1956

Hobbs, Leo. S., "The Aircraft Engine," Pratt & Whitney *Bee-Hive,* Fall, 1954

Howard, Fred, *Wilbur and Orville,* Ballantine, NY, 1987

Jacobs, Eastman; Ward, K.; Pinkerton, R., *Char. of 78 Airfoils, NACA Rep 460*

Jane's *Encyclopedia of Aviation*, London, 1980

Jones, Lloyd S., *US Bombers—B1 to B70*, Aero Pub., LA, 1962

Lee, Arthur Gould, *No Parachute*, Harper & Row, NY, 1970

Littlewood, Wm., "Tech. Trends in Air Transp.," *Jour. of Aero. Sc.*, Apr., 1953

Loudy, *Metal Airplane Structures*, Henley, 1938

Mansfield, Harold, *Vision,* Duell, Sloan and Pearce, NY, 1956

National Advisory Committee for Aeronautics, *First Annual Report, 1916*

Page, Victor W., *Modern Aircraft*, Henley, NY, 1928

Perkins, Courtland D., & Hage, Robert E., *Airplane Performance,* Wiley, 1949

Prichard, J.L., "The Dawn of Aerdynamics," *Jour. Roy. Aero. Soc.,* Mar. 1957

Quill, Jeffrey, *Birth of the Spitfire*, Quiller Press, London, 1986

Raymond, Arthur E., "A Well Tempered Airplane,"*Aviation Week*, Oct., Nov. 1951

Raymond, Arthur E., "Forecast," *Aviation Week*, June 16, 1952

Rise and Fall of the German Air Force, St. Martin's Press, NY, 1983

Schlaifer, Robert, *Development of Aircraft Engines*, Harvard, Boston, 1950

Serling, Robt. J., *Eagle, The Story of American Airlines*, St. Martin's, NY

Setright, L.J.K., *The Power to Fly*, Allen & Unwin, London, 1971

Sharp, Martin C., *An Outline of deHaviland History*, Faber, London, 1960

Shrader, Welman A., *Fifty Years of Flight*, Eaton, 1953

Smith, Geoffrey G., *Gas Turbines and Jet Propulsion*, Aerosphere, NY, 1944

Tuchman, Barbara, *The Guns of August*, Bantam, NY, 1980

von Karman, Theodore, *Aerodynamics,* Cornell, 1954

von Karman, Theodore, *The Wind and Beyond*, Little Brown, 1967

von Ohain, Hans, *History of the HS3 and the Heinkel He178*, Unpublished

Walkowicz, T.F., "Birth of Sweepback," *Air Force Magazine*, Apr., 1952

Warner, Edward F., *Aerodynamics,* McGraw Hill, 1927

Whittle, F.W., "Early History of the Whittle Jet," *Inst. Mech Eng.,*1946

Whittle, Sir Frank, *Jet, the Story of a Pioneer,* Fredrick Muller, London, 1953

Wright Brothers, *National Park Service Handbook,* Series No. 34, 1963

Younger, *Structural Design of Metal Airplanes*, McGraw-Hill, 1935

General Index

Trippe, Juan, 236, 242
Turbo Supercharger, 74-77, 83, 115
TWA, 44, 45, 49-57, 230, 243, 256

United Aircraft Corp., 45, 63
United Airlines, 44-47, 50, 53, 63, 228, 243

Vdolek, Alex, 262
Vega Co., 88
Verville, Alfred, 28
Voight, Woldemar, 203
Volta Congress, 133
von Karman, 52, 126-128, 137, 140
von Kluck, Gen.,13
von Ohain, Hans, 101, 109-114, 148, 254, 266

Warden, Col. H.E., 100, 154, 193, 199, 202-204, 208, 228, 260, 266
Warren, Glen, 117
Washington, Univ. of, 27, 38, 76, 126, 152, 171

Wasp Engine, 30, 47
Wells, Ed, 67, 153, 154, 161, 204, 244, 246, 260
Wenham, F.H., 123
Westinghouse, 116, 131, 202, 247
Westover, Gen. Oscar, 64
Whitcomb, R.T., 257, 261
Whittle, Frank, 101-107, 109, 114, 116, 148, 239, 254, 255, 266
Williams, R.D., 103
Withington, H.W., 128, 149
Wolfe, Gen. K.B., 193, 194, 266
Wright Bros., 1, 3, 5-7, 10, 11, 15, 64, 97, 122, 124, 265, 267
Wright Co., 29, 30, 31, 33, 47, 53, 57, 78, 79, 85, 116, 229, 230
Wright Field, 42, 65, 68, 70, 73, 145, 151-54, 162, 193, 196, 201, 203, 204, 222

Yeager, Chuck, 185-187

Zeppelin, 19

Airplane Index

Piston Bombers

MB-2, Martin, 64
Y1-B7, Douglas, 52
XB-8, Fokker, 40
Y1-B9, Boeing, 37, 40-45, 64, 66, 72
B-10, Martin, 42, 48, 64-66
B-12, Martin, 66
XB-15, Boeing, 65-67, 77
B-17, Boeing, 52, 63, 67-78, 131, 140, 161
B-18, Douglas, 66, 73
B-19, Douglas, 78
B-24, Consolidated, 76, 77, 80, 161
B-29, Boeing, 77-84, 149, 174, 186
XB-30,* Lockheed, 78
XB-31,* Douglas, 78
B-32, Consolidated, 78-82
XB-33,* Martin, 83
B-36, Consolidated, 80, 199, 227
XB-54,* Boeing, 180, 193, 194
  *Proposed, not built

Jet Bombers

Arado (Germany), 139, 162
Junkers 287 (Germany), 139-141
XB-43, Douglas, 118, 146
B-45, North American, 146, 147, 164
B-46, Convair, 146, 147, 164, 191, 217
XB-47, Boeing, 131, 142, 148-213, 218, 220
XB-48, Martin, 146, 148
XB-52, Boeing, 201, 204, 211-213, 221, 254
XB-55, Boeing, 204-209
XB-60, Convair, 204

Piston Fighters

Taube (Germany), 15
Sopwith Camel (Britain), 14
SPAD (France), 14, 19, 26
SE-5 (Britain), 19, 26

Albatros, 26
D-1, Fokker, 18
V11, Fokker, 18, 21, 26
V111, Fokker, 23
Me-109 (Germany), 66, 98, 140
P-38, Lockheed, 81
P-51, North American, 26, 98
Spitfire, 66, 92
Hurricane, 66
Zero, 79

Jet Fighters

Me-262 (Germany), 112, 137, 139, 153, 203
Meteor (Britain), 107
Vampire, deHaviland, 237
P-59, Bell, 116, 145
P-80, Lockheed, 107,109, 161, 163, 176
P-84, Republic, 118
F-86, North American, 118, 120, 141, 142, 178, 179, 196
F-94, Lockheed, 196
MiG-15 (Russian), 121

Piston Transports

247, Boeing, 37, 41, 42, 56, 63, 215, 238
Fokker Tri-Motor, 1, 33, 34
Ford Tri-Motor, 33, 34
80, Boeing, 34, 47, 72
Condo, Curtiss, 34
C-46, Curtiss, 217
DC-1, Douglas, 43, 45, 47, 49, 51-56
DC-2, Douglas, 42, 51, 63, 66, 70, 238
DC-3, Douglas, 42, 45, 51, 56, 224
DC-4/C-54, Douglas, 55, 60, 227
DC-6, Douglas, 58, 59, 224, 230, 236, 241, 245
DC-7, Douglas, 230, 232, 238
Model 10, Lockheed, 57
Constellation, Lockheed, 57, 59, 176, 228-240

Turbo-Prop Transports

Jet Transports

Single-Engine Piston Miscellaneous

--- --- --- --- --- --- --- --- --- ---

Please send me _____ copies of **The Road to the 707**

I enclose $17.95 x _____ books _____

Shipping and handling ___ $2.00 ___

Washington residents add $1.47 for each book _____

Total enclosed _____

Name_____

Address_____

City_____State_____Zip_____

Send order and payment to: TYC Publishing Company
875 Shoreland Drive S.E.
Bellevue, WA 98004